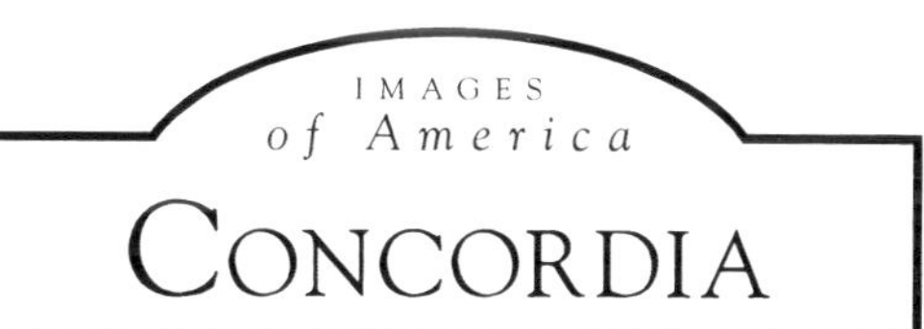
IMAGES
of America
CONCORDIA

On the Cover: Diners gather at West Side Inn in 1947. The popular café at 232 West Sixth Street was owned by Harlan "Woody" Woods and his wife, Helen Woods, who had purchased it the previous year from Roy Brownell after moving to Concordia from Emerson, Iowa. The couple ran the business, which originally opened in 1926, for the next 32 years before retiring and selling it to Leo Householder in 1978. From left to right at the counter are Shorty Blackburn, Roy Brownell, Dorothy Brownell, and Helen Woods. Behind the counter are Ruth Rittle and Bessie Penabaker. Householder kept West Side Inn open for another 10 years. (Courtesy of Sue Vignery.)

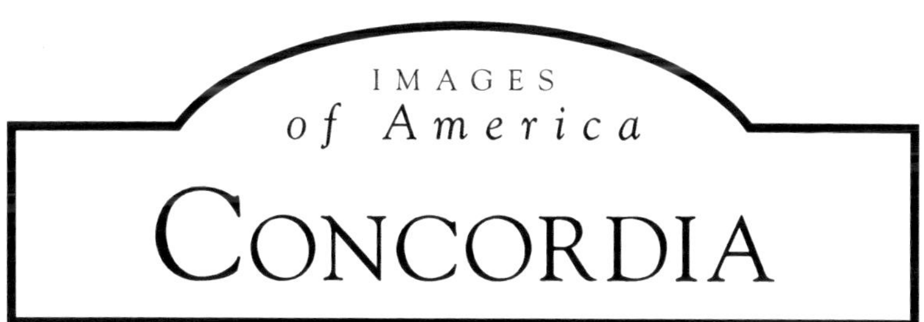

Dena Bisnette and Joe Gilliam

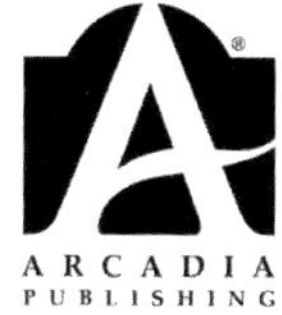

ISBN 978-1-4671-1329-8

Published by Arcadia Publishing
Charleston, South Carolina

Printed in the United States of America

Library of Congress Control Number: 2014958233

For all general information, please contact Arcadia Publishing:
Telephone 843-853-2070
Fax 843-853-0044
E-mail sales@arcadiapublishing.com
For customer service and orders:
Toll-Free 1-888-313-2665

Visit us on the Internet at www.arcadiapublishing.com

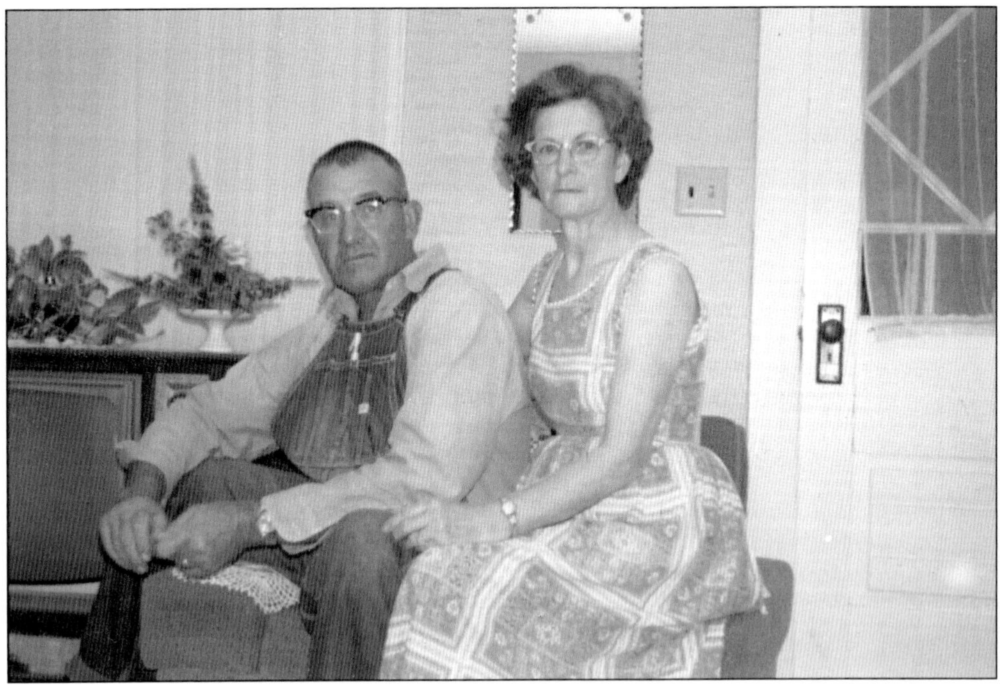

We dedicate this book to Dena's grandparents John and Edith Bisnette of Concordia and to our dear friends Jake and Belle, who both died during this project.

Contents

ACKNOWLEDGMENTS

We thank the folks at Cloud County Historical Society Museum for their assistance, including curator Cindy Riemann, Aline Luecke, Marilyn Johnston, and the many volunteers and board members who helped us. We appreciate the following individuals who provided images and information: Jim Bell, Jim Buoy, Kim Buoy, Arlan Campbell, Dan Chaput, Guy and Karla Chizek, Arlene F. Clayton, Marie Dochow, Anson Edwards, David Erickson, Sandi Davidson Foster, Joseph D. Grimm, Lori Halfhide, Dan Harris, Susie Haver, Margo Hosie, Sarah Jenkins, Charles B. Johnson, Marilyn Johnston, Kurt Kocher, Richard Larson, Jean Leon, Aline Luecke, Everett Miller, Dallas Nading, Sr. Bernadine Pachta, Mary Ann Palmquist, Gladys Peterson, Cindy Riemann, Paul Rimovsky, Harold G. Severance, Art Slaughter, Mardell Snavely, Charles Switzer, Robert A. Thomas, Virginia Thull, Sue Vignery, and Tom Walker. We also thank the Frank Carlson Library, Susie Haver and Tammy Britt at Cloud County Tourism, Pamela Campbell at Cloud County Medical Center, Cloud County Chamber of Commerce, Sisters of St. Joseph Concordia, Brown Grand Theatre, National Orphan Train Museum and Research Complex, POW Camp Concordia Museum, and Cloud Ceramics. Thanks go to KNCK Radio and *Concordia Blade-Empire* for publicity, Beverley Buller for additional proofreading, the folks at Jitters for letting us do an impromptu photograph scanning there, and Janet Pease Emery and Clarence Paulsen for what he left behind. And special thanks go to my cousin Anson Edwards and my mother, Dorothy Bisnette.

INTRODUCTION

I was three days short of 12 years old in 1971 when Concordia, Kansas, celebrated its centennial. That was when I first asked dad how Concordia came to be, and he told me about James Manny Hagaman.

Having heard stories about settlements based on discoveries like good drinking water, oil, and gold and about special-purpose places like factory towns, railroad towns, mining towns, cowtowns, and the like, I expected a similar tale. I did not expect a story about a man who got angry at another town and founded his own town as a result, but that is exactly what J.M. Hagaman did, and he did not even name it after himself.

Concordia lies on the south side of the Republican River in Cloud County in the hills of North Central Kansas, which the locals just call NCK. Today, it is a neat, compact town full of churches, schools, shops, small industries, and mostly older homes. It has a hospital and a college. In Hagaman's day it was just prairie, grasses on rolling hills, rocks, a few homesteads along creeks, and that sometimes-wild river, which was even mentioned in *Around the World in Eighty Days* by Jules Verne.

Nearby, across the river, is another town called Clyde. Hagaman came to Kansas in 1860 with his wife, son, and two friends, J.M. Thorpe and August Fenskie. They had settled near the river by the time Clyde became temporary county seat for a new county called Shirley County in 1866. Hagaman was appointed county clerk but wanted to be the first state representative for the new county. John B. Rupe defeated him and then promptly tried to do two things Hagaman hated. Rupe was unsuccessful in the first one, which would have split the county in half and let the halves be absorbed by Ottawa County and Republic County, but he was successful in changing the name of Shirley County to Cloud.

Hagaman took another shot at political office, running and winning by a slight margin in 1868. He decided to buy land in Clyde and build a hotel on the government road through town. Clyde was the obvious choice for permanent county seat, and visitors would need lodging. Local leaders liked the idea and offered him the land he wanted at a price that pleased him, but before arrangements were finished, they raised the price and substituted an acre that was not as good. Hagaman was angry and declared that he would personally make certain Clyde would never become county seat.

First, he chose and bought a quarter section of land south of the Republican River in Lincoln Township. He knew most voters lived in the smaller section of the county north of the river and decided to build a road from Junction City to his own homestead to make traveling to the southern part easier. He paid for the survey himself but used his political skills to get the state to pay for construction. Called 64 Milepost Road because it was 64 miles long, it would bring in stagecoaches and settlers and give farmers a way to market their goods without crossing the Republican River. With partners G.W. Andrews and William English, Hagaman planned his town on paper. Now, they needed a name.

Already campaigning for county seat votes, the partners approached a Solomon Township resident, "Cap" Snyder. He promised votes, so they let him suggest a name. He had once worked in Concordia, Missouri, and liked that name. Hagaman liked it too.

Next came a petition for a county seat election, set for December 21, 1869. There were three candidates: Clyde, a now extinct town called Sibley, and the "paper" town called Concordia. Although the people of Clyde seemed confident their town would be chosen, no one got a clear majority, so a second election was set for January 4, 1870, and Concordia won. Six months later, the US government helped the new county seat prosper when Congress decided to move the Republican District Land Office to Concordia. It officially opened January 16, 1871, to a crowd of hopeful settlers who had camped overnight. One local legend states that a particular settler was so eager to file his claim before anyone else that he took hold of the door handle at dawn and did not let go until the office opened.

The official beginning of Concordia was March 3, 1871, the date the plat of the townsite was filed in the Cloud County Register of Deeds.

Hagaman had indeed kept Clyde from becoming county seat by starting his own town, Concordia, but that was only the beginning of the story. What followed was a period of frantic building and development.

The first real building was a hotel, actually a family home dragged in from elsewhere, and the first thing built was the land office. A French Canadian who had been living in Illinois showed up with his sawmill, and more French followed. The Concordia to Waterville stage line brought all kinds of people into town and then not one, but four, railroads came through. Soon, former New Englanders, many from Vermont, joined the earlier arrivals in town. Germans, English, Swedes, and others arrived, and Concordia was off to a bustling start. Men interested in starting businesses and getting rich arrived and brought their women, because everyone knew that women helped bring culture to a young town. Churches formed, and their congregations met wherever they could until they could afford to build houses of worship, and opera houses opened to make certain everyone was amused.

Fine hotels opened, along with eateries, banks, saloons, public offices, and stores of nearly every kind. Farmers who had settled the land around town brought in their wares to sell, had their corn and flour ground at local mills, and did their shopping. Doctors, lawyers, and politicians opened for business. Fairs, circuses, and traveling acting companies made the town a regular stop. Newspapers came and immediately went to war—with each other.

Concordia certainly was not just a paper town any more.

One

Concordia Becomes a Town

Concordia before 1900 was a bustling place. With stagecoaches and trains passing through and new stores and service businesses being added all the time, Sixth Street must have been a busy place indeed.

Sixth Street serves as a main street for Concordia but is called Sixth Street because Hagaman named his streets for their position relative to the Republican River, and it is sixth from where the river was before it shifted its channel in the 1903 flood. He named some of the perpendicular streets for presidents (Lincoln and Washington), trees (Willow and Cedar), and even a favorite sister-in-law (Olive). He made the business streets wide because he wanted stagecoaches and the trains he anticipated to be able to unload without inconvenience to regular traffic. It was, after all, his town, and he planned to make it a good one.

Hagaman and a small group of Concordia's early settlers were involved in just about every aspect of the town, and he took it so seriously that he served as mayor. Most of them invested money in lots of different businesses and did what they could to make sure the ones they liked would prosper.

The Indian problems were over, but the citizens of the new town still fought fires, floods, and blizzards together. They banded together into churches and communities, and as Janet Pease Emery said when writing about Concordia, they knew "it takes people to make a town."

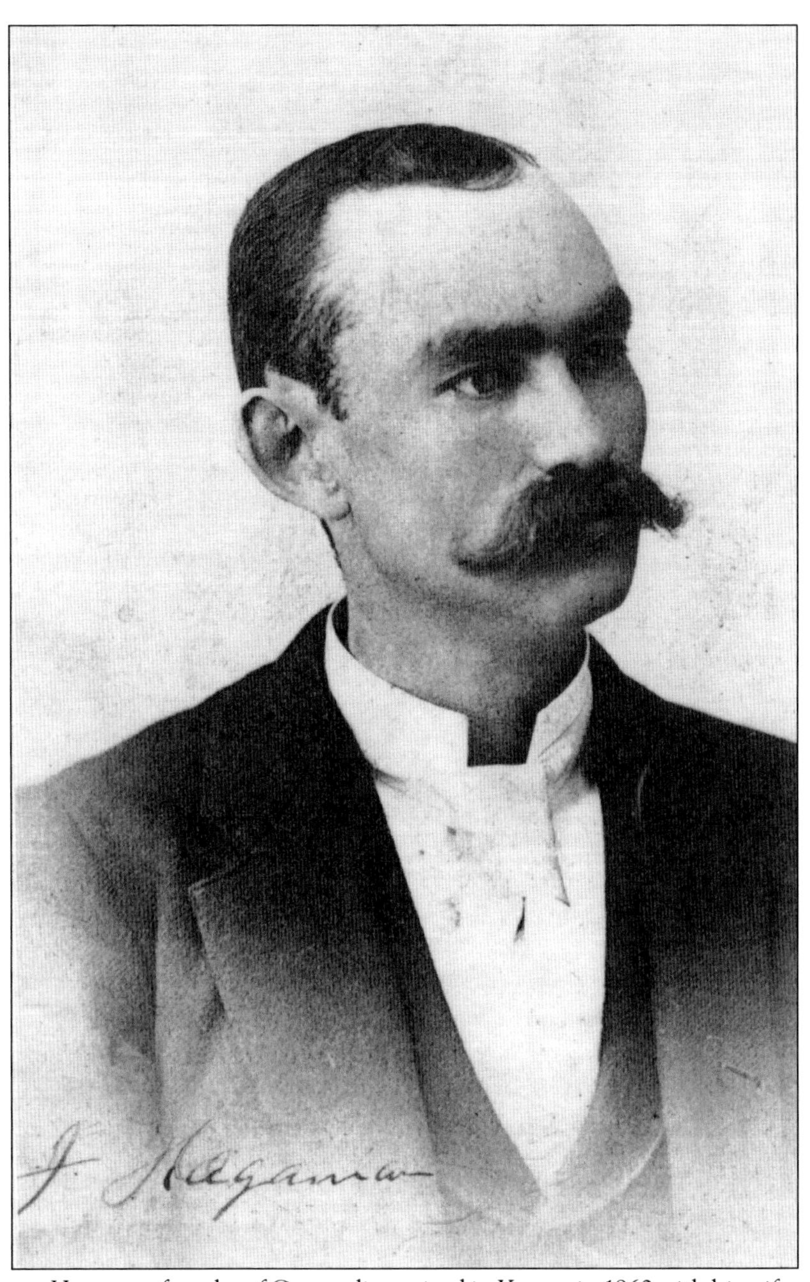

James Manny Hagaman, founder of Concordia, arrived in Kansas in 1860 with his wife and eldest son, James E. Hagaman. They settled on the bank of Elm Creek near J.M. Thorpe and August Fenskie. Hagaman's quarrel with the city fathers of Clyde, temporary county seat of the new Shirley County he had helped to establish, stemmed from a defeat in a legislative race and a failed land deal. What he saw as a bait-and-switch at the last minute for inferior land resulted in his establishment of Concordia south of the Republican River. Hagaman became one of Concordia's most important pioneer citizens and was a land agent, lumber dealer, builder, city councilman, and mayor, and dabbled in other businesses including a newspaper and an early telephone company. In contrast to his active and often temperamental personality, Hagaman lived quietly in his elder years and his grave is unmarked. (Courtesy of Cloud County Historical Society Museum.)

When Rep. John B. Rupe introduced a bill to change Shirley County's name amid rumors that it referred to Jane Shirley, a notorious "woman of ill fame" from Fort Riley, legislators who had served under Col. William F. Cloud, leader of the 2nd Kansas Cavalry in the Civil War, honored him by renaming it Cloud County. Territorial legislator D.L. Chandler actually named Shirley Township in 1854 after a Massachusetts governor. (Courtesy of Cloud County Historical Society Museum)

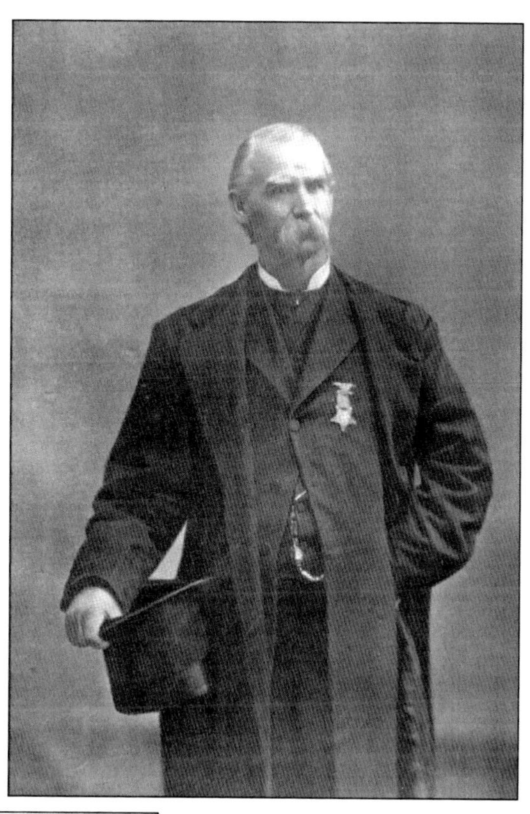

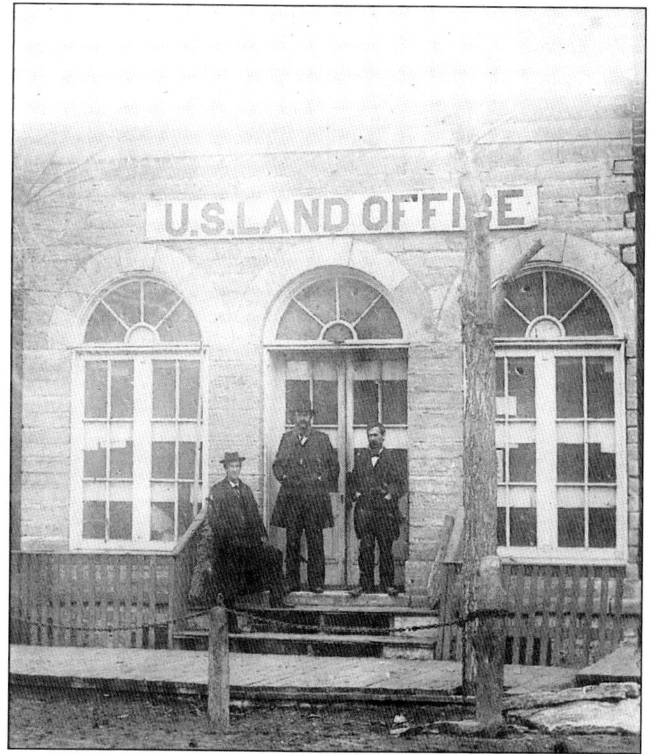

Local photographer H.S. Mulit captured this image of the US Land Office in Concordia in 1881. This stone building replaced the original wooden office in 1873. Although the men are not identified, Evan J. Jenkins was receiver, serving until 1884. He was succeeded by Thomas Wrong in 1884 and A.A. Carnahan in 1886. The office closed after consolidating with the land office in Topeka in 1889. (Courtesy of Sandi Davidson Foster.)

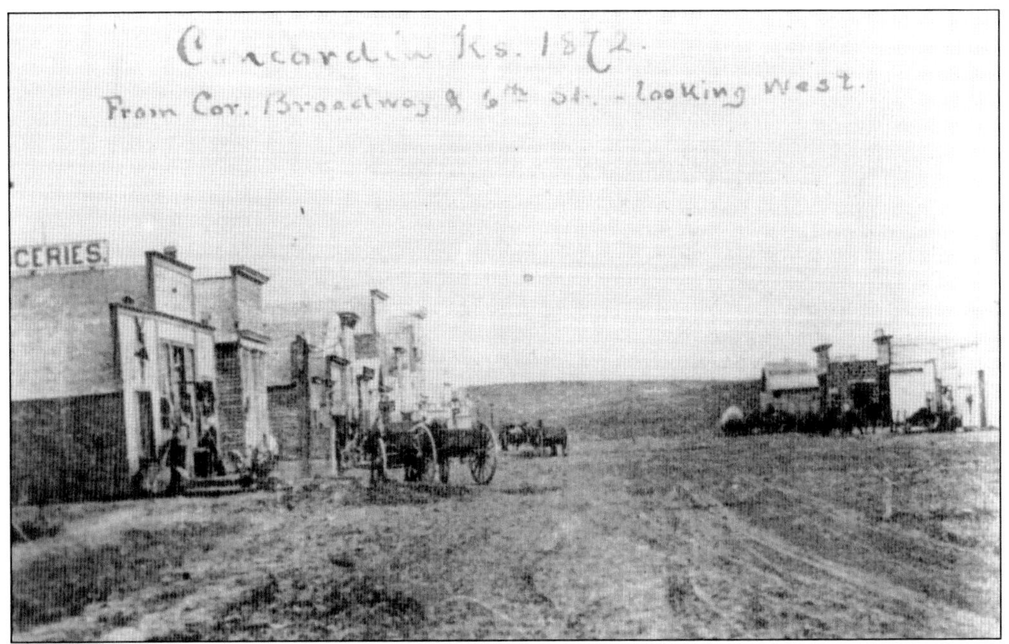

The 1872 photograph of Concordia above was taken from the corner of Broadway and Sixth Street, looking west. Albert T. Reid, son of a stagecoach line owner, was the third white child born in Concordia. He became a noted artist who served as president of the National Artists Professional League, president and lifetime honorary member of the Artist's Guild, and 1949 recipient of the Gold Medal of Honor, the country's highest art award. Below, Reid's painting, *Concordia Main Street in 1872* was based on boyhood memories and a photograph. This painting depicts the Waterville-Concordia stage. The 8-by-5.5-foot painting was purchased by the Concordia Branch of the American Association of University Women and now hangs in the Cloud County Historical Society Museum. (Both courtesy of Lori Halfhide.)

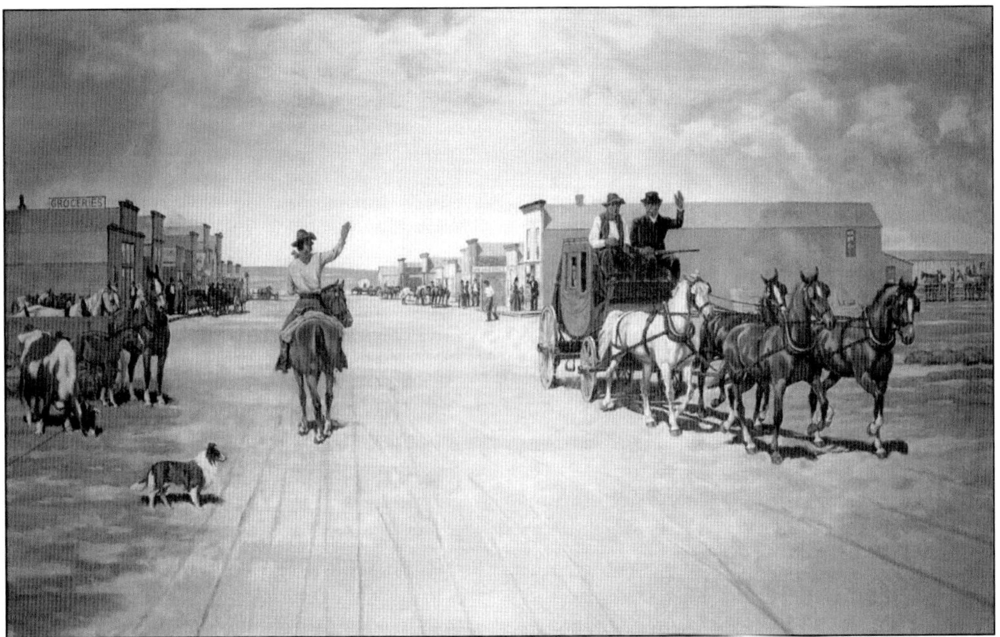

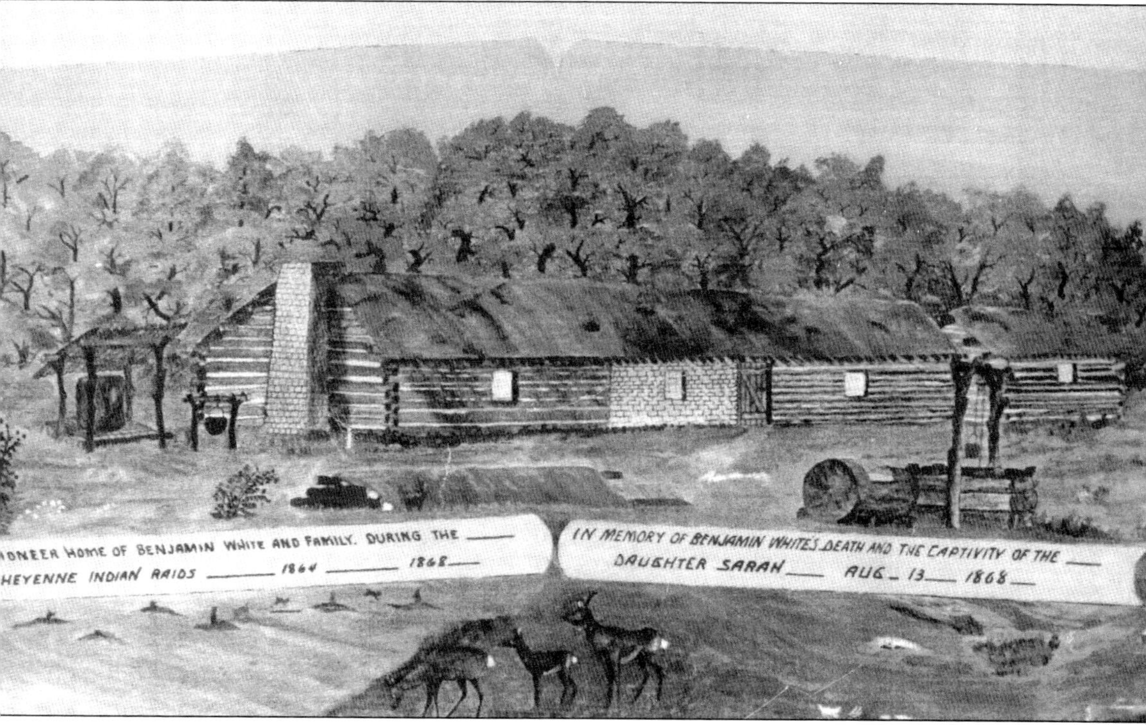

Despite a history of Indian troubles before Concordia existed, Sarah White was the only white woman ever kidnapped by Indians in Cloud County. Sarah's father, Benjamin White, established claims for himself and his eldest son in 1866 on Granny Creek, now called White's Creek. Indians had visited White before the incident and had stolen horses, begged for food, and tried to trade for Sarah. In August 1868, Benjamin was collecting hay with his sons when Indians, probably Cheyenne dog soldiers, surprised and killed him. His son Martin was wounded, but his other two boys escaped unhurt with help from nearby settlers. Indians broke into the house and took Sarah, but her mother, Mary, and the three youngest children escaped. Sarah was captive for seven months before Gen. George A. Custer in Texas rescued her and Anna Morgan in March 1869. Sarah became a teacher, married Erastus Otis Brooks, had six children, and died at age 89 in 1939. This drawing by Martin White shows the White homestead. (Courtesy of Cloud County Historical Society Museum.)

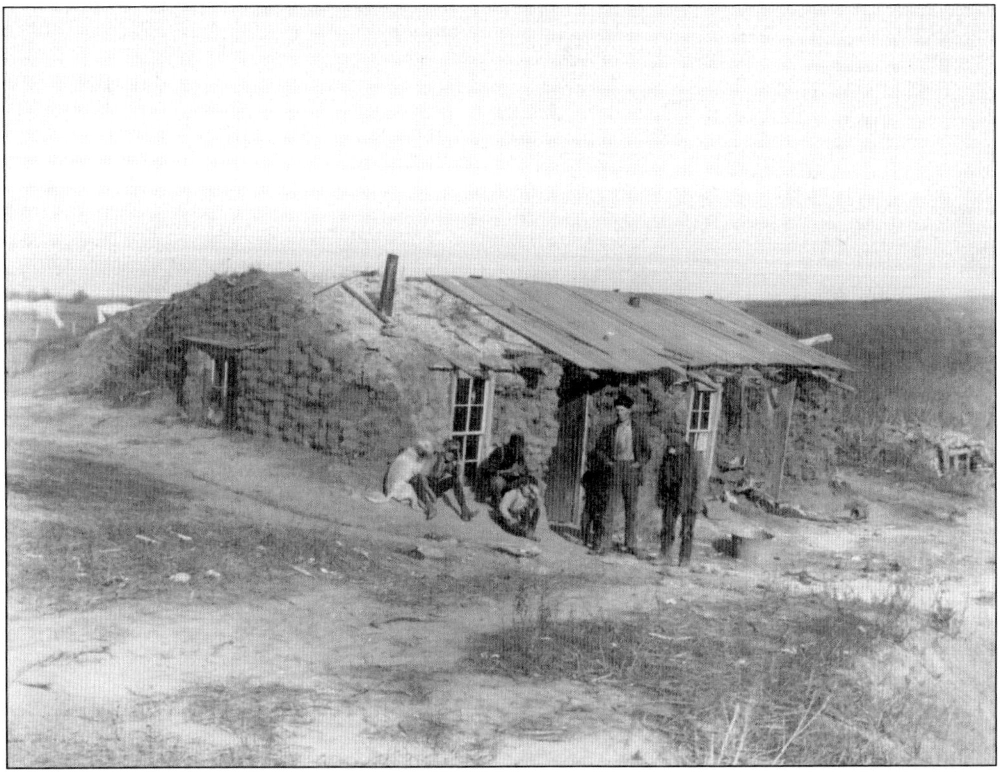

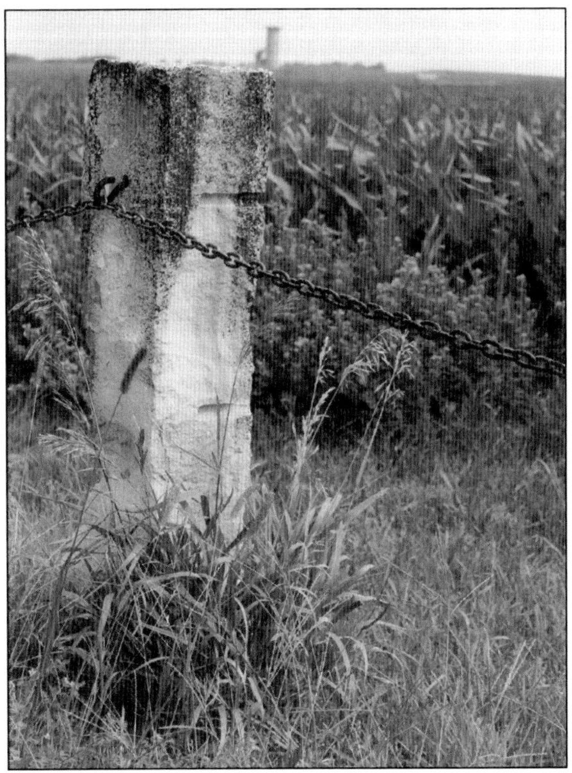

Dugouts, also called soddies, had roofs of earth and sod. Averaging 10 to 15 square feet, these temporary homes were built into a hillside or ridge. Wooden poles, logs, or rocks braced the walls. A wooden ridgepole supported the roof. The front wall, made of available materials, had the only door and windows. Inside, dirt floors were leveled and swept until they became hard and clean. This house belonged to Bill Smith. Nearly everything required adaptation. The shortage of lumber and abundance of rock in North Central Kansas led to the invention of the postrock, a stone fencepost. To split the rock, settlers drilled holes in it, poured in water, and let it freeze. Most surviving postrocks have been recycled into address markers or yard ornaments. (Above, courtesy of Cloud County Historical Society Museum; left, photograph by Dena Bisnette.)

Charles Avery photographed Aletha Smith Avery in 1907 at the old Dutton well. The Duttons, early homesteaders in Cloud County, lived near Granny Creek when Sarah White was kidnapped by Indians in 1868. Most versions of the story list one of the Dutton families among others who helped her mother and siblings to safety and rode with the search party. (Courtesy of Cloud County Historical Society Museum.)

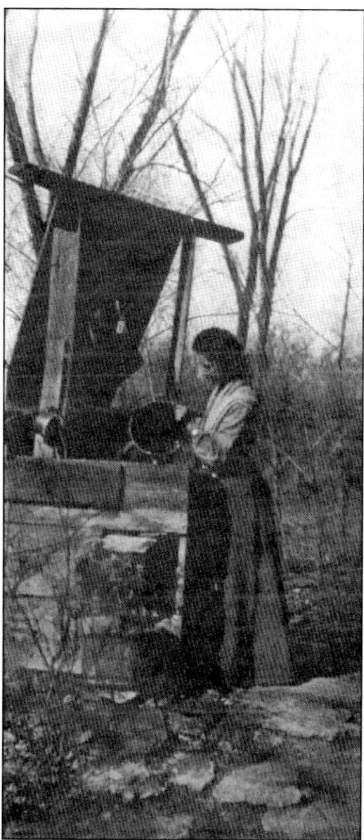

Sorgatz Pharmacy and Bookstore started as Sorgatz and Gilmer in 1873. F.F. Sorgatz added books to his merchandise about 10 years later, after his partner left. In a 1914 directory, the store's address was listed as West Sixth Street. (Courtesy of Cloud County Historical Society Museum.

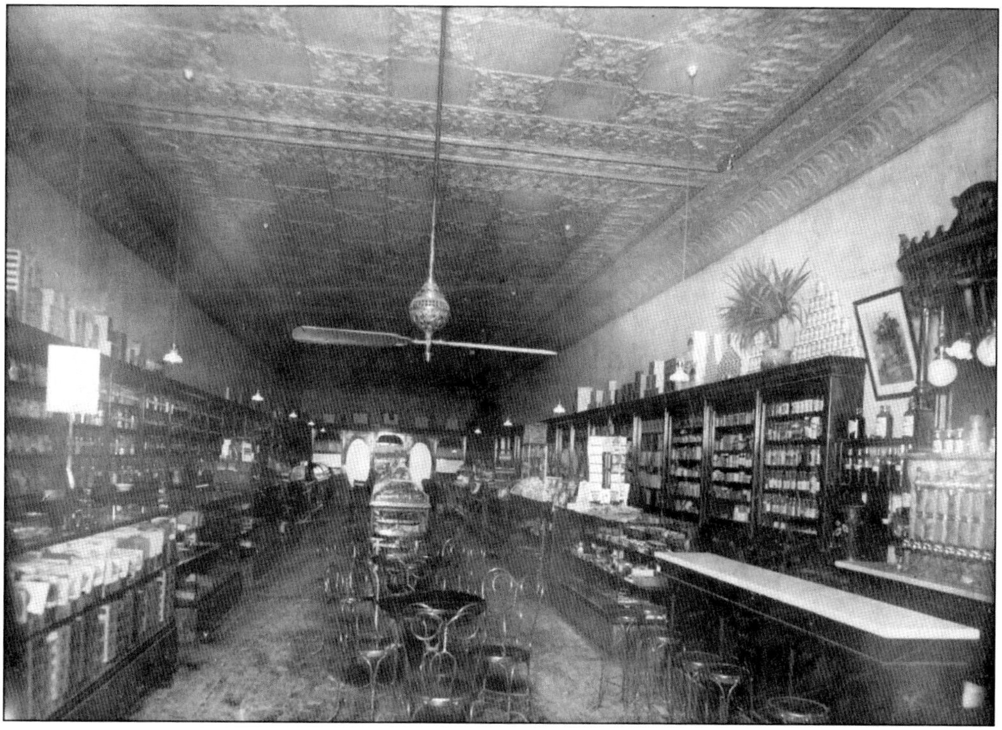

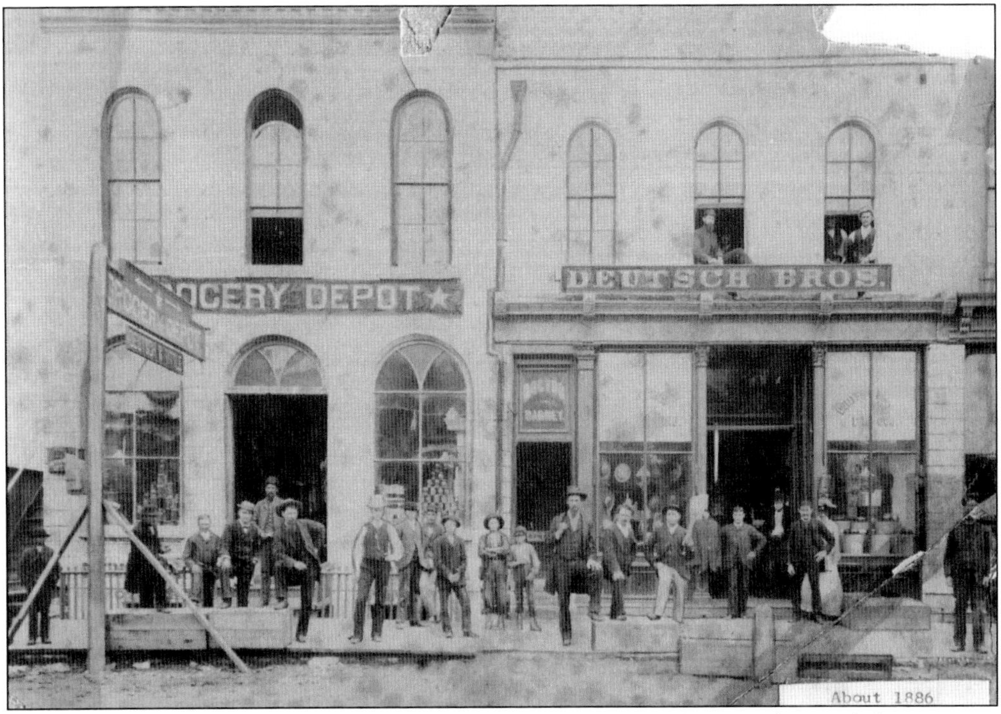

This is one of Concordia's early businesses, Deutsch Brothers, a general mercantile, in 1886, the year electric lights became available in town. Grocery Depot appears to be in a separate but adjoining building, a common style of the times. Concordia had board sidewalks by then, but paved streets were still in the town's future. (Courtesy of Cloud County Historical Society Museum.)

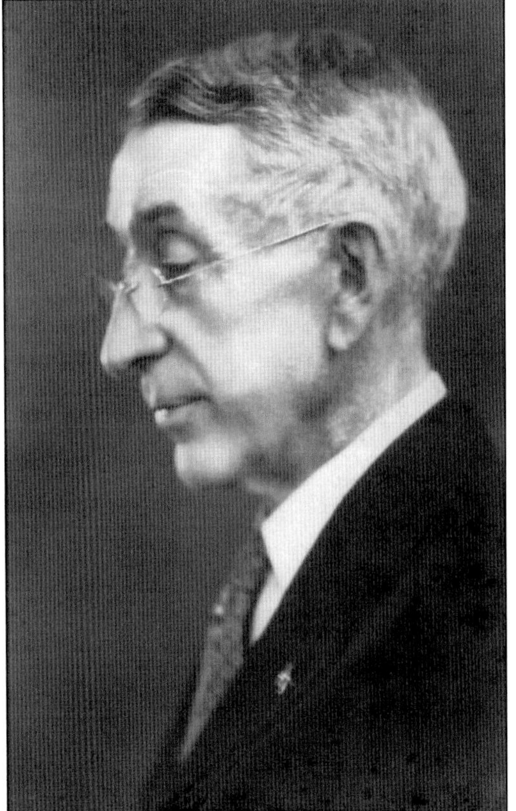

C.A. Betournay moved to Concordia from Kankakee, Illinois, following other French Canadians. Janet Pease Emery, in her book, *It Takes People to Make a Town*, called him a "factotum" who was involved in every aspect of the town. Betournay opened a grocery, creamery, and two icehouses, gave up the store to build a cold storage plant, and then invested in other businesses. (Courtesy Cloud County Historical Society Museum.)

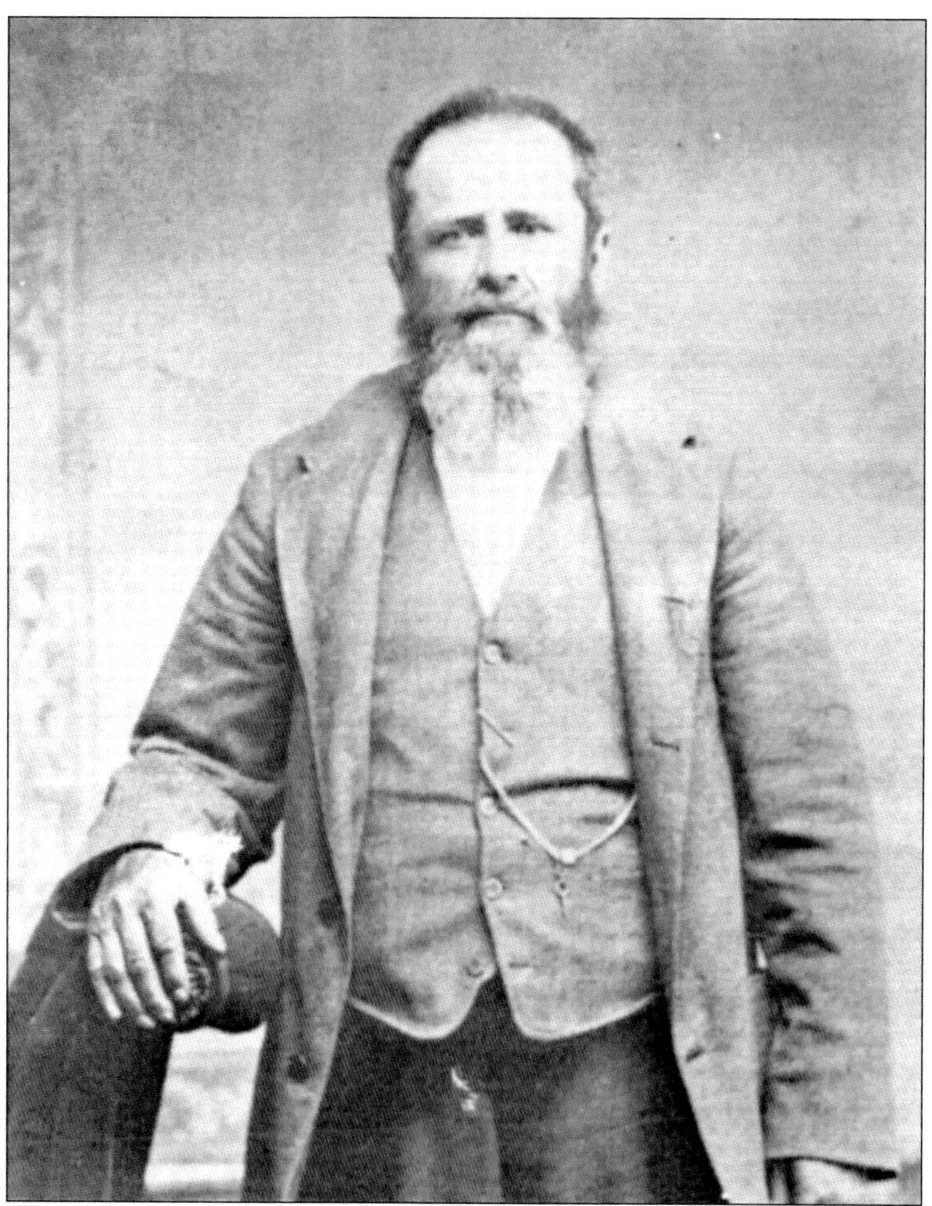

Hilaire Lanoue, one of the first French Canadians in Concordia, opened his sawmill beside the Republican River and soon became involved in Concordia's civic affairs. He started his first gristmill in 1871 and produced the first flour made in Concordia. Steam was expensive, so he decided to generate power from the Republican River. An ordinary spring flood destroyed his first dam and mill in 30 minutes. He rebuilt and was flooded out twice more. The fourth time, financially empty, he found partners, but the river destroyed what he had built the day it was completed. Lanoue moved, opening a general store in St. Joseph. His partners rebuilt the mill a fifth time, also generating power to run dynamos for H.M. Spaulding's electric company, which produced electricity from sundown to midnight on weekdays, but not Sundays. Power failures were referred to as "another fish caught in the wheel." None of it lasted. In 1903, the Republican River flooded again and changed course, leaving both without power. The entire operation had to be rebuilt and converted to steam. (Courtesy of Cloud County Historical Society Museum.)

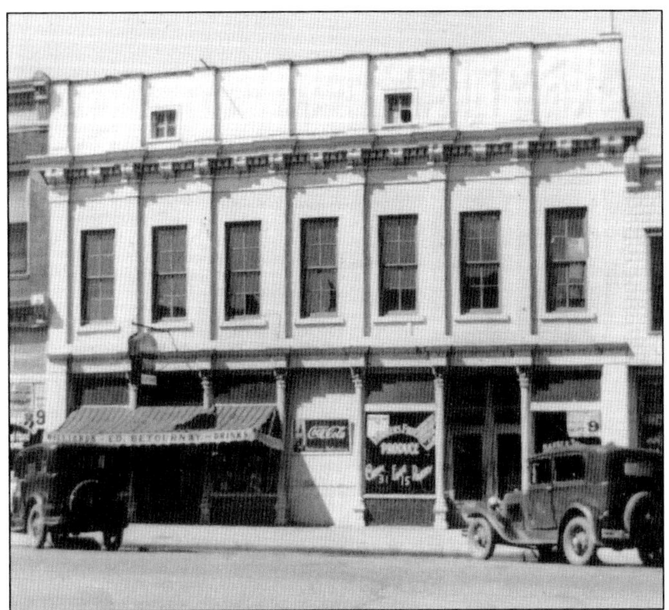

LaRocque's Opera House, founded by Joseph and Fred LaRocque in 1878, occupied the second and third floors at 105 East Sixth Street and featured benches in its balcony and moveable seats on its main floor to accommodate dances when no shows were scheduled. It doubled as a meeting hall and hosted some of the first Catholic Masses celebrated in Concordia. (Courtesy of Our Lady of Perpetual Help Catholic Church.)

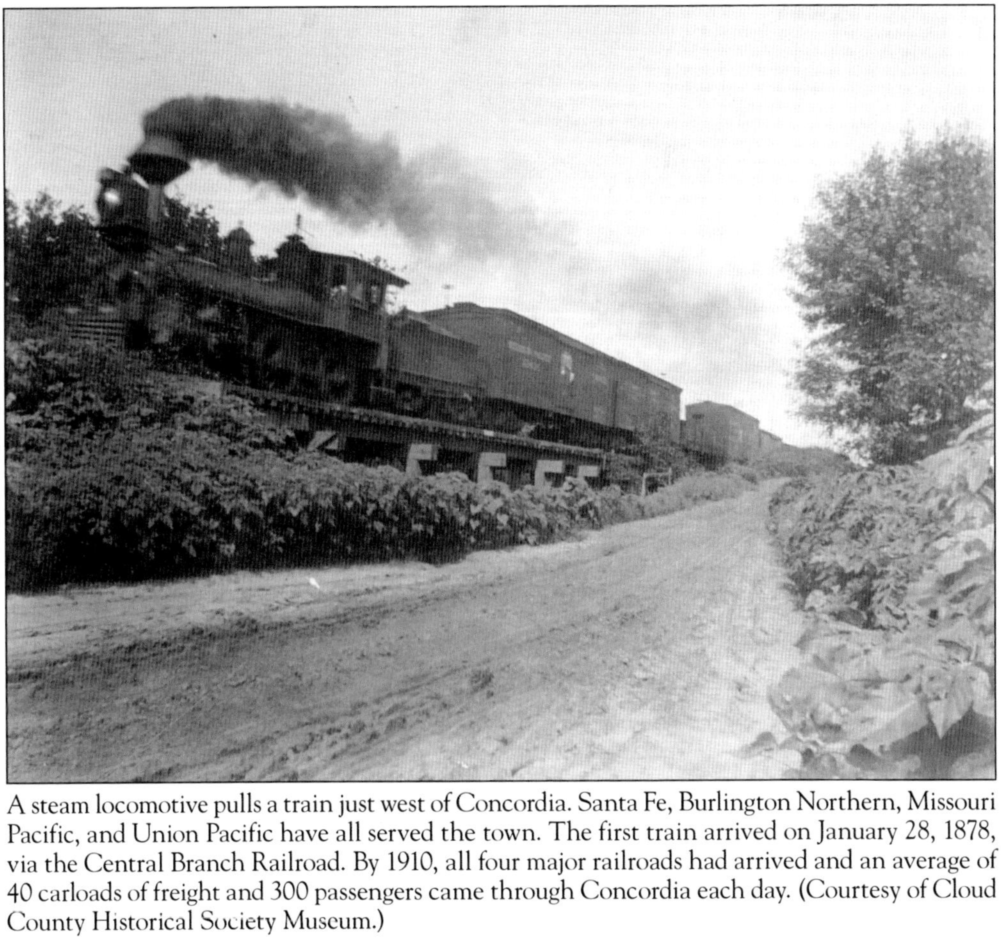

A steam locomotive pulls a train just west of Concordia. Santa Fe, Burlington Northern, Missouri Pacific, and Union Pacific have all served the town. The first train arrived on January 28, 1878, via the Central Branch Railroad. By 1910, all four major railroads had arrived and an average of 40 carloads of freight and 300 passengers came through Concordia each day. (Courtesy of Cloud County Historical Society Museum.)

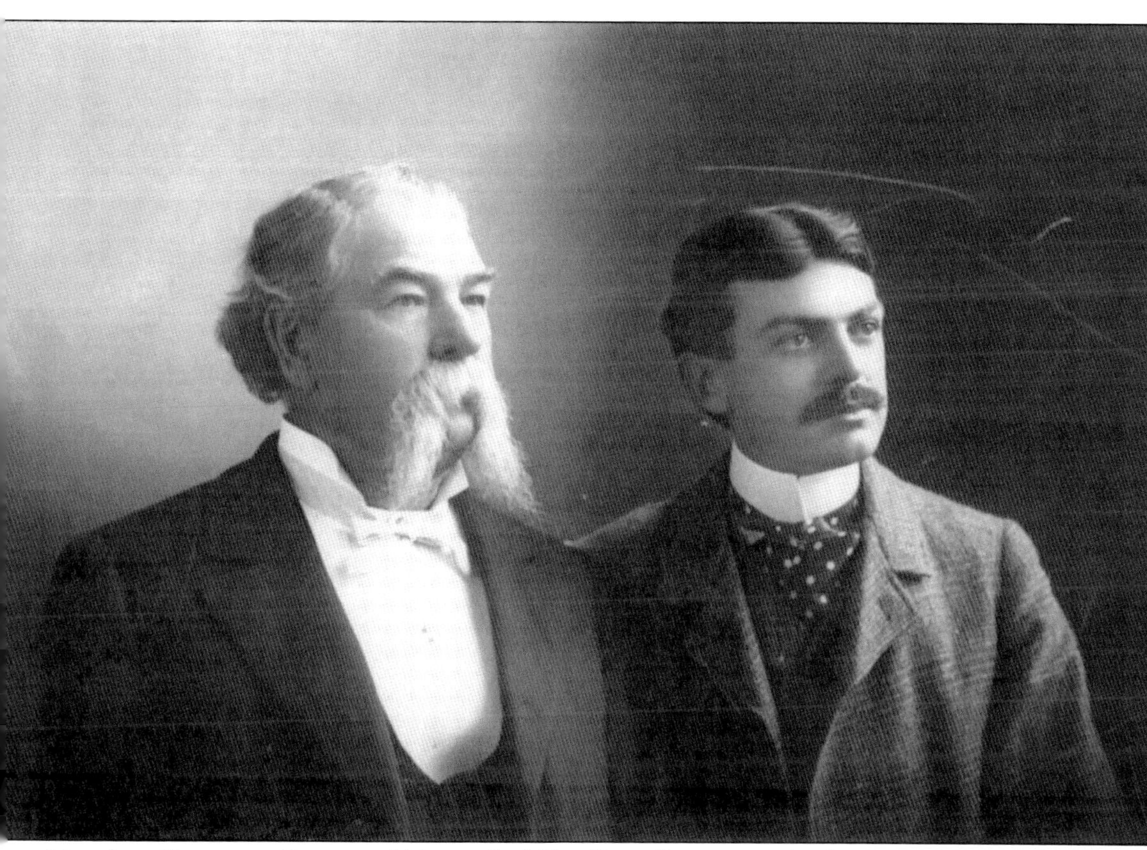

Napoleon Bonaparte Brown and his son Earl Van Dorn Brown were both active in civic and business affairs in Concordia. The elder Brown, a former doctor, lawyer, and landowner, arrived in Concordia from Missouri in 1876 calling himself "Colonel" and carrying a carpetbag full of money. He convinced friends B.F. Poston and John Elliott to follow him. Certain the railroad would soon reach Concordia, he built a stone and brick building at Sixth and Washington Street and opened a privately owned, and therefore unregulated, bank. He gave Elliott a small share for running it and added W.H. Taylor as bookkeeper. Despite his high interest rates, Brown prospered. By 1878, he ran N.B. Brown & Co. and was silent partner in many investments. In 1883, he liquidated his business and retired to his residence, Brownstone Hall. He died in 1910. Earl Van Dorn Brown interrupted college to join the Navy during the Spanish-American War, then attended Kansas Wesleyan University and Harvard before marrying Gertrude Whittredge. He died in 1911 without descendants. (Courtesy of Cloud County Historical Society Museum)

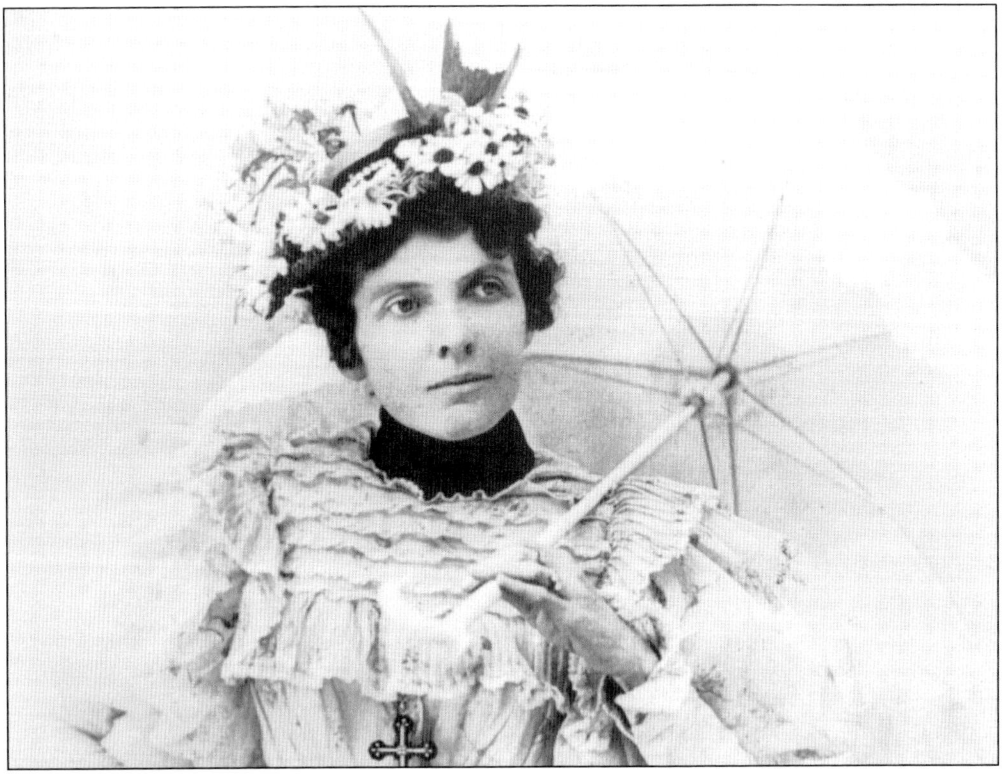

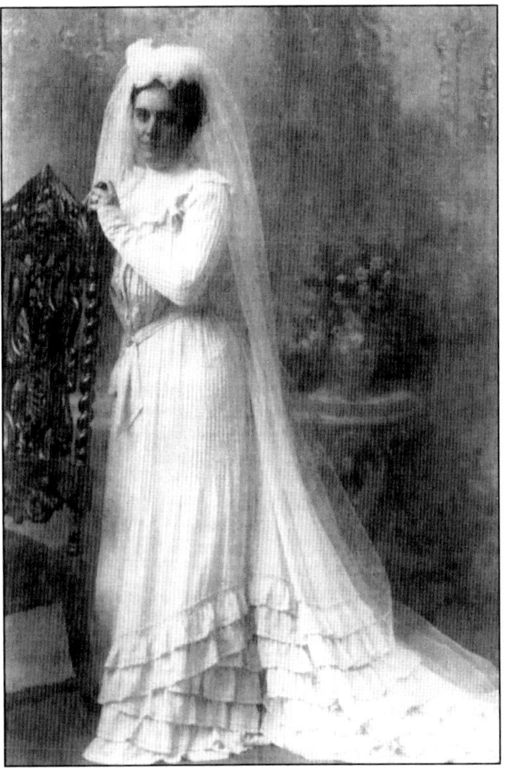

The Brown family included two women important to Concordia's history. Katharine Frances Fitzgibbons Brown, above, the second wife of Colonel Brown, married him in 1870. Brown sent her to boarding school to learn how to be a proper society wife. She soon became the most recognizable woman in Concordia, leading ladies' social activities with Mollie Peck, wife of banker W.M. Peck, and Lucy Sawhill, wife of school-superintendent-turned-editor T.A. Sawhill, who ran the *Empire* newspaper. When Earl Brown wed Gertrude Whittredge (at left) in 1901, Katharine disliked Gertrude but allowed the couple to live in basement rooms in Brownstone Hall. After Earl's death in 1911, Gertrude married Ray Green, editor and half owner of the *Blade* newspaper. She promptly bought him the other half. (Both courtesy of Brown Grand Theatre.)

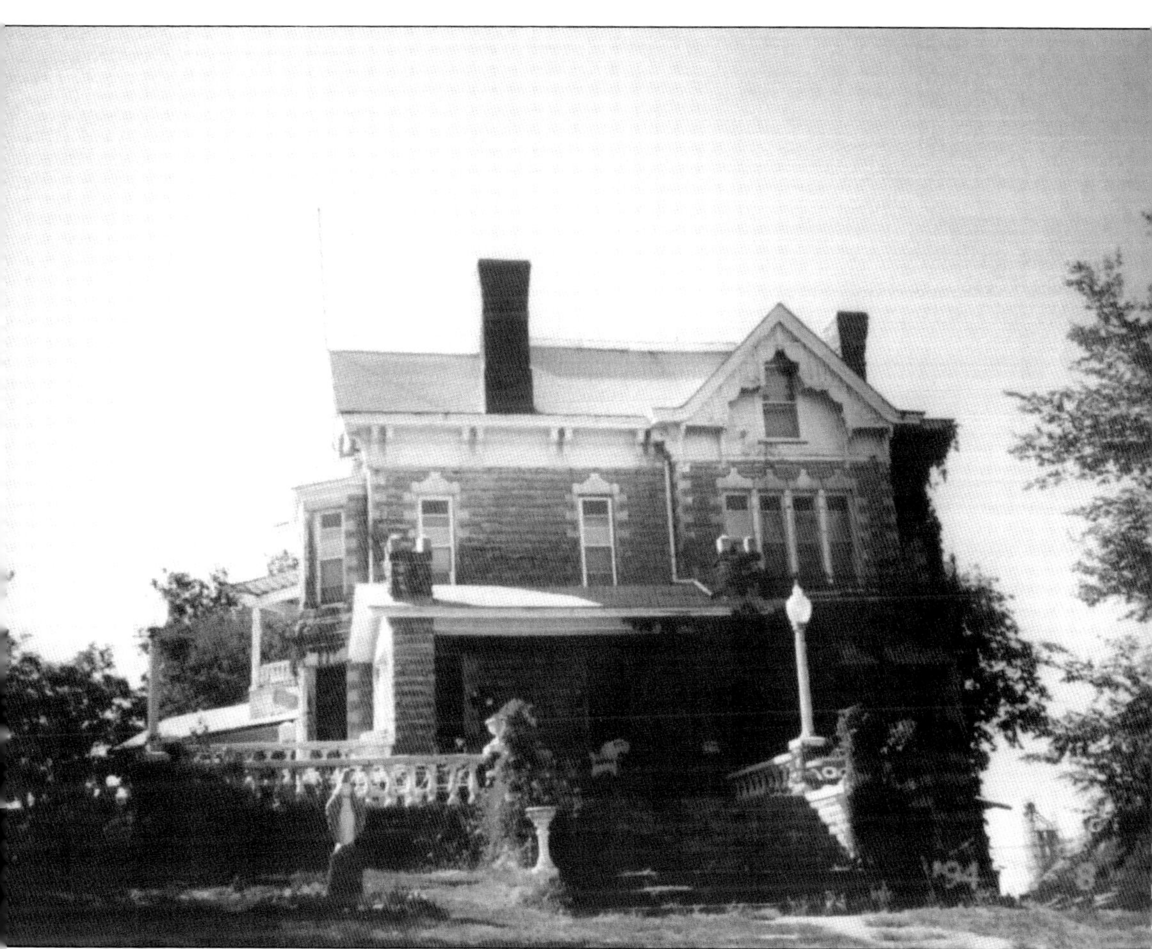

The elegant home called Brownstone Hall sits at the highest point of Sixth Street and remains a private residence today. Colonel Brown had the house built in 1882 by W.T. Short, who later supervised the opera house construction. The house had seven fireplaces, 41 stained-glass windows, Tiffany lights, separate bedrooms for Brown and his wife, Katharine, and the first indoor toilet in town, which local legend says was reserved exclusively for the colonel's use. In Brown's day, a portrait of Napoleon Bonaparte decorated the great room. Much of the house has been restored, and the exterior looks the same as it did when Brown lived there but lacks its original tower. Native stone was incorporated into the construction. (Courtesy of Brown Grand Theatre.)

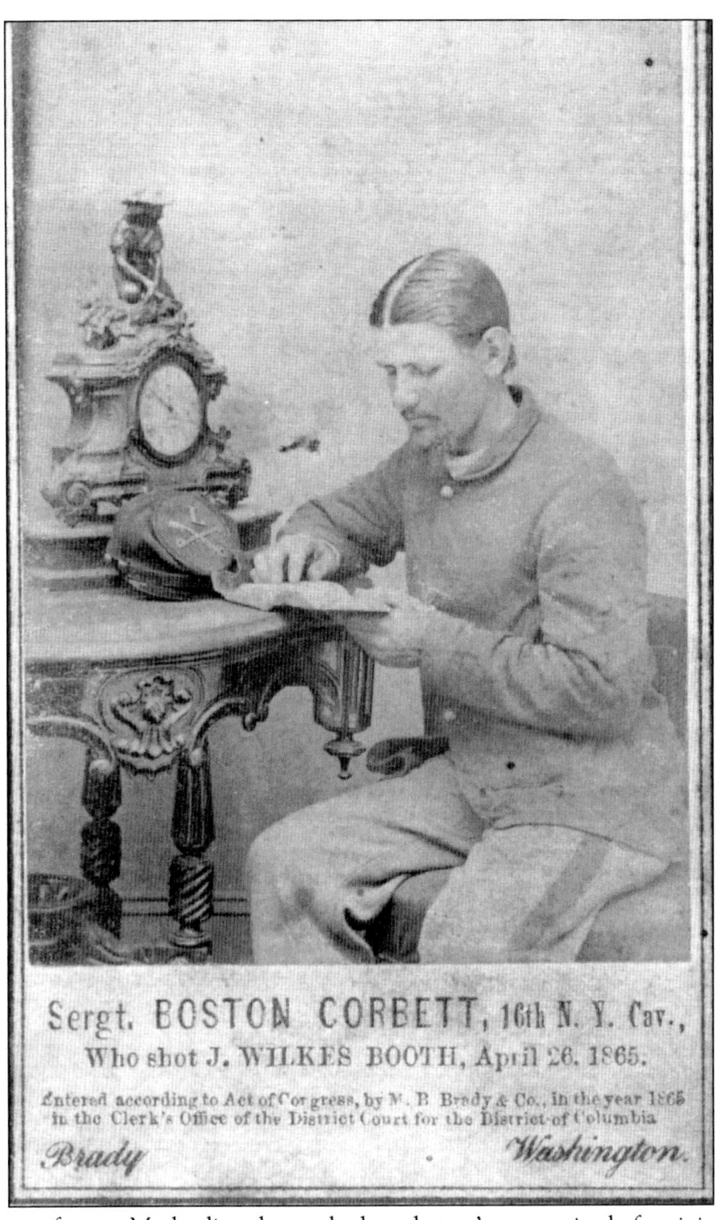

Boston Corbett, a fervent Methodist who worked as a hatter's apprentice before joining the Army and probably suffered from mercury poisoning, became part of history when he shot Lincoln assassin John Wilkes Booth in a Virginia barn. He insisted that "God directed the bullet" but was denied a reward because Booth was supposed to be taken alive. Corbett vanished, then reappeared living in a dugout just outside Concordia in 1878. Rev. Horace Bushnell of Concordia's Presbyterian church and Prof. T.A. Sawhill persuaded him to speak on August 23, 1883, but were publicly embarrassed when Corbett gave a random religious lecture instead of talking about his military service. In November 1885, Corbett was arrested for assault after shooting over the heads of boys playing ball on his property on a Sunday. In court, he drew a pistol and left. Corbett began threatening people while working as a doorkeeper at the state legislature in Topeka. Committed to the state mental asylum, he escaped by stealing a pony in 1888, and disappeared forever. (Courtesy of Cloud County Historical Society Museum.)

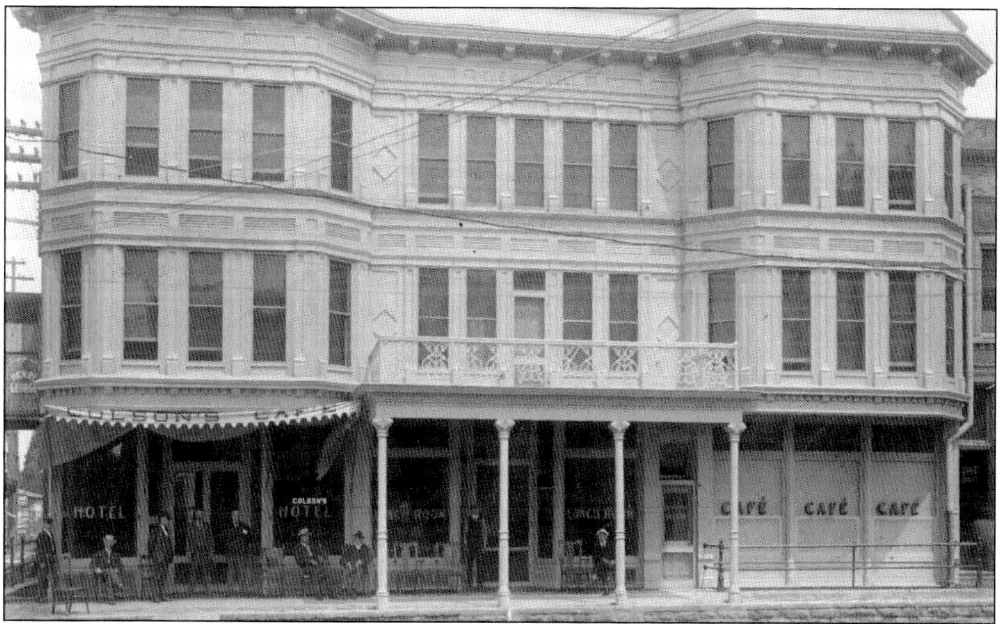

Colson Hotel on Washington Street was torn down in 1926 to make room for the Caldwell Building. The hotel's heyday was in the 1890s, when it was known for its popular host, Al Colson, and the Colson Café, which had fresh seafood shipped in ice to what Eastern newspapers called "the little café in the Kansas desert." Upstairs, upper-class young men of Concordia gambled, and the ballroom presented elegant parties. The Colson hosted 21 traveling men for eight days when trains could not reach Concordia during the 1903 flood and still kept its reputation for good food. The hotel lunch counter served 800 people in one day, not counting those who ate in the dining room, when the Ringling Bros. Circus visited in 1901. Below is the Colson Café. (Both courtesy of Cloud County Historical Society Museum.)

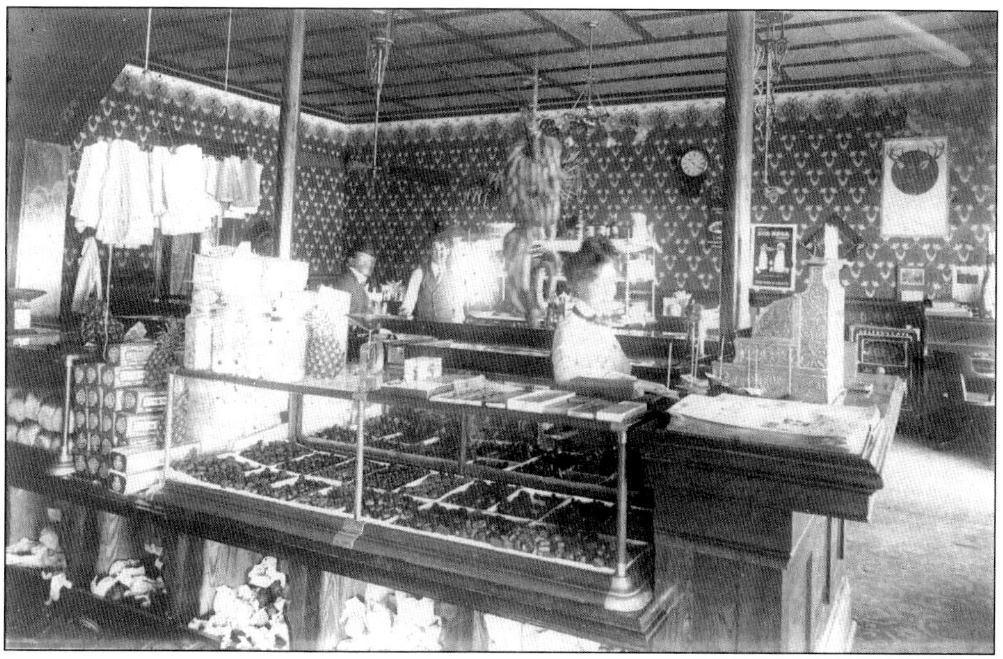

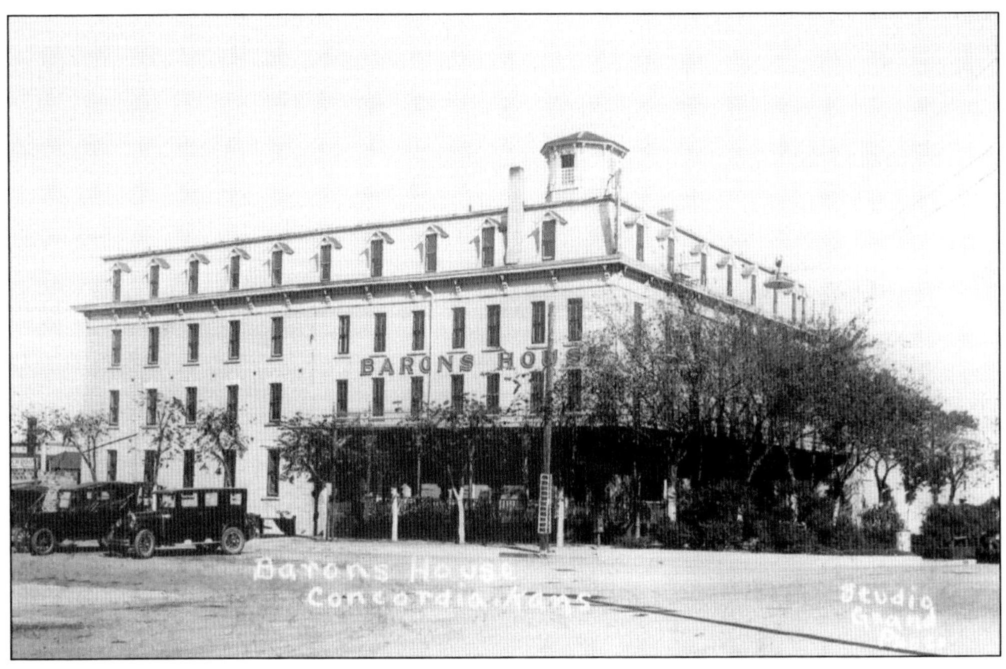

Baron's House, another fine hotel, opened in 1888 at the corner of Fifth and Washington Streets where partners Crill and Zimmerman had a hotel in 1870. Samuel H. Barons, a retired railroad man from New York, rebuilt the hotel with stone, which cost $80,000 and took five years. He added ironwork on porches, hot and cold water, a gas plant, and a livery stable. Barons died in 1901 and his widow sold the hotel to C.H. Martin, who passed it down through his daughter, Marceline Martin Ward, to Norman and Adele Lewis. The couple took over in 1955 and sold it in 1962. New owners sold the furnishings and building in separate auctions. Baron's House was later demolished. Below is a letterhead from the hotel's stationery. (Above, courtesy of Lori Halfhide; below, courtesy of Cloud County Historical Society Museum.)

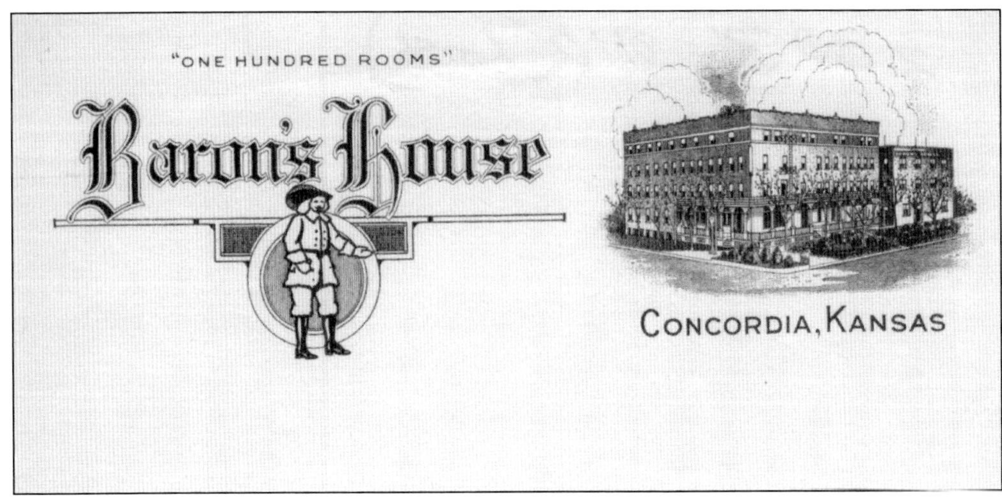

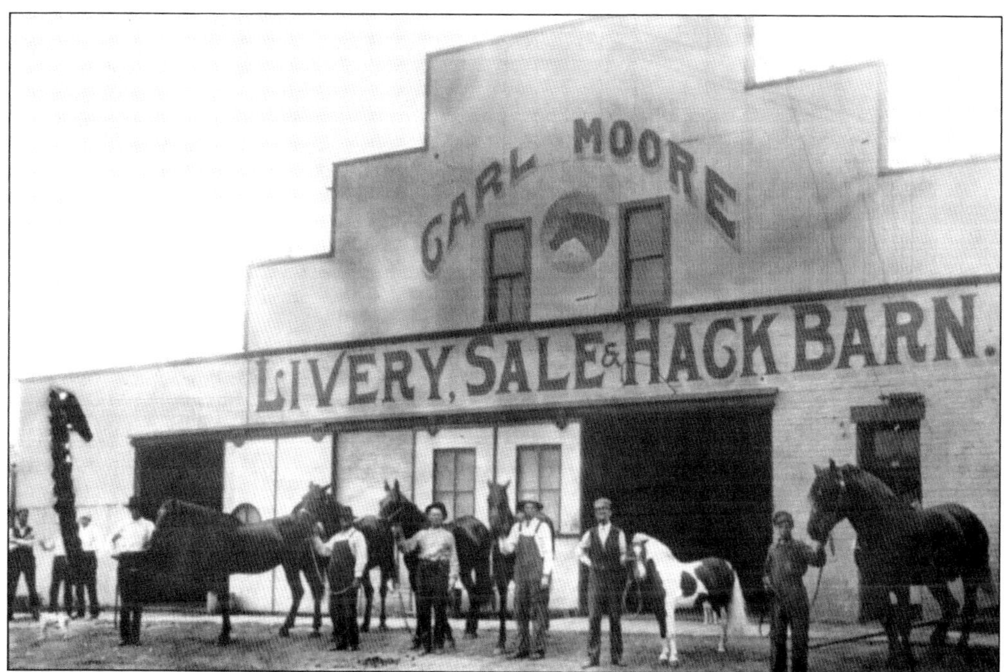

Above, Carl Moore Livery, Sale & Hack Barn stood near Fifth Street and Broadway. A customer could board a horse, rent a saddle horse or a horse and hack (a type of wagon), or purchase a horse. Below, Moore and Poole Auto and Livery, shown about 1908, served as a livery barn for Baron's Hotel. By 1914, horses could no longer be tied on Sixth Street. The last downtown hitching lot, on Fifth Street, closed in 1929, leaving no place to tie up horses in Concordia. With changing times, many livery stables and blacksmithing shops across the country became garages and automobile repair shops, although a few of the blacksmiths continued in the business of shoeing horses. (Both courtesy of Cloud County Historical Museum.)

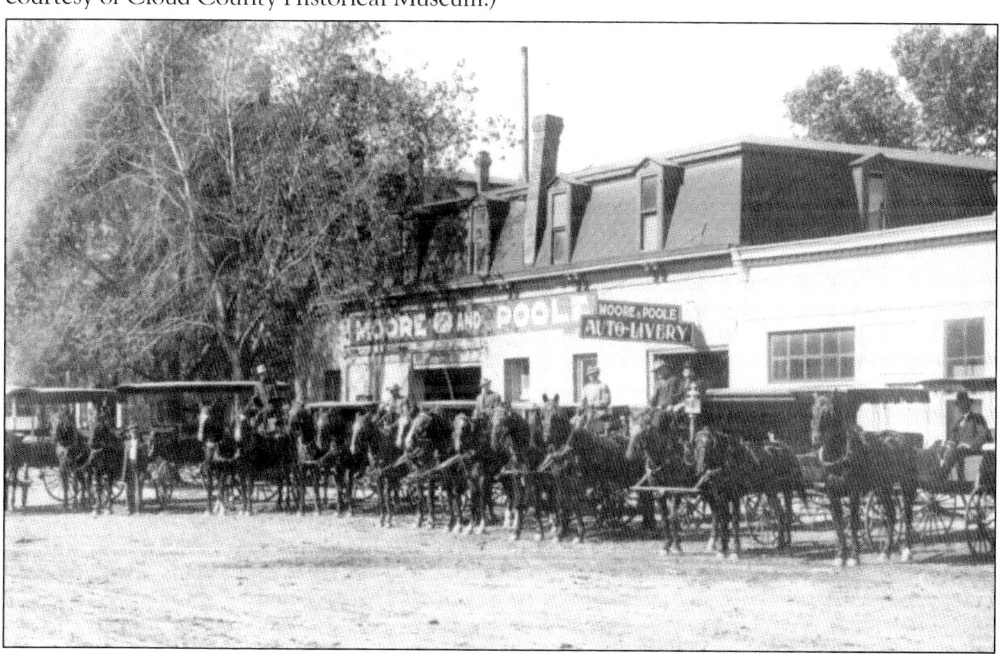

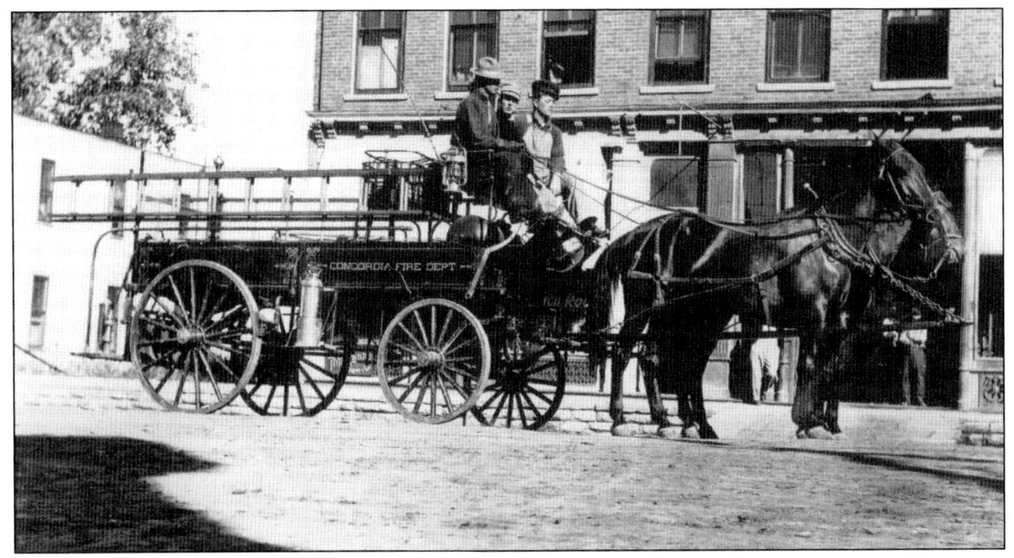

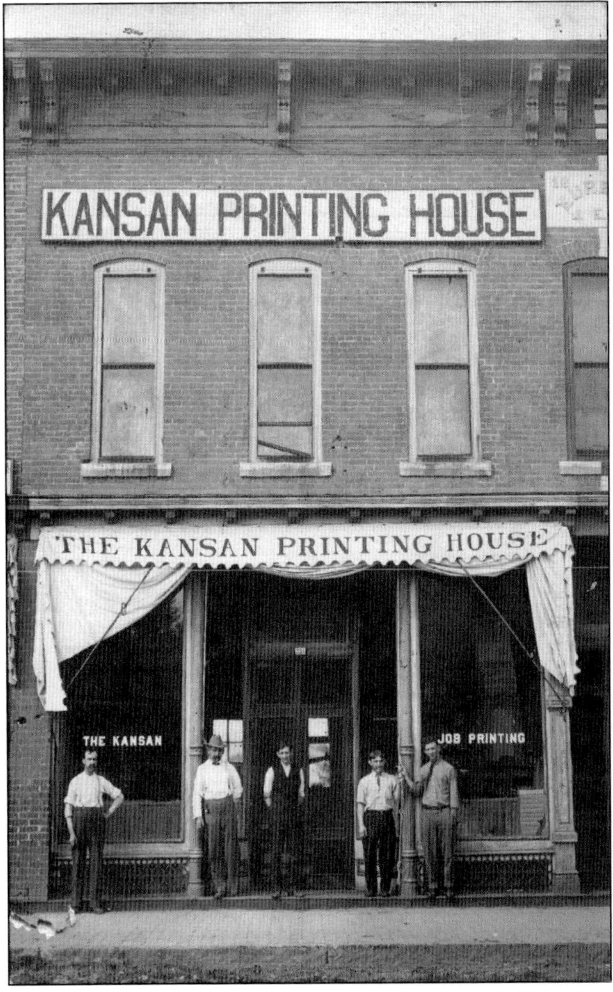

Concordia was protected by a volunteer bucket brigade until establishing its first hook-and-ladder company in February 1876 with 14 members. D.W. Williams was captain. A note on this photograph said Frank R. Ward, father of Vada Ruth Ward Lantz, had a shoe repair business in Concordia at 601 Broadway in 1939. Ward may also have been a member of the fire department. (Courtesy of Cloud County Historical Society Museum.)

The Kansan Printing House was the headquarters of the *Kansan* newspaper and relocated a couple of times downtown, but in this photograph, it was on the ground floor in J.E. Dey's Eureka Building. The paper was established in Jamestown in 1881 and moved to Concordia in 1895, where it lasted until 1988, when its last owner, Dallas Nading, closed it. (Courtesy of Dallas Nading.)

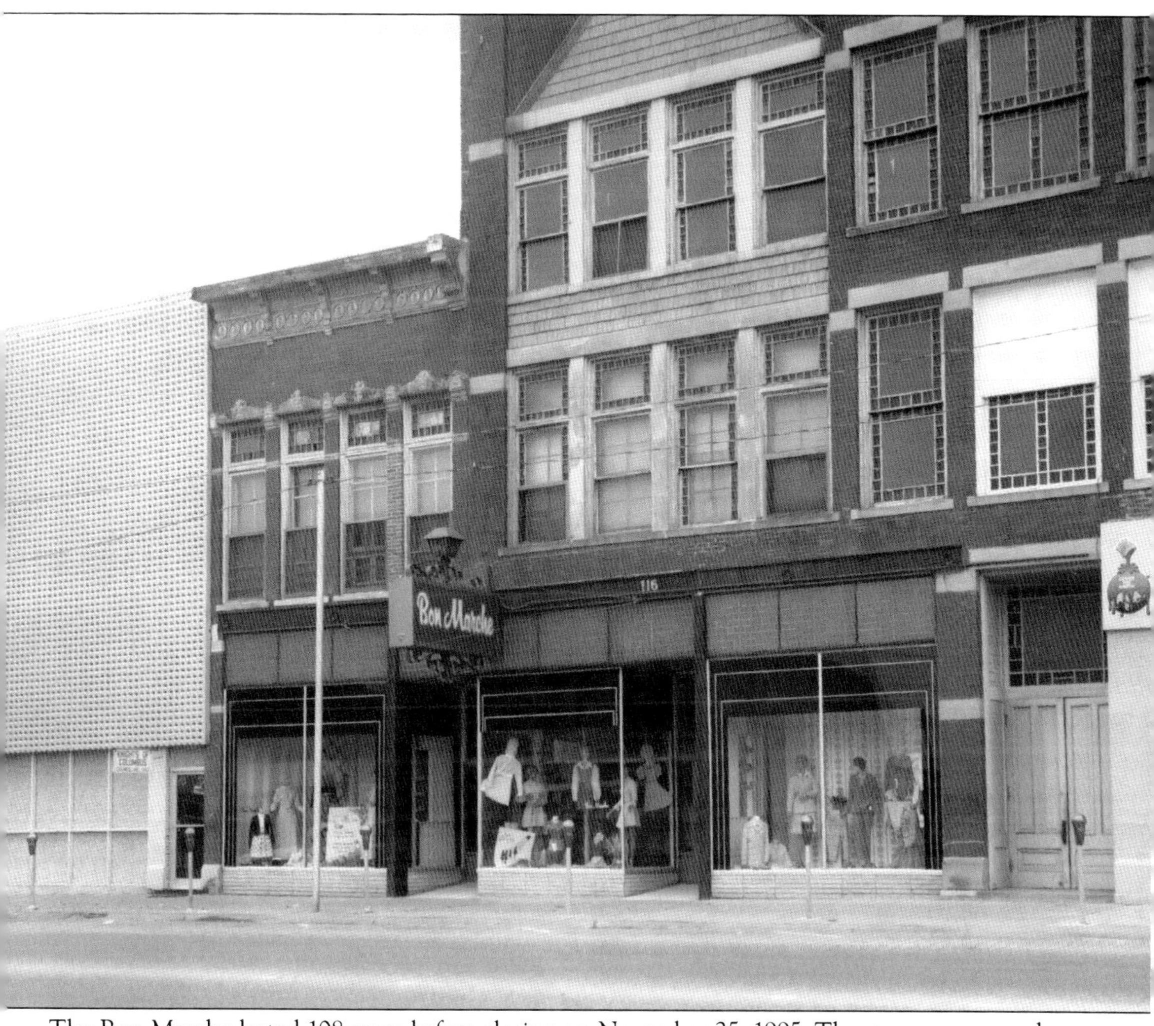

The Bon Marche lasted 108 years before closing on November 25, 1995. The store was opened at 116 East Sixth Street on October 7, 1887, by A.E. and C.E. Lasnier, two French Canadians who came from Kankakee, Illinois, to build it with C.A. Betournay. The three-story building expanded in 1907 when archways were cut through the connecting walls into the former Wiard Building. A.E. Lasnier retired in 1906 due to ill health. C.E. Lasnier later turned it over to his sons, Edmond and Alfred, who was called Pat. They took over in 1937 and ran the store together until 1950, when Edmond retired. Pat Lasnier and his wife, Marguerite, sold it to Robert and Betty Anderson and Richard and Elaine Walters in 1970. During the entire time, a single register that had been purchased around 1906 was used. The last manager was David Walters, who took over in 1991. (Courtesy of Cloud County Historical Society Museum.)

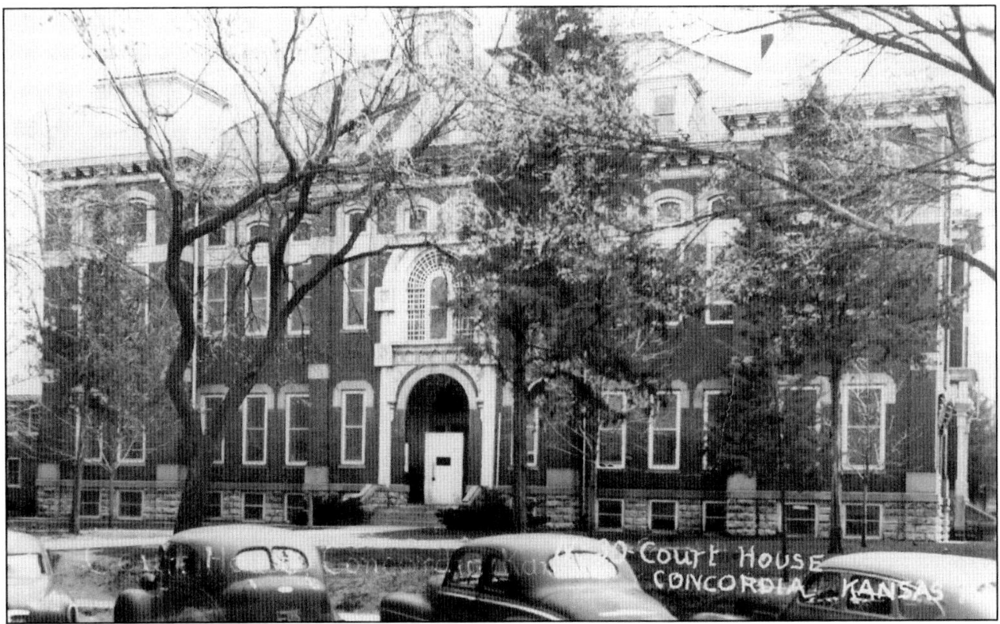

The Cloud County Courthouse, built in 1887 and 1888, cost over $50,000, including cost overruns. Designers were W.H. and Howard C. Parsons, the same architects who designed Nazareth Convent and the Maddox Building at Sixth Street and Broadway. Actual plans were more elaborate, but the courthouse was never finished. The building was demolished in the late 1950s to make room for a new courthouse. (Courtesy of Lori Halfhide.)

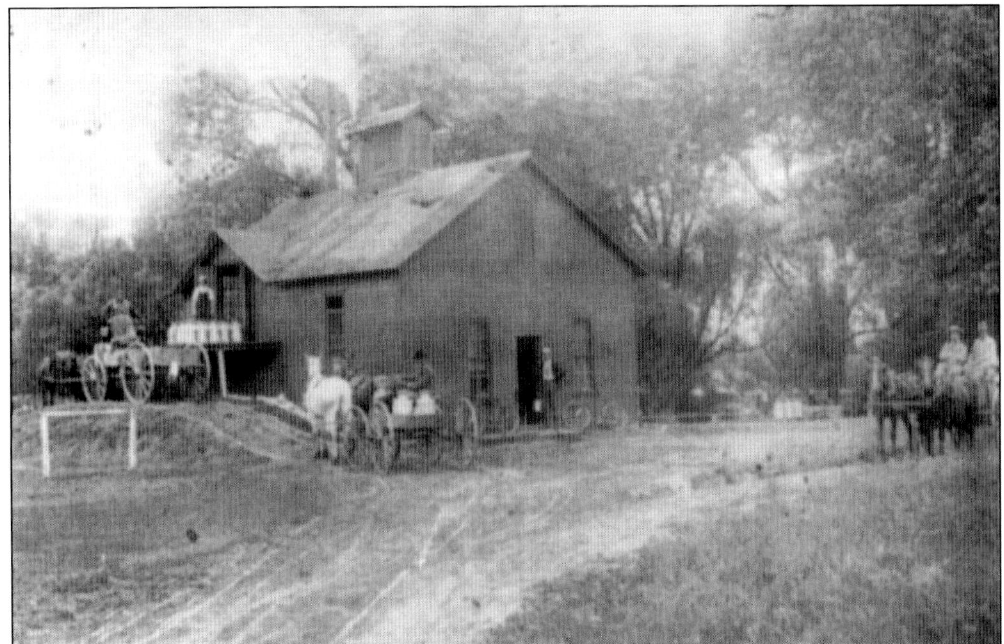

Chris Hanson and his brother Peter owned this creamery in northwest Concordia where the city water department later located one of its pump houses. The photograph was taken around 1897, and only Chris Hanson, standing in the doorway between the two bicycles, is identified. (Courtesy of Cloud County Historical Society Museum.)

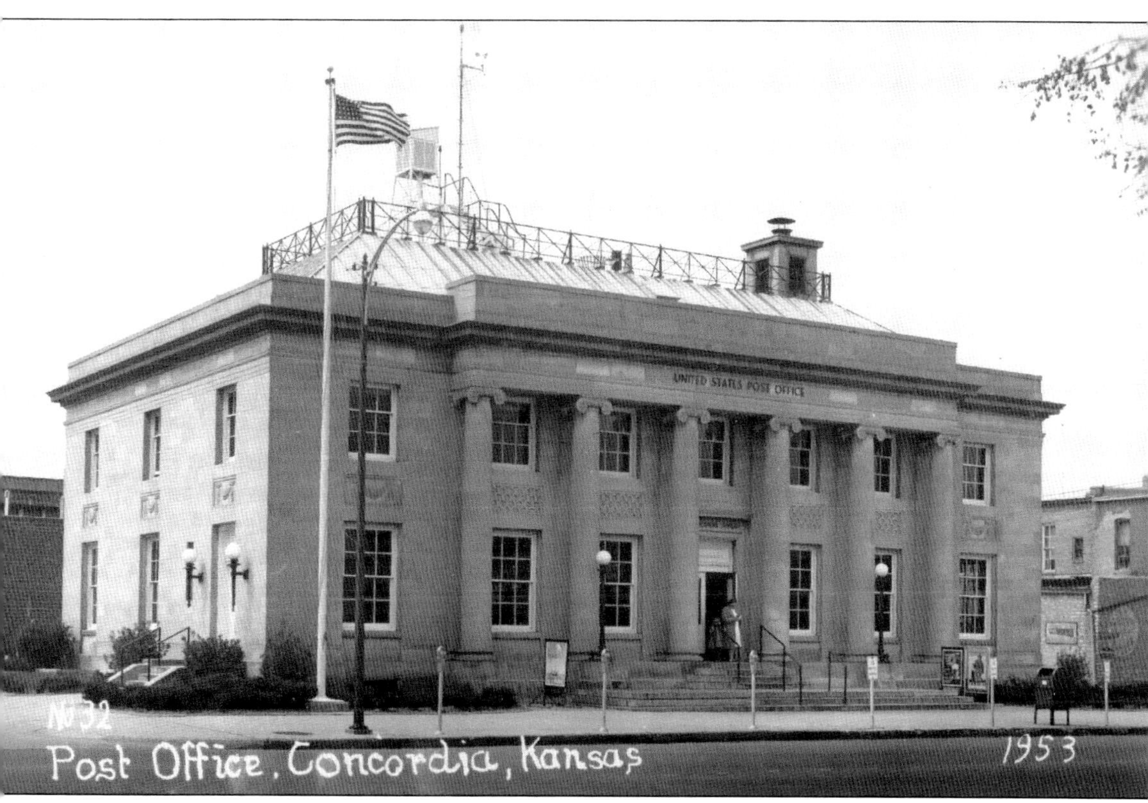

A US Signal Service station, the old name for a weather station, was established on top of the Concordia Post Office in April 1885, with P.J. Cahill in charge. Daily weather reports from all parts of the United States were sent by wire, and the observer hung various flags from the tower on the top of the post office at Washington and Seventh Streets to warn residents of a weather change. When this post office replaced the old one in 1915, a weather station was built on top of it as well. Later, when new technology became available, the weather station was moved to Blosser Airport. This post office is still in use. (Courtesy of Cloud County Historical Society Museum)

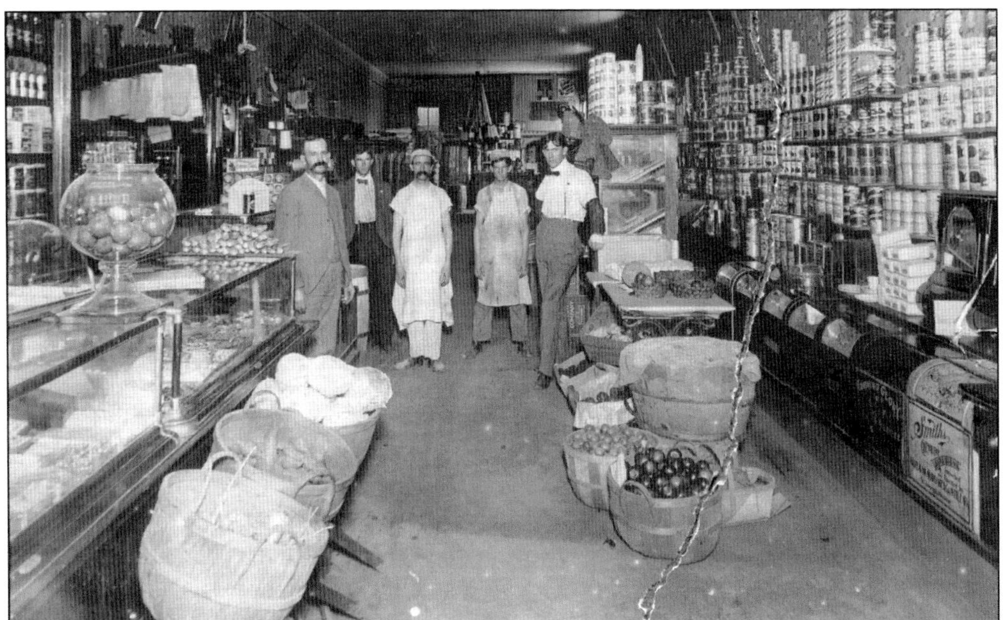

G.C. Wilson Grocery supplied seasonal produce, canned goods, and other products. The five employees pictured here show the range of work involved by the different ways they are dressed. The two men in jackets would take customers' orders, and the ones in aprons did the packing, while the fellow on the right with sleeve guards was most likely an accountant. (Courtesy of Cloud County Historical Society Museum.)

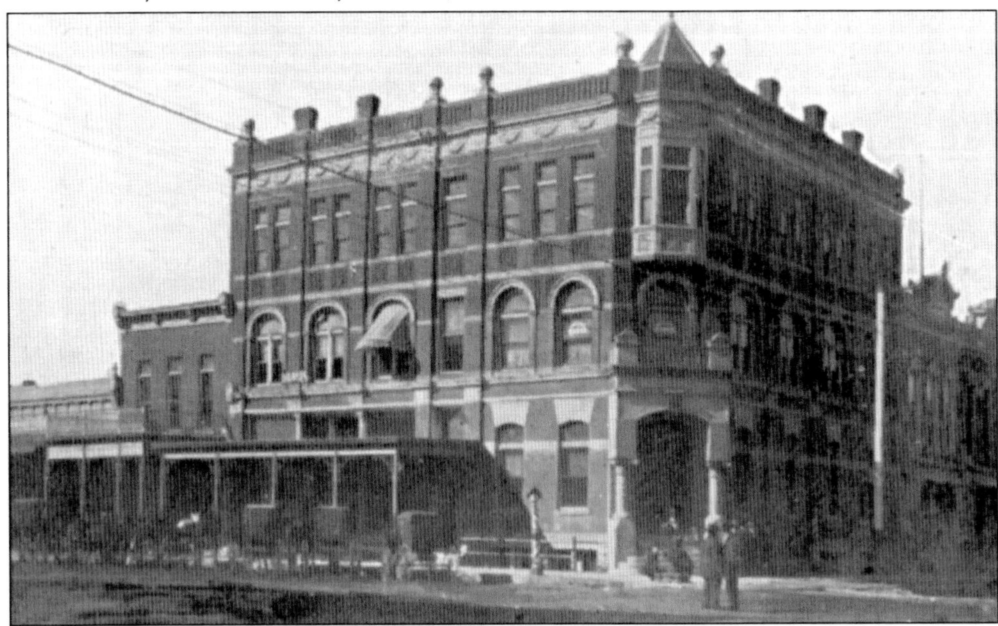

The three-story Caldwell Building was built on the property known as the old Maddox Block at Sixth and Washington Streets for Caldwell Investment Company. (The term "block" used to refer to a business building.) The Caldwell Building was razed in 1962 to make room for a new building for Central Savings and Loan, which moved in after Caldwell Investment Company closed. (Courtesy of Dallas Nading.)

Two

Concordia Enters the 20th Century

The 20th century brought all kinds of changes for the world and Concordia. Old businesses and customs went out of style, with new inventions replacing them.

Ida Wiard brought the first automobile to Concordia in 1905, starting a trend that would eventually end passenger train service. In 1909, a broom factory operated in town, and Dr. Asa Weaver built a hospital. A flood in 1911 involved both the Solomon and Republican Rivers, bringing water into homes and businesses in Concordia and Glasco. World War I took some of the town's men. By 1915, the town had a new fairgrounds, new city hall, and new post office. A country club followed four years later.

The 1920s roared. Movies talked. Prohibition failed in Concordia and everywhere else. The Concordia Travelers baseball team were champions in 1927. Bankers worried through the Great Depression. One bank was robbed. A flood in 1935 washed out the Highway 81 bridge, which, stuck and acting as a dam, compounded the problems Mother Nature had caused. The Republican River flooded again in 1941. Dust storms blew in from Oklahoma. World War II started, and men went again. Folks who stayed behind did their parts.

The Civilian Conservation Corps (CCC) camp and the sight of German troops getting off trains and being loaded onto trucks headed for Camp Concordia became memories. Some things, like shopping at Everitt Hardware or Bon Marche, seemed as if they would last forever. But change, good and bad, happens. In the 1950s, things settled down. In the 1960s, the town got a college. In the 1970s, old landmarks closed, and new businesses opened. In the 1980s, downtown changed forever when fire destroyed a commercial building at Sixth Street and Broadway.

Changes can still be a little hard to see sometimes, and in some moments, walking down Sixth Street, one suddenly expects to see cars with tail fins and whitewall tires, and men wearing hats. Then the illusion of a simpler time is interrupted by the sight of a student in a Cloud County Community College shirt, bringing back the present—another good image.

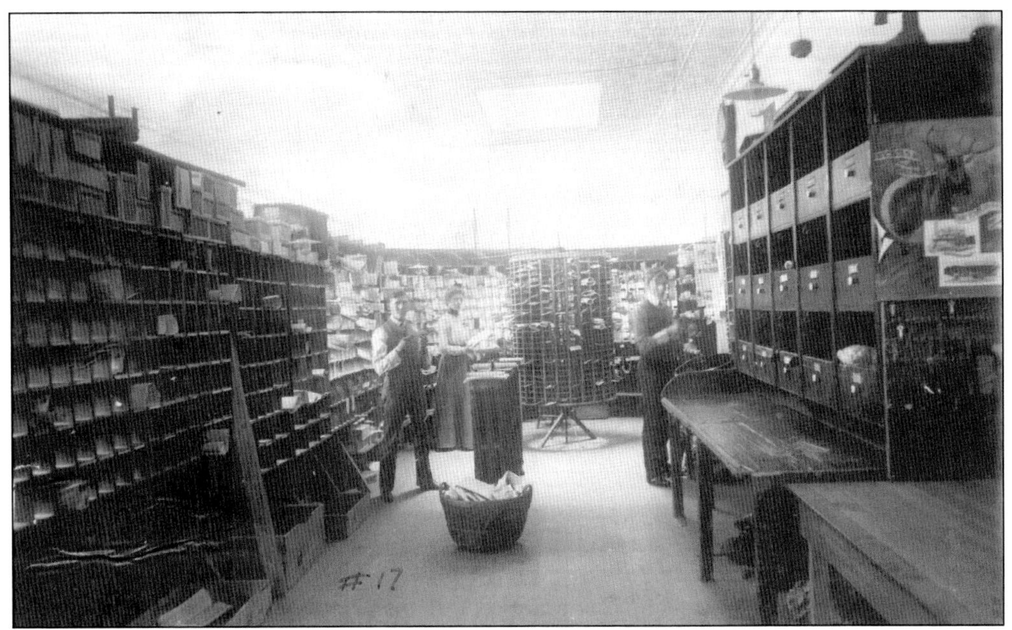

Mail was sorted by hand before the US post office developed automation, and in this photograph, a sorting crew works in the Concordia Post Office around the turn of the century. The employees are unidentified. (Cloud County Historical Society Museum.)

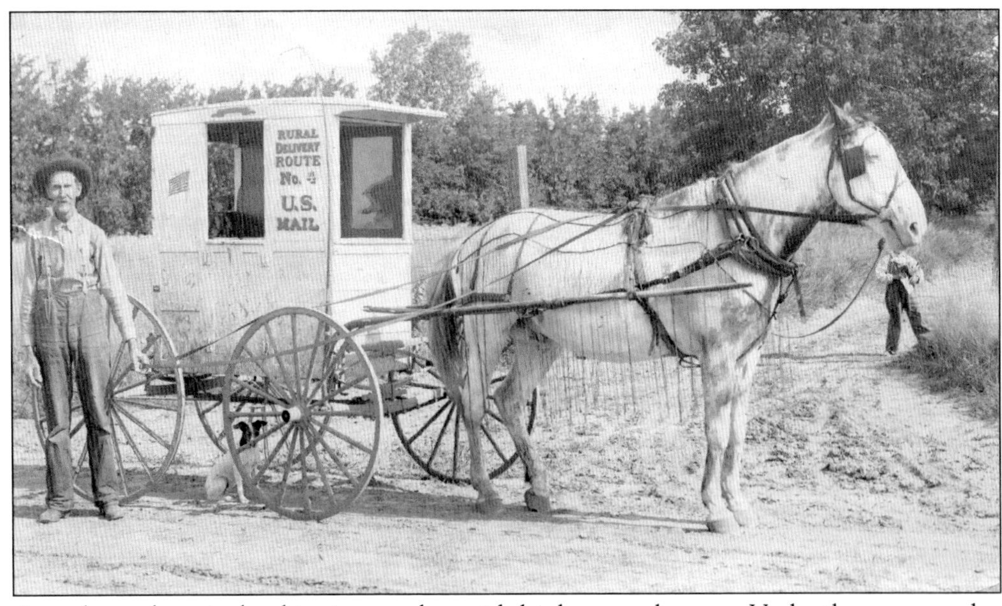

A rural postal carrier has his picture taken with his horse and wagon. Under the wagon, a dog joins the photograph session. This picture may have been taken in summer because the horse wears fly netting. The swinging strings were supposed to shoo flies away. Rural postal delivery out of Concordia began in 1903. (Courtesy of Cloud County Historical Society.)

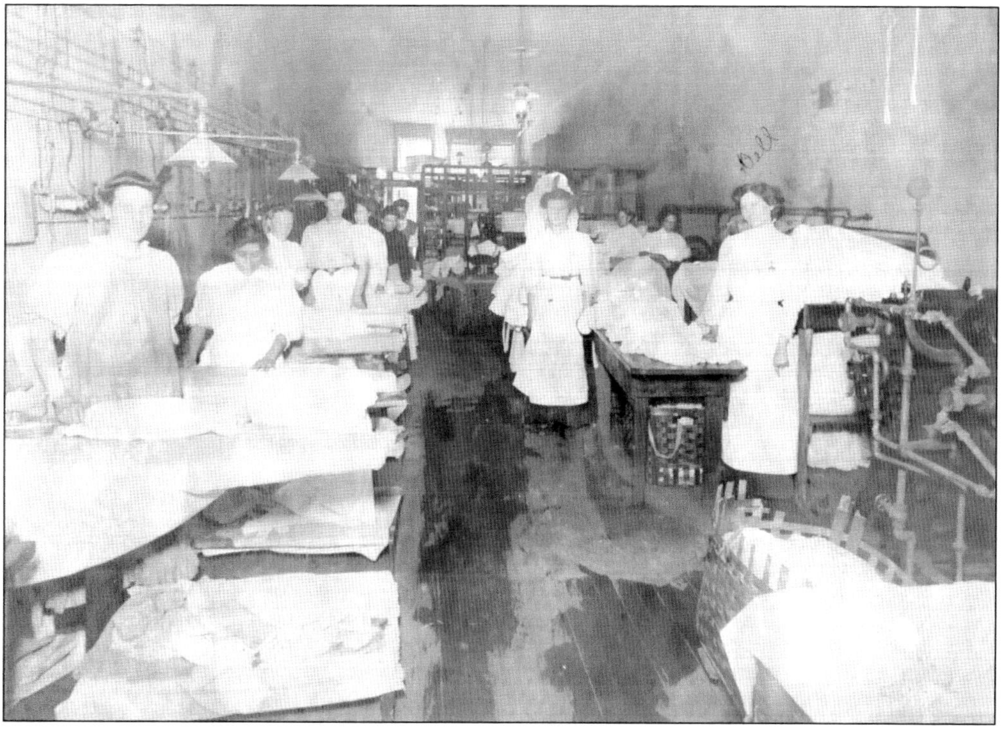

In 1900, Concordians could get clothes and linens cleaned at Concordia Steam Laundry. Inside, women work at the tasks still to be done after washing is finished. Outside, employees pose for a photograph. The light-colored square above the heads of the women to the right of center is actually a sign instructing the customer: "if closed, drop your bundles in here" with what appears to be a small door. (Both courtesy of Cloud County Historical Society Museum.)

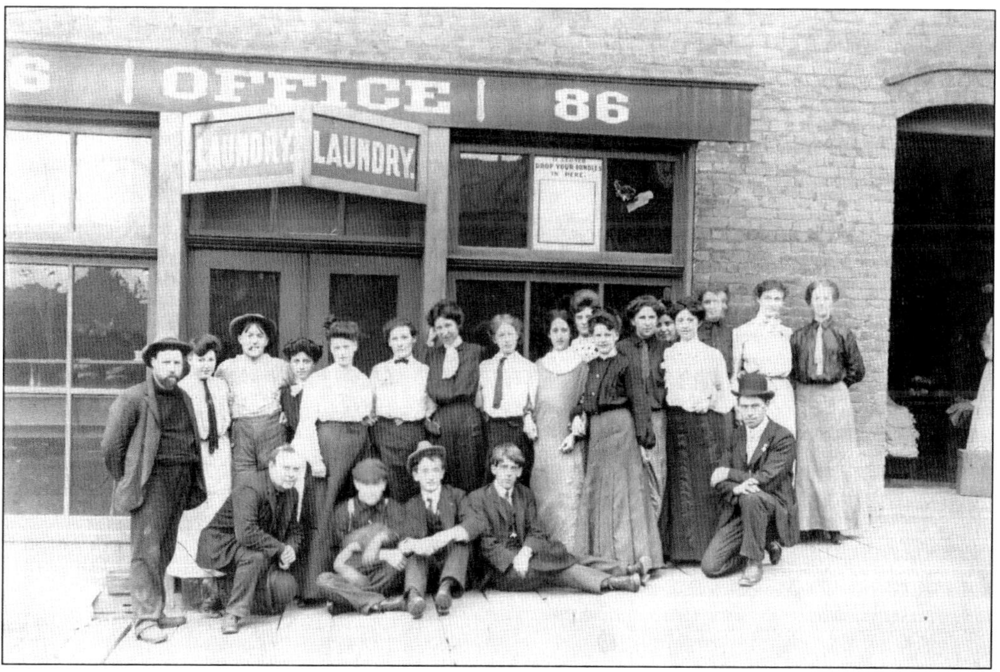

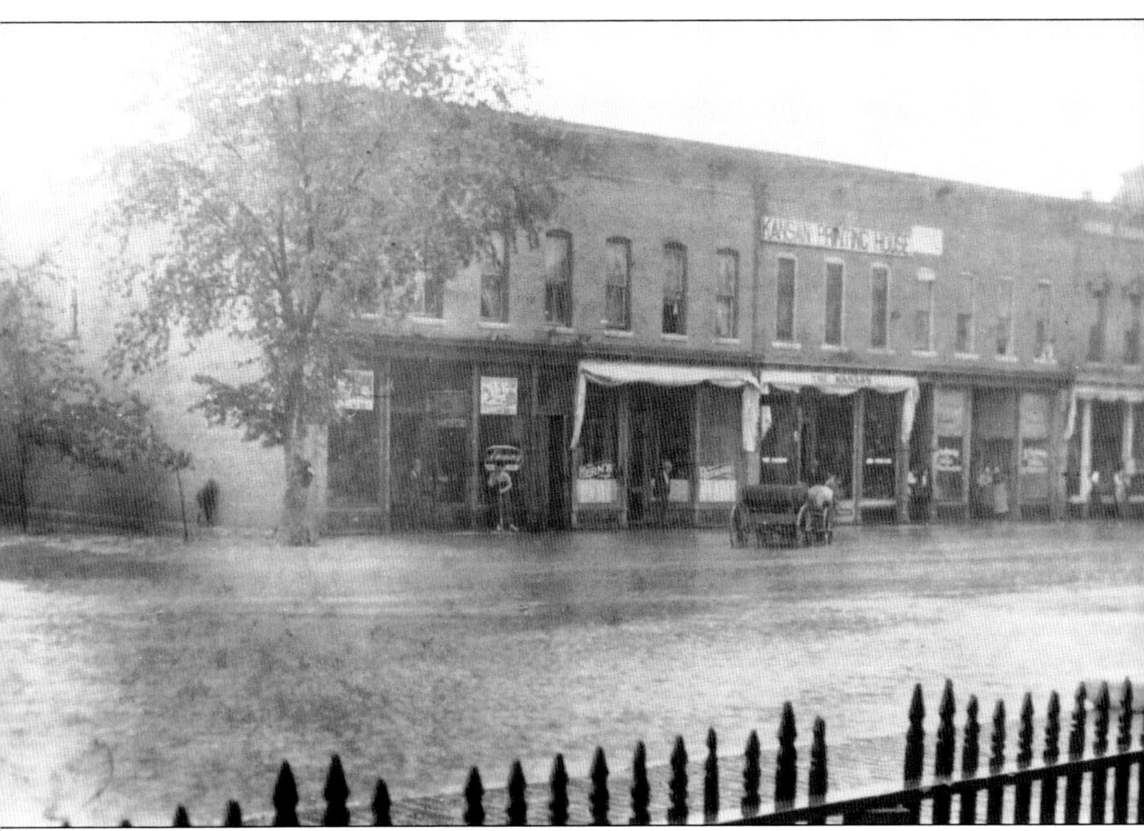

The Republican River has flooded several times in Concordia's history and has more than once changed its channel. One major flood occurred in July 1903, when the nearby Solomon River also flooded. Newspaper reports of the time mentioned water getting into downtown buildings and several nearby farms being ruined. The Missouri Pacific Railroad's track washed out at Yuma, about four miles west of Concordia. Electrical power was lost when the water-powered electrical plant originally built by H.M. Spaulding and the former Lanoue gristmill were left dry because the river shifted its course a mile and a half to the northeast of where it had been. Both had to be rebuilt and converted to steam power. Here, in a photograph that may date from that flood, water rises in the street in front of the Kansan Printing House, and the proprietors of the businesses prepare to fight it. (Courtesy of Dallas Nading.)

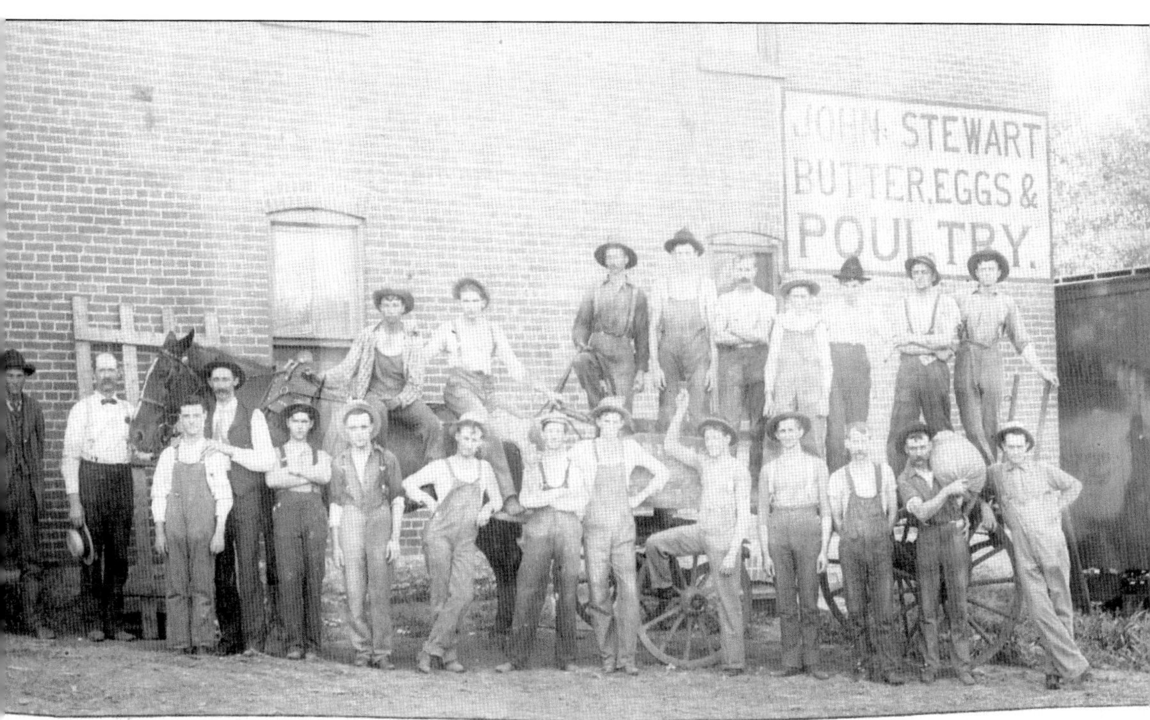

HN STEWART PRODUCE HOUSE CONCORDIA
EST OF UNION PACIFIC DEPOT
FT TO RIGHT: UNKNOWN TRAMP, JOHN STEWART, BILL
RANAHN, UNKNOWN, JOE DUMAS, PATTY MARTIN, ON
RSE: FRED FISHER & CHARLIE WEAVER, ON GROUND BY
RSE: RAY BROWN, NEWT SHORT, ED JINKINS, UNKNOWN,
C GODFREY, ANDY TANKERSLY, ED LOPSHIER, UNKNOWN.
ANDING IN WAGON: JACK HARRIS [GOT HIS HORSE SHOT
OM UNDER HIM AT THE BATTLE OF WOUNDED KNEE IN
KOTAS] ELMER SHROUF, TIM LOCKWOOD, JIMMEY
CRACKEN, OTE BROWN, LEW CRUM, UNKNOWN
DONOR: NEWELL SHORT 1969-016-1

John Stewart Produce House stood just west of the Union Pacific Depot. Employees took a casual approach to their group portrait and allowed an unidentified tramp to join them. Information with the photograph also notes that Jack Harris got his horse shot from under him at the Battle of Wounded Knee. The business was one of several produce houses serving Concordia. (Courtesy of Cloud County Historical Society Museum.)

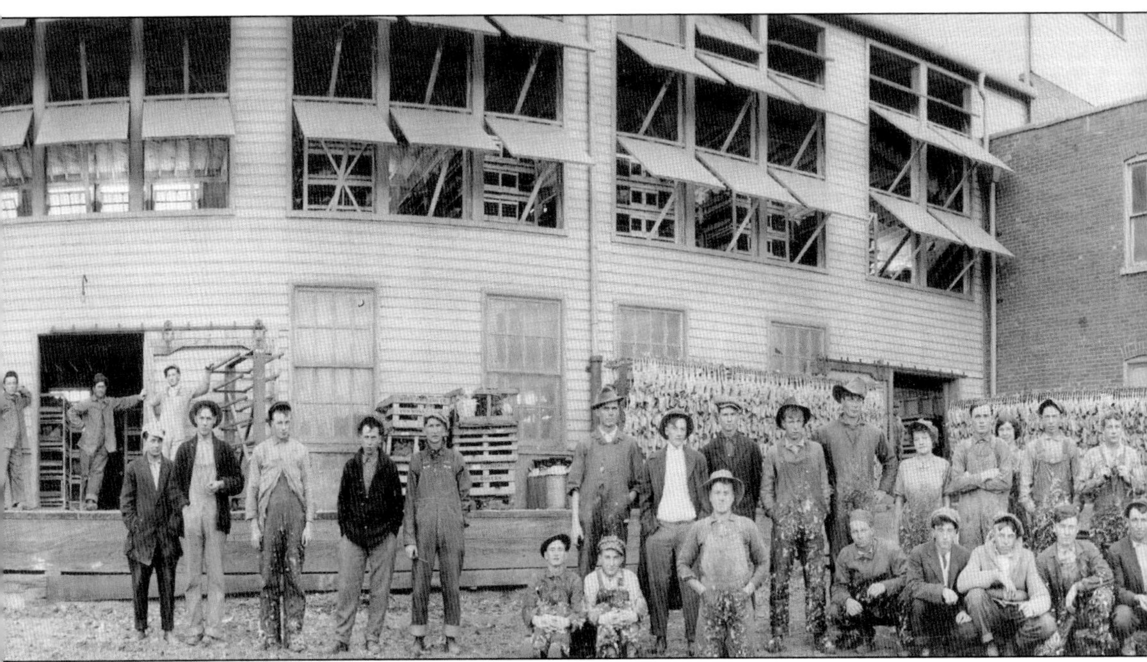

Workers, many covered with feathers, pose in front of Metz Packing Company in the early 1900s. The plant was on State Street between Third and Fourth Streets, with the Union Pacific depot at the east end of the block and several rail lines nearby. Also known as W.F. Metz Butter, Eggs

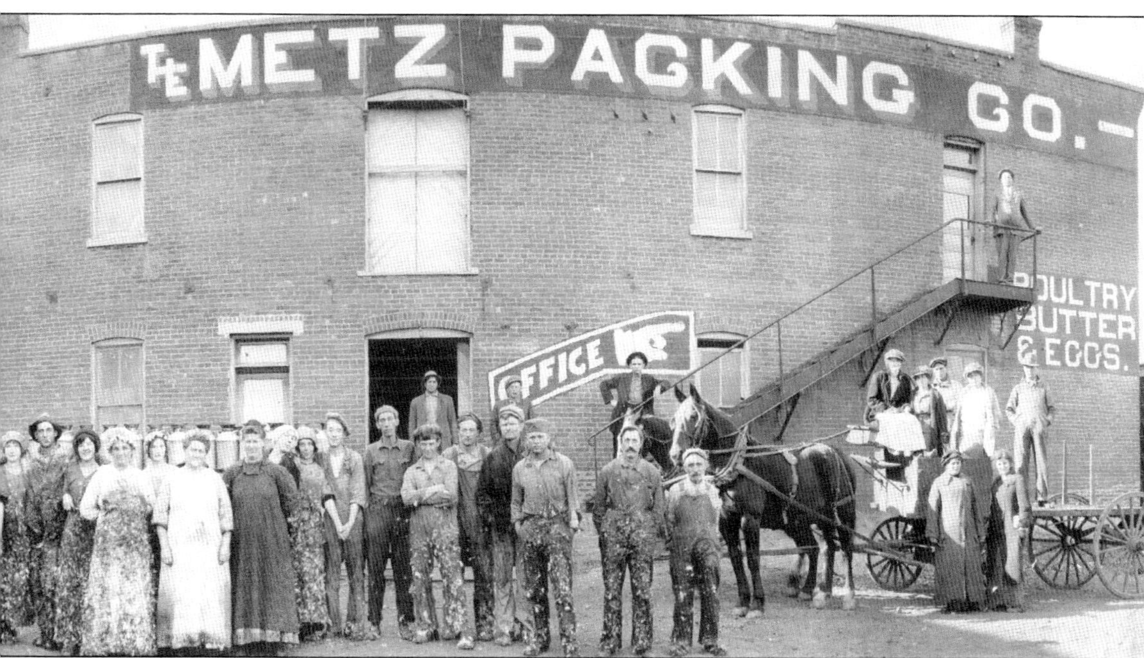

and Poultry Company, it was sold to Seymour Packing Company, and shipments began by truck rather than rail. It closed in the mid-1960s, and the building burned in the 1970s. (Courtesy of Cloud County Historical Society Museum.)

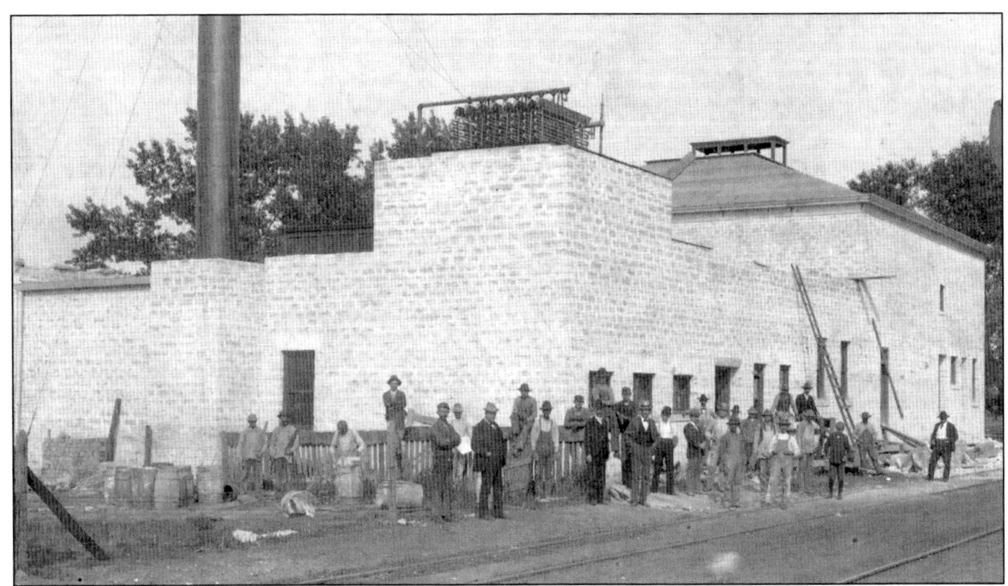

Concordia Ice and Cold Storage Company opened in 1902. The native stone building insulated with cork and sawdust cost $35,000. The plant produced 15 tons of ice daily for Concordia, nearby towns, and refrigerated railcars. C.A. Betournay owned, managed, and was treasurer of the business. Its water supply came from a well that never ran dry, which the city of Concordia tapped during droughts. Betournay sold the company to George and Ezra Huscher in 1918. The last owner was Ernest Huscher. The *Kansan* reported the building had been vacant about three years when it burned November 7, 1972. It was torn down in 1984. Shown below are Wilbur Betournay, Ezra Huscher, and Russell Sturges at the plant in 1913. It was one of two ice companies in town. (Both courtesy of Cloud County Historical Society Museum.)

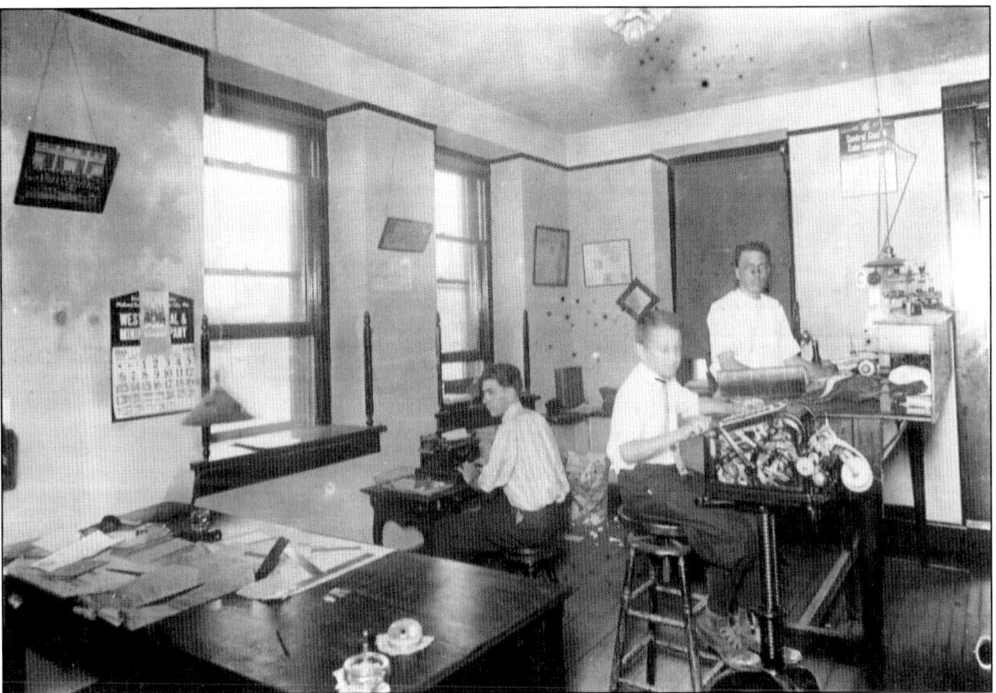

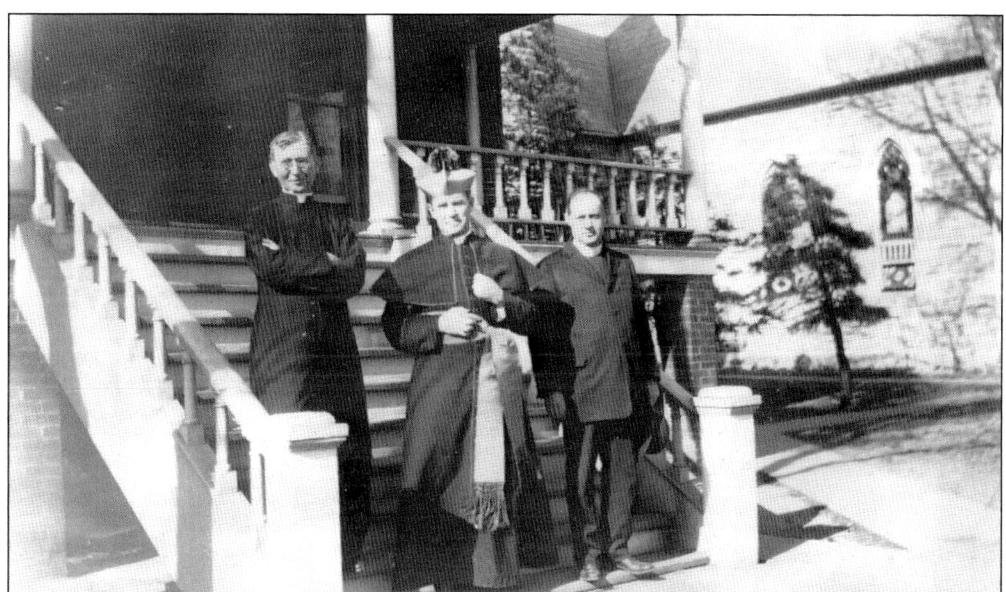

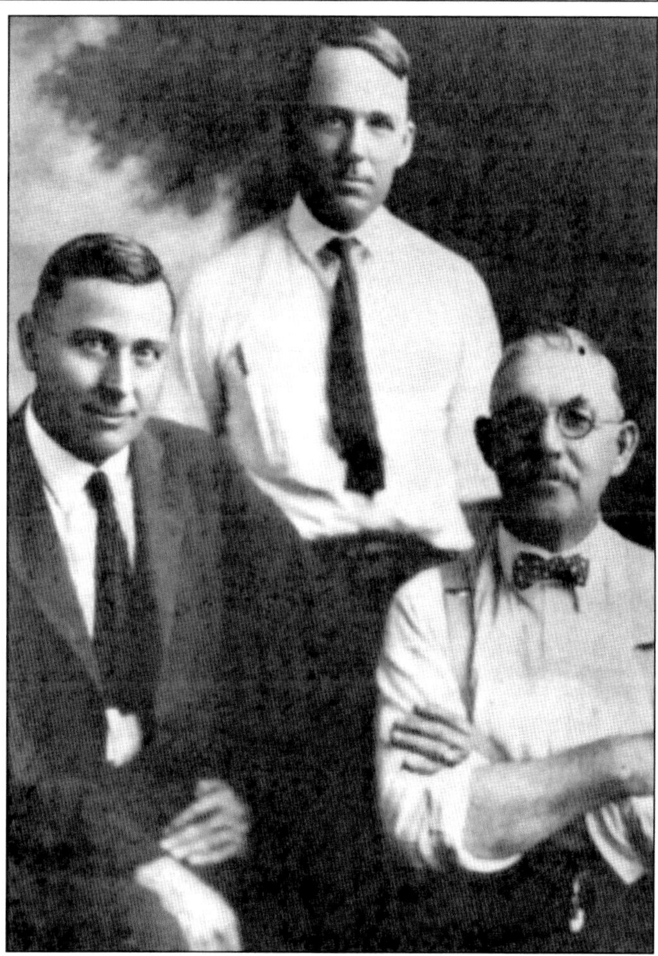

The Ku Klux Klan arrived in Concordia in 1922. They ordered Baron's House to fire black employees, threatened city officials and the editor of the *Blade-Empire*, and made Catholics their next target. Fr. Adolphus T. Ennis of Our Lady of Perpetual Help Catholic Church, pictured above on the left later when he was a monsignor, appealed to the editors of Concordia's three newspapers for help. *Kansan* editor Gomer Davies, on the left at right, was a sworn enemy with Green, in the center. William Danenbarger, at right, edited the *Press*. Green's janitor drank, and the editors sent him, sober but acting drunk, to the next Klan meeting to record the names of all who attended. All three papers ran an editorial the next day promising to publish the names "at an appropriate time." The Klan left Kansas in 1925. (Above, courtesy of Our Lady of Perpetual Help Catholic Church; right, courtesy of Dena Bisnette.)

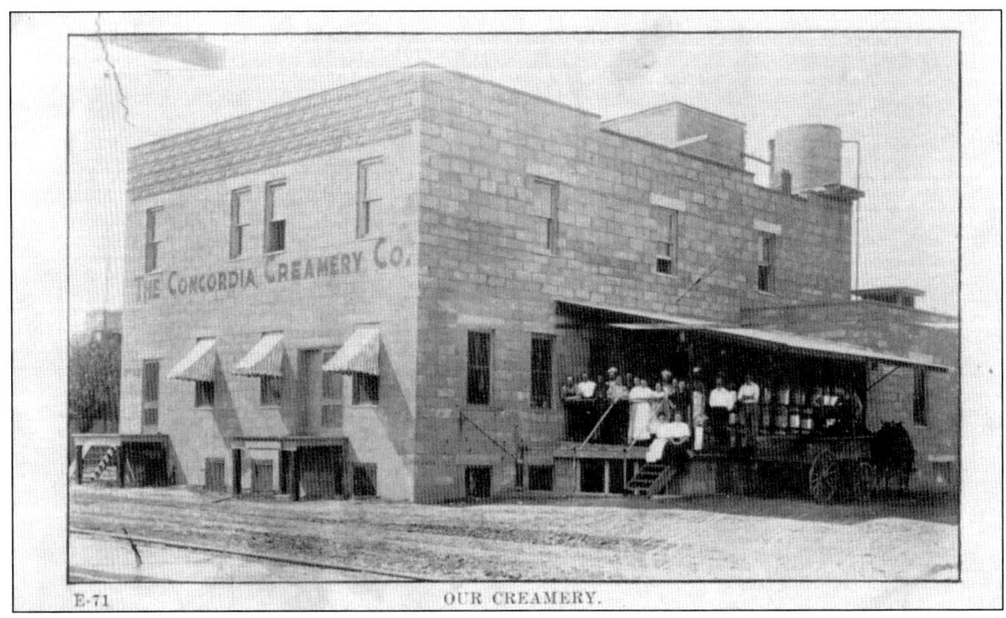

Concordia Creamery Co., pictured above with employees, milk cans, and a wagon at the side of the building, was sold to Fairmont Foods in 1929. Produce was also processed there until the plant was remodeled and handled only dairy again. Shown below in 1928 are, from left to right, Matt ?, Ray Thompson, Bill Cox, Ralph Davidson, John Fazel, and Clarence (Slim) Thompson. The company also operated a dairy store. The business was sold to Roberts Dairy in 1979 and the Concordia office closed in 1988. (Both courtesy of Cloud County Historical Society Museum.)

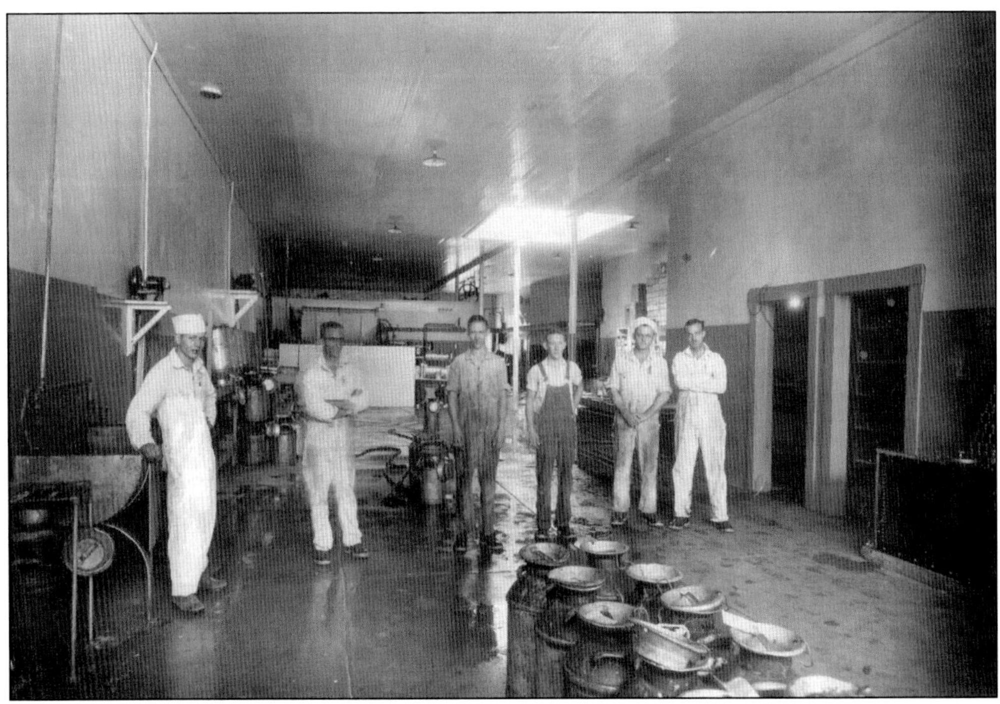

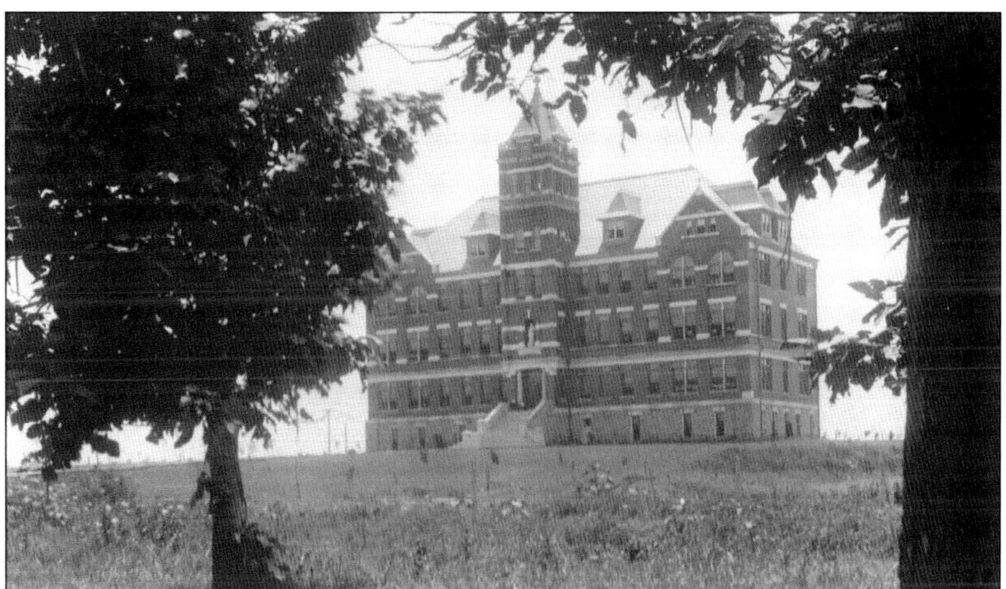

When the Sisters of St. Joseph arrived in Concordia at the request of Fr. Joseph Perrier in 1884, they established Nazareth Convent and Academy, but quickly outgrew their original quarters on East Fifth Street. On May 15, 1902, the cornerstone was laid for the brick building that has been their home since 1903. Wings added in 1906 and 1907 included a new chapel and music wing. The academy moved to Salina in 1922, but the motherhouse remains open and Nazareth Convent still serves the Sisters of St. Joseph and the community. Listed in the National Register of Historic Places since 1973, it is noted for its art collection and stained-glass windows. Above, the building is shown as it appeared in 1903. The photograph below was taken after the chapel and music wing were added. (Both courtesy of Sisters of St. Joseph Archives.)

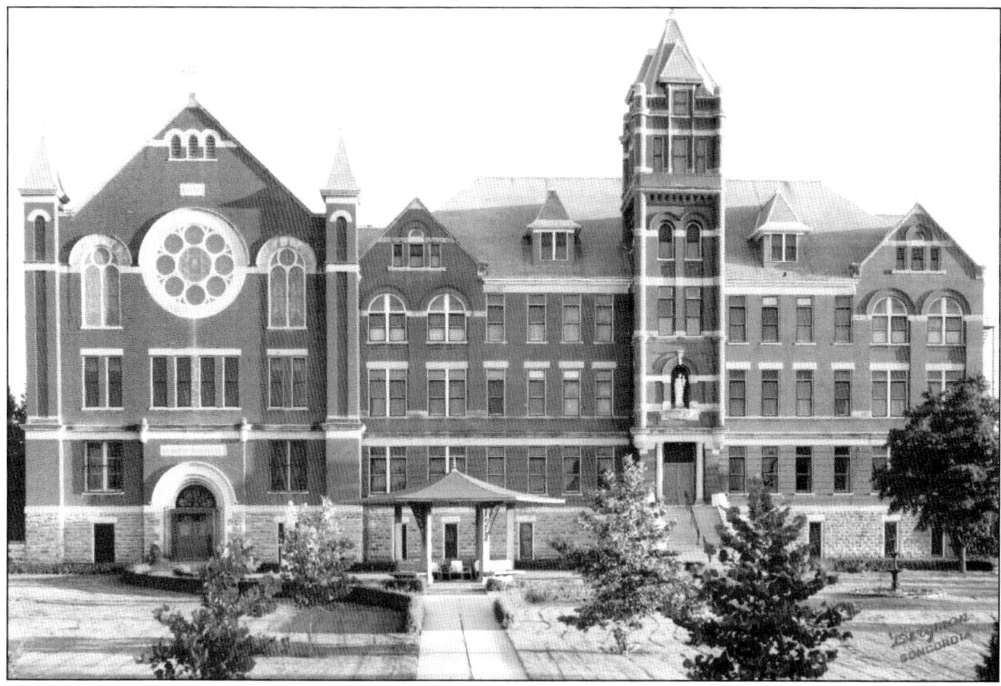

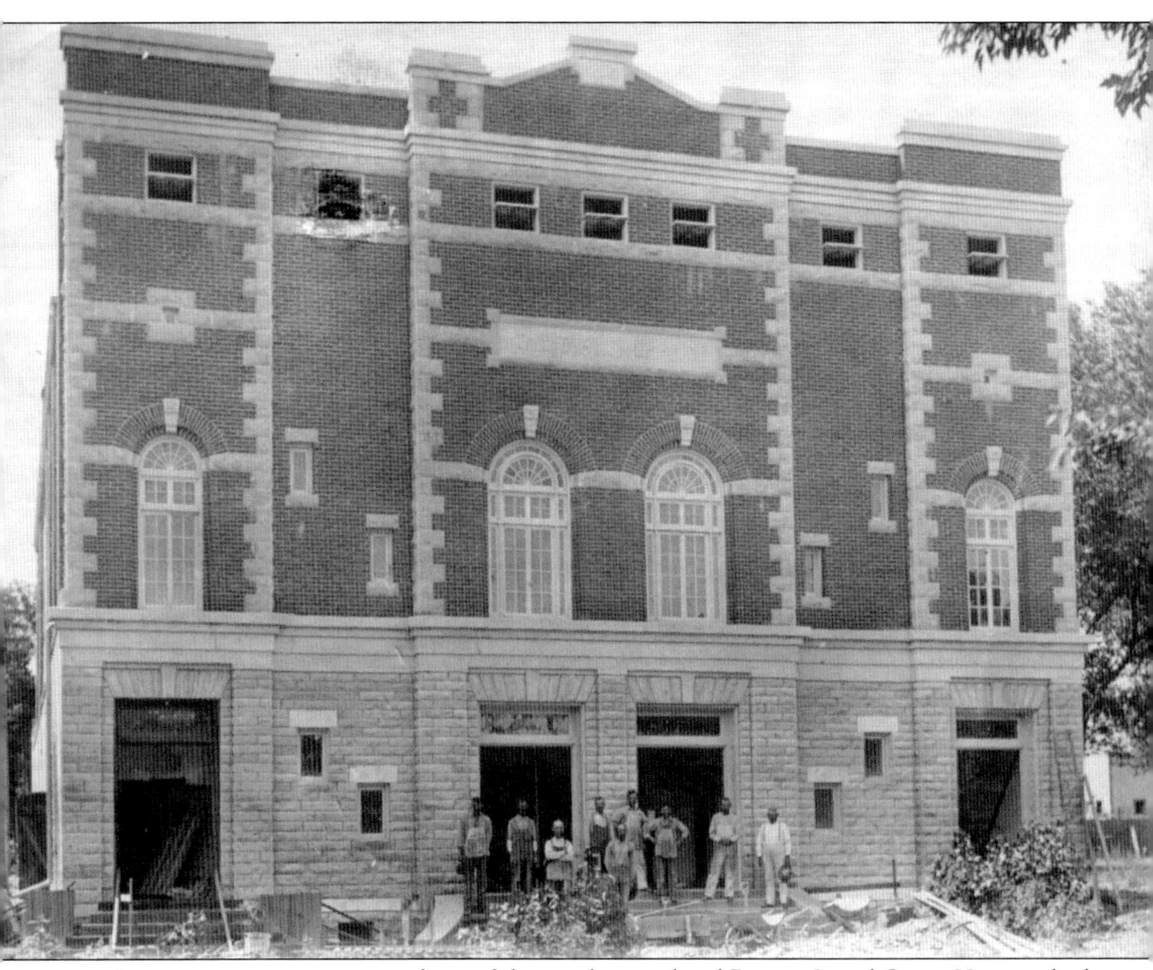

A construction crew poses in front of the nearly completed Brown Grand Opera House, which opened September 17, 1907. Col. Napoleon Bonaparte Brown, a Concordia banker, commissioned construction in 1906 and assigned the $40,000 project to his son, Earl Van Dorn Brown. The younger Brown used local materials and labor and hired Concordia native W.T. Short to supervise construction. The opera house became a movie theater from 1925 to 1974 before being purchased by Everett Miller and donated to the city as a bicentennial restoration project. It is listed in the National Register of Historic Places. The Brown Grand reopened in 1980 and still hosts performances, tours, and rentals. The opulent decor inside includes luxury boxes, original paint colors, and a chandelier in the ladies' restroom. S.N. Westover is fourth from left, but the others are not identified. (Courtesy of Cloud County Historical Society Museum.)

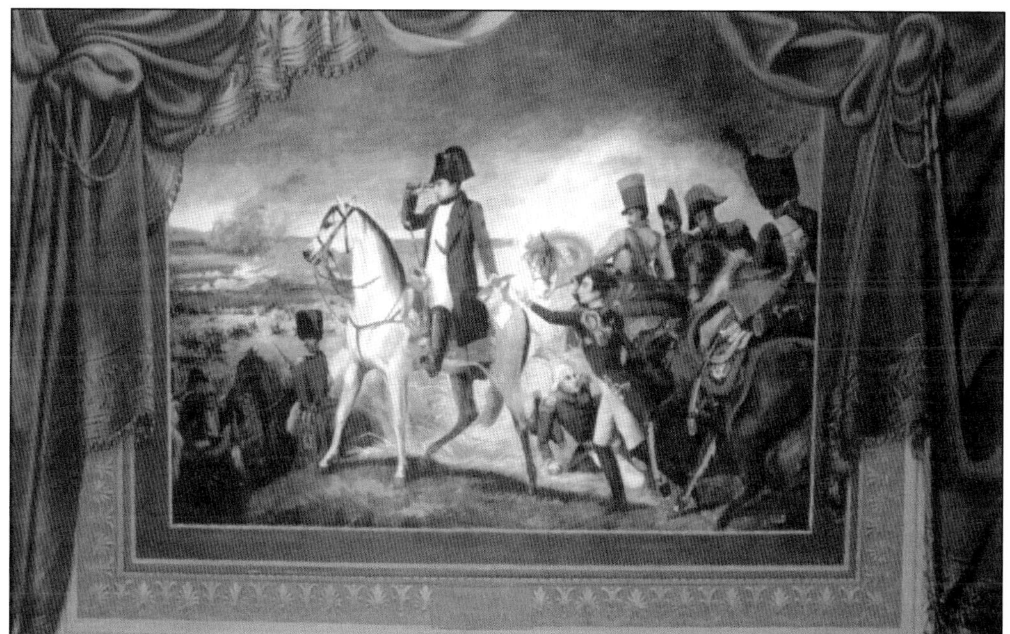

On opening night, September 17, 1907, Earl Van Dorn Brown gave his father the Napoleon Drape for his Brown Grand Opera House. During restoration of the Brown Grand, workers found the badly damaged drape. Twin Cities Scenic Company of Minneapolis–St. Paul, Minnesota, which painted the original, copied it for the restoration. It was their last drape made before the company burned in 1980. (Courtesy of Brown Grand Theatre.)

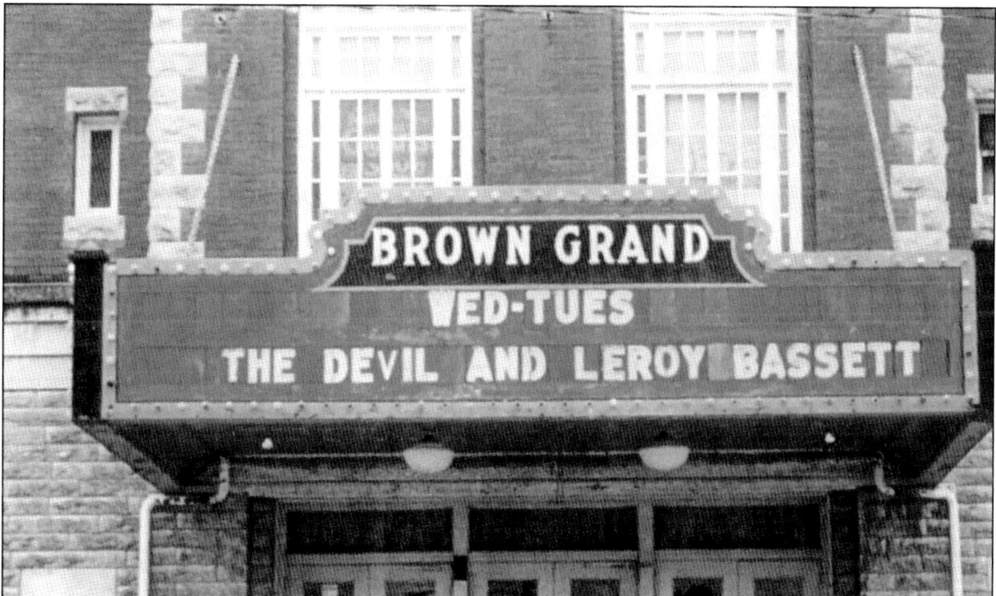

After Colonel Brown died, his widow gave Brown Grand Opera House to the city in 1912. Concordia officials returned it to the family in 1916. Sold to Concordia Amusements, it served as a movie theater for over 50 years, closing with the world premiere of *The Devil and Leroy Bassett*, directed by former Concordia resident Robert Pearson, on September 10, 1974. (Courtesy of Brown Grand Theatre.)

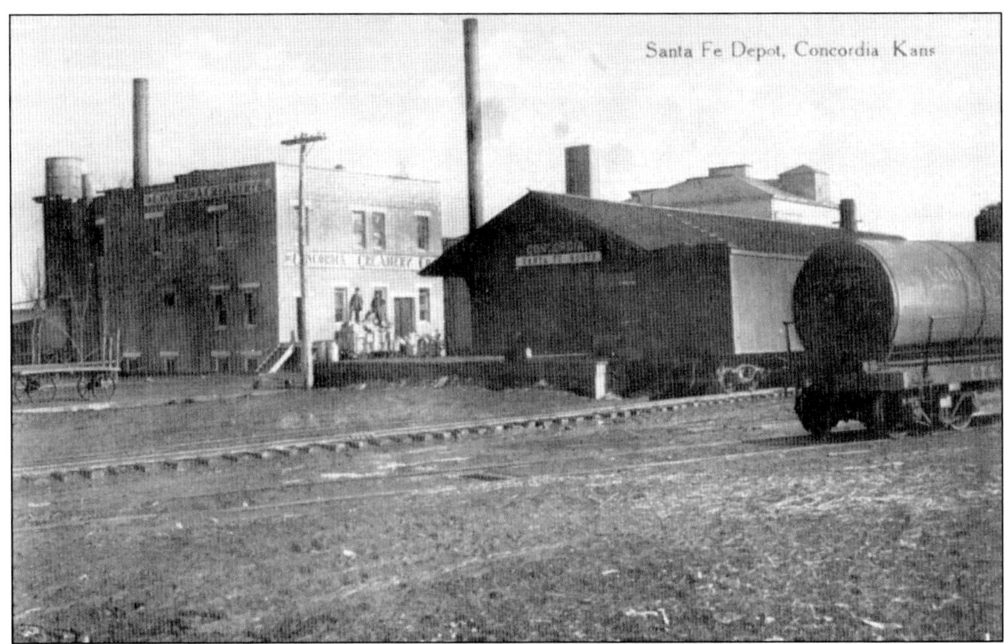

The Santa Fe Railroad Depot, at right, was across from Concordia Creamery. The Santa Fe started as the Atchison, Topeka & Santa Fe Railroad, one of four rail companies serving Concordia, but eventually discontinued passenger service. Its freight division merged with Burlington Northern. Engines with the old orange-and-gold Santa Fe colors are still seen sometimes in North Central Kansas. (Courtesy of Cloud County Historical Society Museum.)

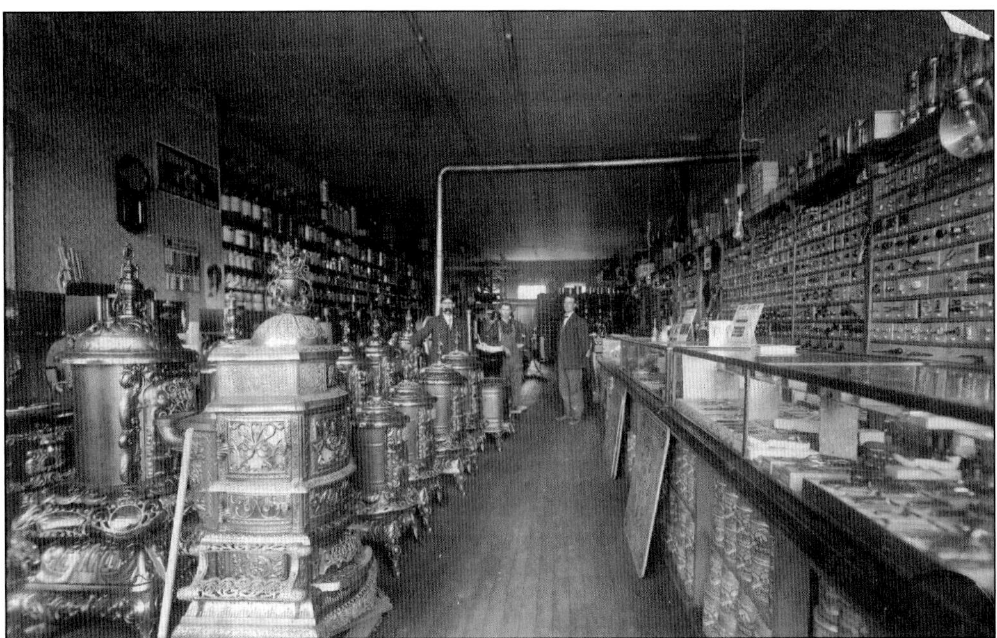

Employees Ed Fitch, John McDonald, and Ed Rose ran Linville Hardware Store at 214 West Sixth Street in 1909. The store stocked a wide range of tools, hardware, paint, and even stoves. (Courtesy of Susie Haver.)

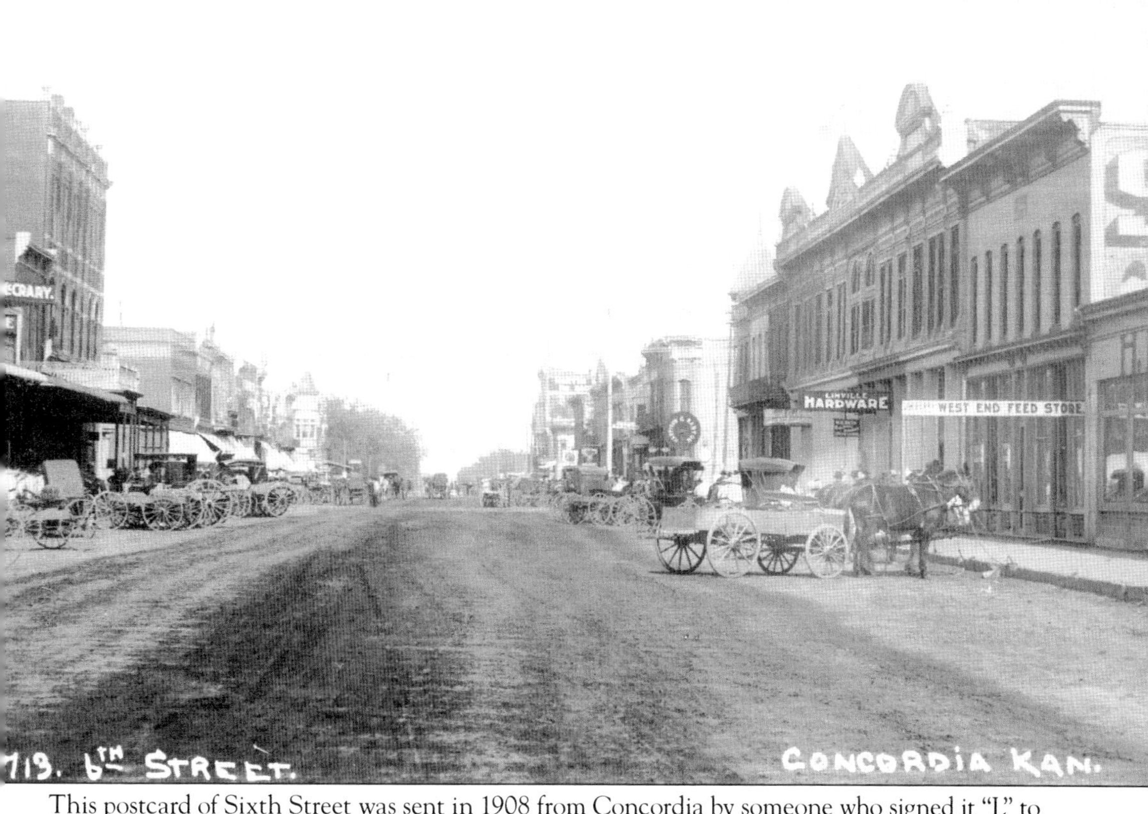

This postcard of Sixth Street was sent in 1908 from Concordia by someone who signed it "L" to a man in Glasco, Kansas, to inquire about the health of a rooster; the sender mentioned plans to pick up the bird "in a few weeks, as this is leap year, you know." Sixth Street has wagons parked at both sides, and businesses with signs include, at left, Robinson-McCrary, the *Daily Blade* newspaper, and Martin Brothers Racket Store. At right are West End Feed Store, Linville Hardware, and W.G. Reid Real Estate Insurance and Farm Loans, Frank Schmidt's Sincerity Store, Harrison and Barton, and a tailor shop. The street is still unpaved. (Courtesy of Cloud County Historical Society Museum.)

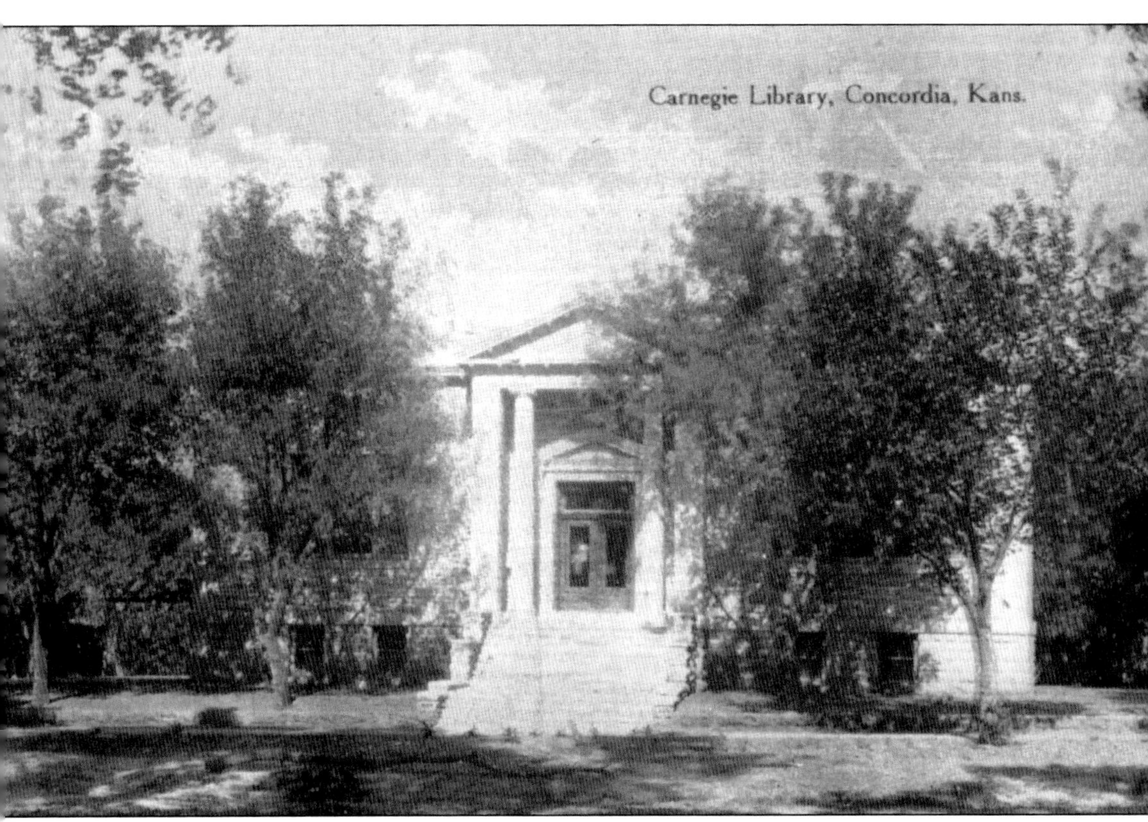

When the Concordia Ladies' Library Association formed in 1892, Caroline Dudley and Augusta Wilfong earned money for the town's first public library in six weeks by sharpening scissors on a grindstone. Two years later, the library moved from a room in the Young Men's Christian Association to what later became Brown's Shoe Store. In 1907, Concordia accepted philanthropist Andrew Carnegie's offer of funds for a public library. This Carnegie Library, completed in 1909, has been replaced by the Frank Carlson Library. The Carnegie building and its additions currently house Cloud County Historical Society Museum, where every item has ties to Cloud County and shows life from pioneer times to now. The eclectic collection, started in 1959 in the courthouse basement, now includes airplanes hanging from the ceiling and a windmill. Re-created rooms in the permanent exhibit include several shops, a railroad station waiting room, a broom factory, Lester's, and Marion Ellet's study. The museum annex on Sixth Street features antique vehicles and shares space with Cloud County Tourism. (Courtesy of Dena Bisnette.)

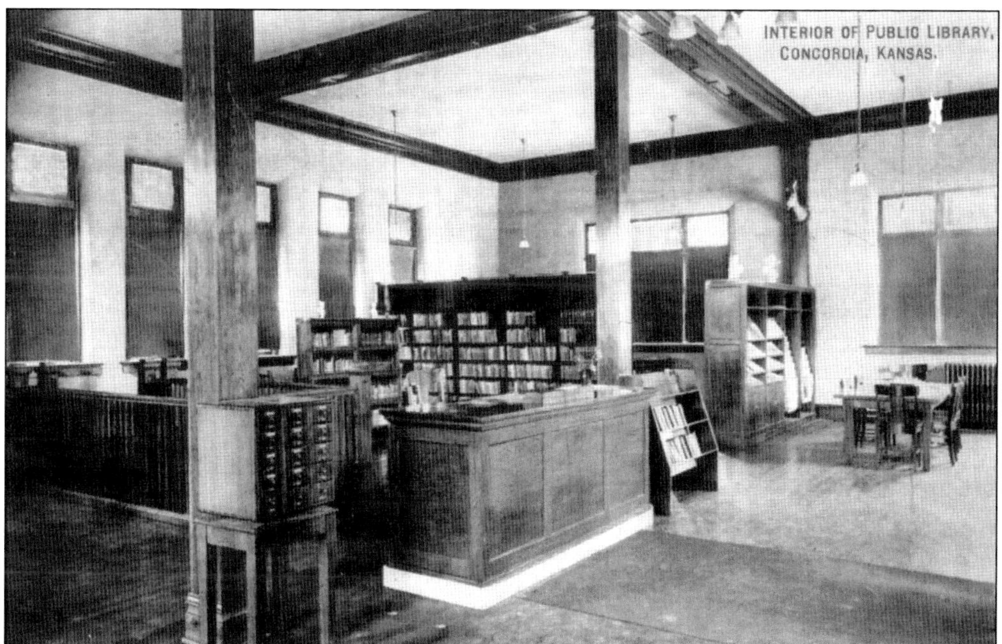

This photograph shows the interior of the Carnegie Library before it became the Cloud County Historical Museum. Before the city had an official library, Ed Linney, who had the very first general store in Concordia in 1870 and was also postmaster for a time, operated a small lending library out of his combination store and post office. (Courtesy of Lori Halfhide.)

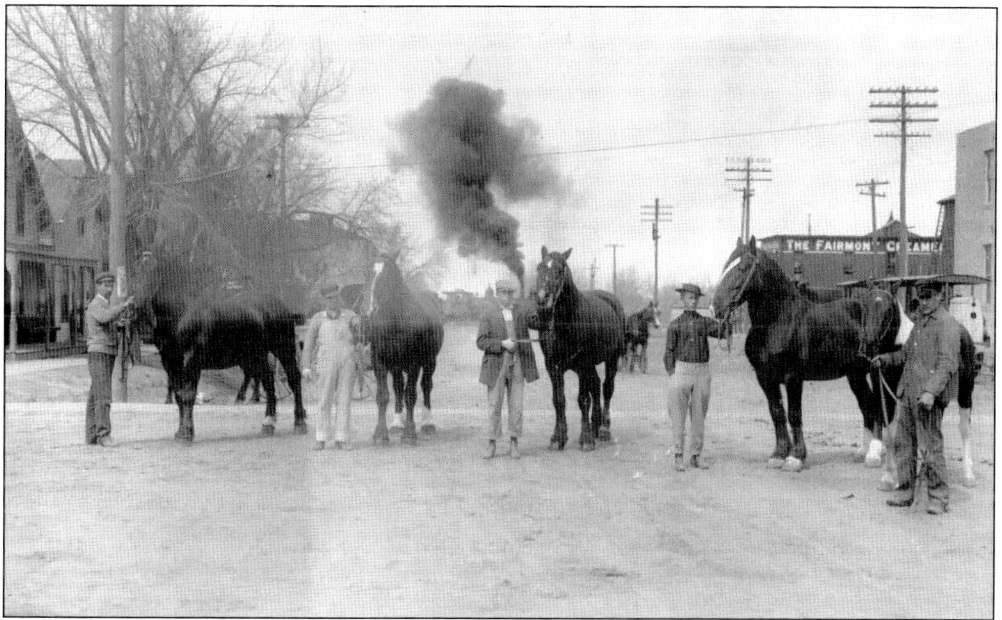

International Harvester in Concordia provided equipment for farmers nearby. Here, in 1910, employees show off some of the company's breeding horses on the Broadway side of the building. The men include, from left to right, Grant Hall, L.J. Cox, Bill Swafford, ? Hinks, and J. Decker. The smoke behind them comes from a passing locomotive. (Courtesy of Cloud County Historical Society Museum.)

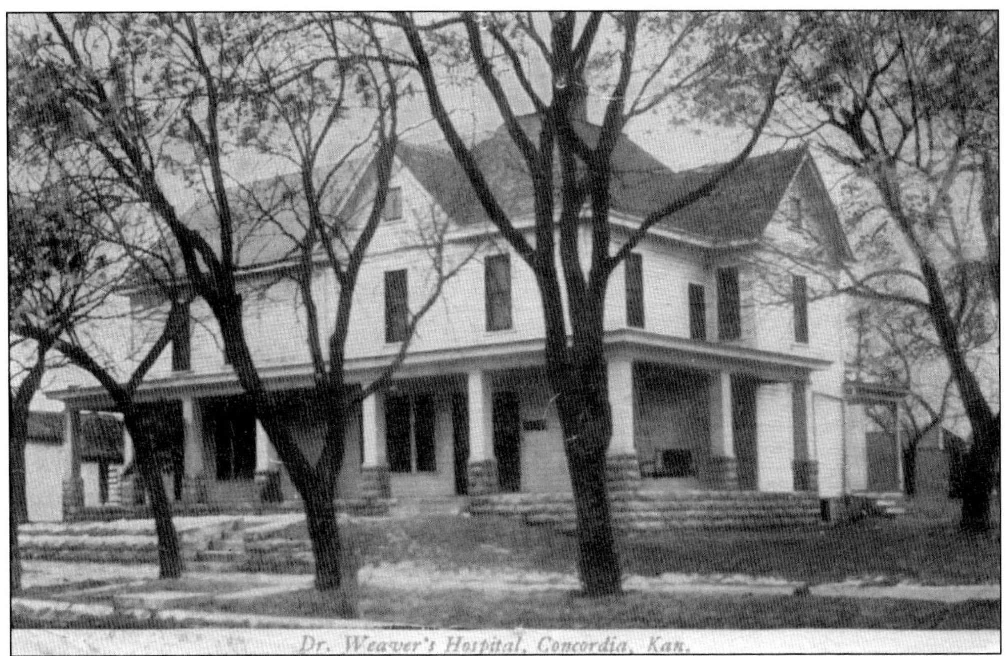

Dr. Asa J. Weaver opened this hospital on the southeast corner of Ninth and Washington Streets in 1909. Some of his predecessors in Concordia arrived in the 1880s and included William F. Sawhill, Dr. Samuel C. Pigman, and several others. Dr. Wilson A. Priest had a reputation for treating medicine as a business and built the elegant home shown below at Seventh and State Streets. Some of the first surgeons in town, Dr. Hugh Roberts St. John and Dr. Otto Keine, arrived in 1914 and 1915. Most of them were among the staff members at St. Joseph Hospital, which the Sisters of St. Joseph opened in 1903. Weaver's building was later split into two separate structures. Both are now residences. (Both courtesy of Dena Bisnette.)

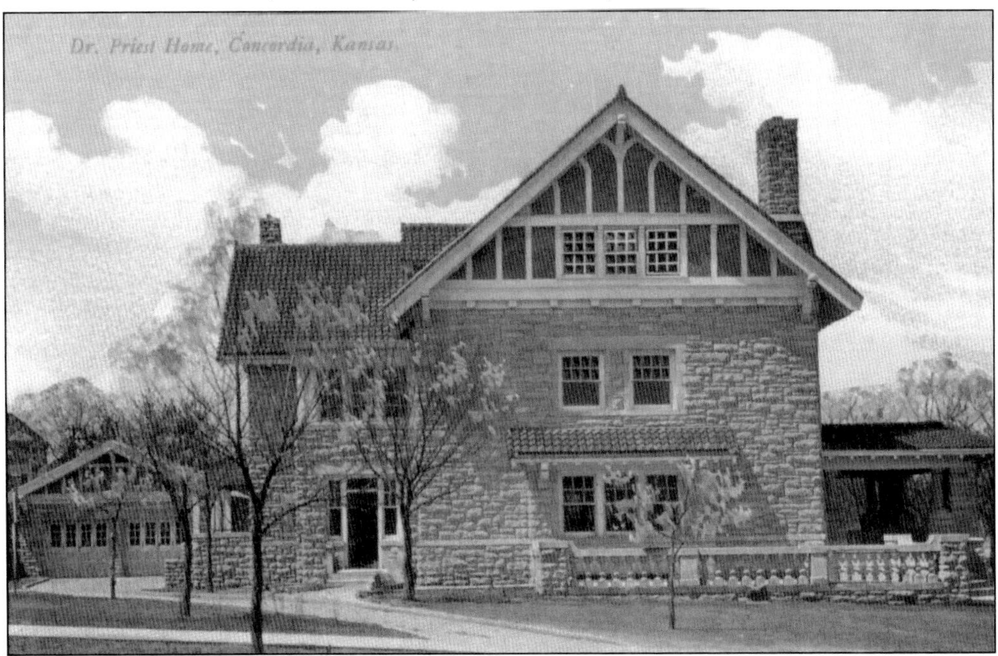

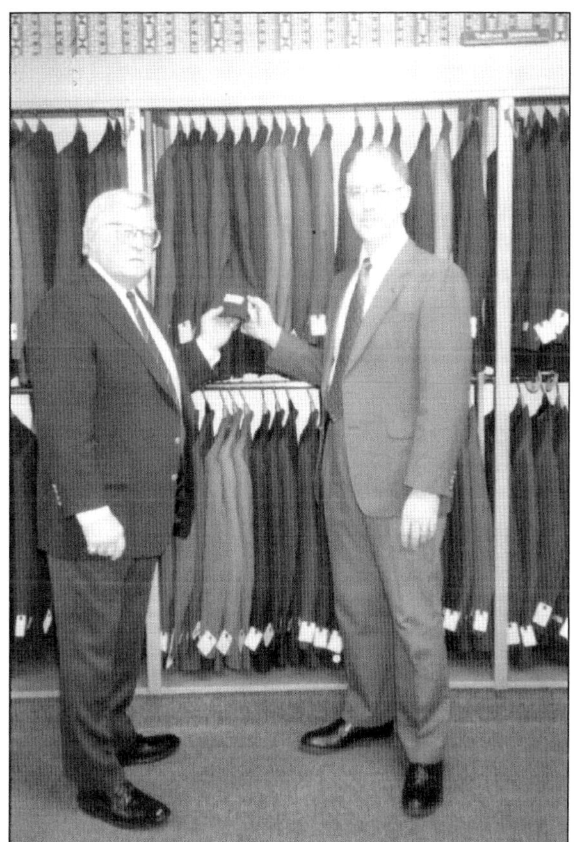

Daylight Clothing Company acquired its name around 1910 when Ernest Swanson had skylights installed in the roof of the building, then known as Marshall and Barton on Sixth Street, and a customer told him it looked just like daylight inside the store. From 1950 to 1953, the name was changed to Oscar Allen Inc. after a stockholder, but was renamed the New Daylight Clothing Company after Allen sold his stock. Art Slaughter, who joined the company in 1956, was the last owner of Daylight Clothing Company. Slaughter is on the right in the photograph at right. In the older picture below, the store is visible at right behind Concordia's first newsstand, operated by Chas McDonald. (Both courtesy of Cloud County Historical Society Museum.)

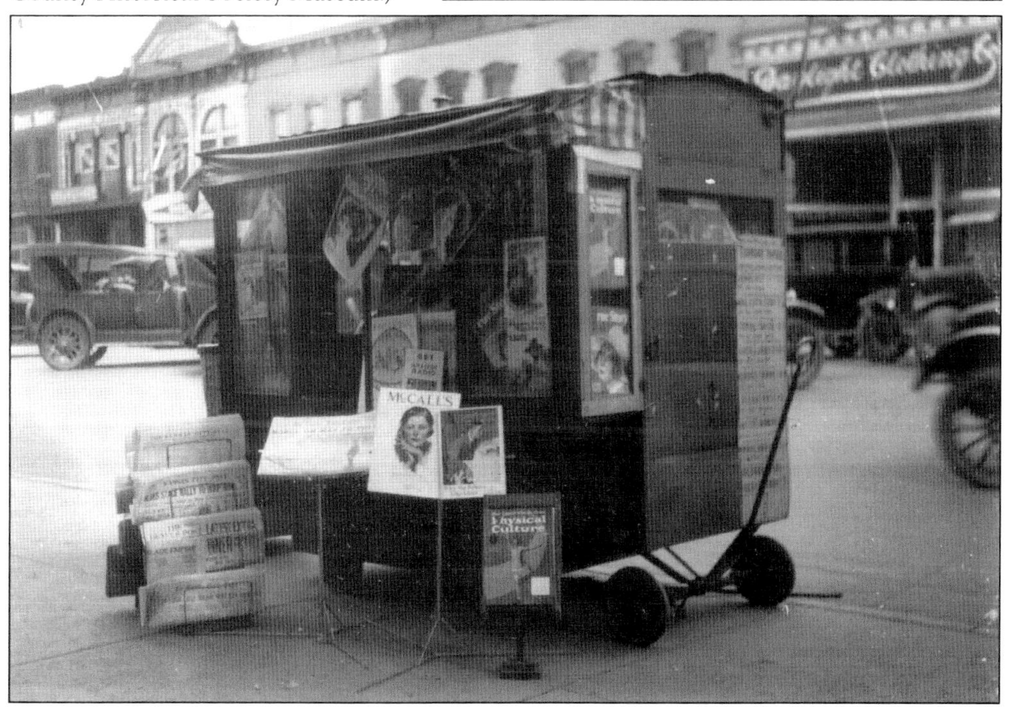

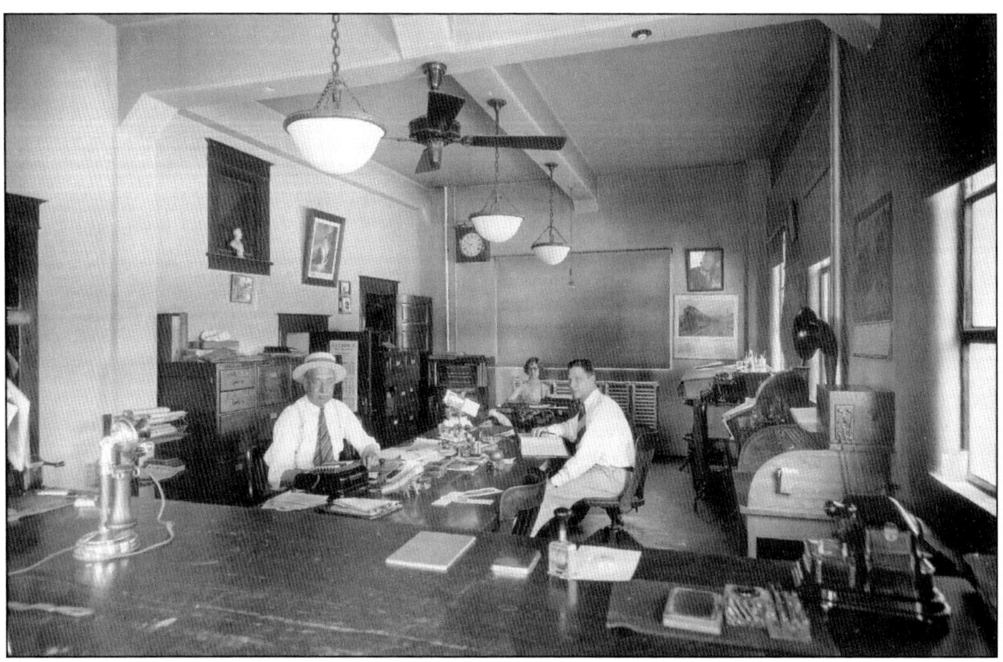

Shown in the office at Concordia Milling Company are Bill Bennett and his son Jack Bennett, who owned the mill when Concordia turned 100 years old in 1971. The woman is unidentified. The business is the descendant of Lanoue's Mill and was built in 1912 to grind wheat and corn into flour. (Courtesy of Cloud County Historical Society Museum.)

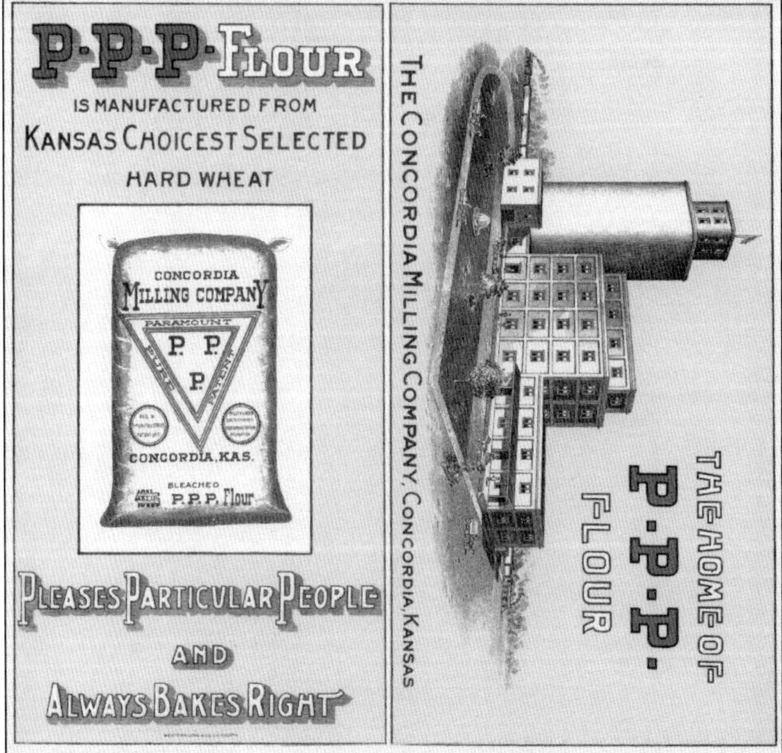

According to this advertising folder for Concordia Milling Company's P.P.P. Flour, the three Ps stood for Pure, Paramount, and Patent, and also for Pleases Particular People. The advertising line was first used in 1886 when the mill was owned by the partnership of Spaulding and Cline. (Courtesy of Dena Bisnette.)

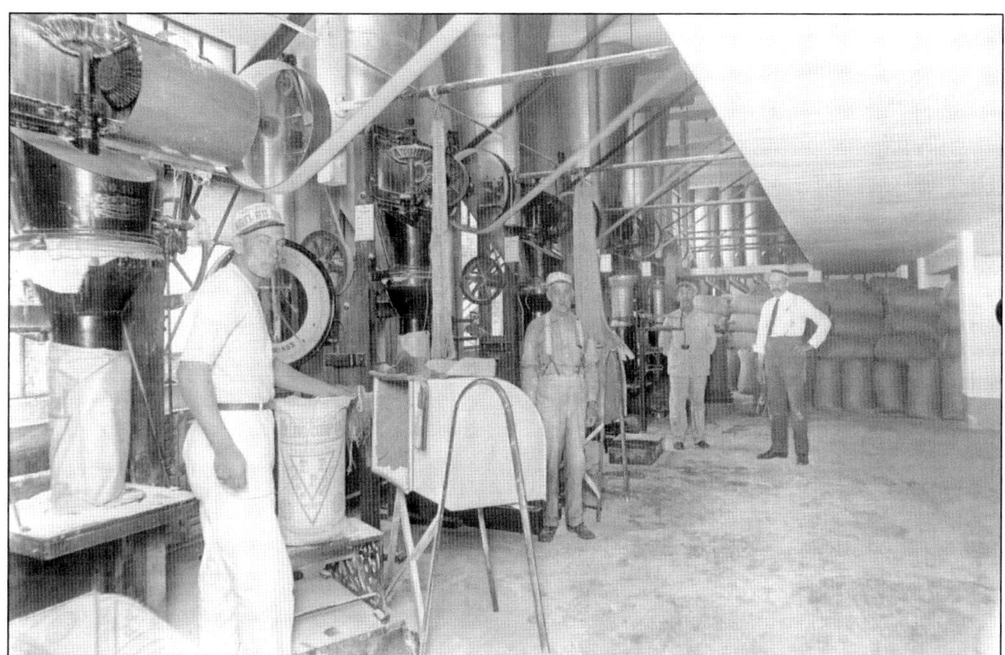

Concordia Milling Company packing room employees interrupt their work to have their photograph taken for a magazine feature in *American Miller and Processor* in 1948. The man at left has weighed a bag of the company's P.P.P. Flour and is sewing the top of the bag shut. (Courtesy of Cloud County Historical Society Museum.)

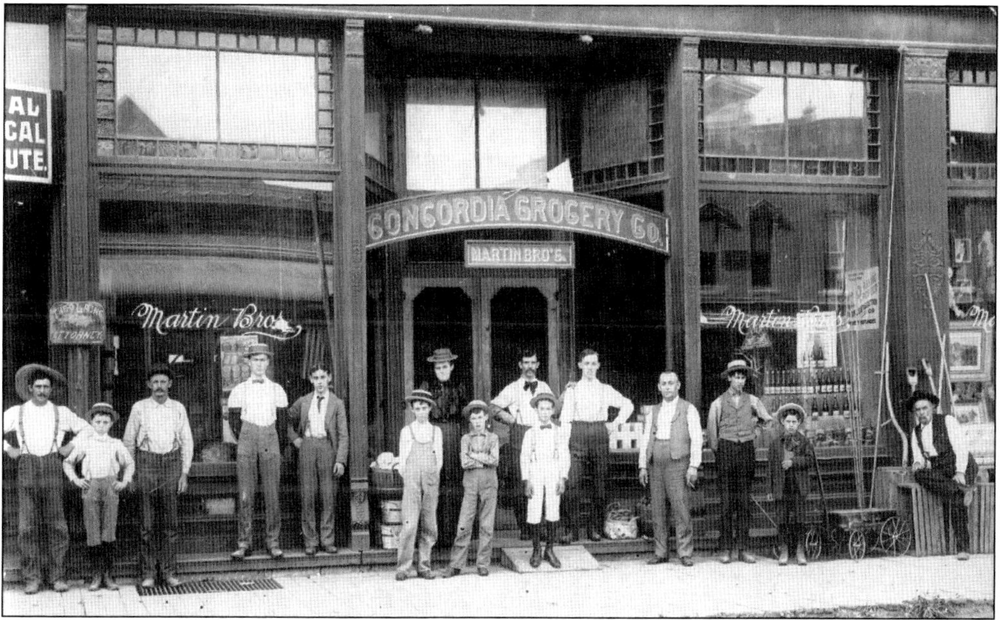

Everyone turns out for a photograph at Martin Brothers' Concordia Grocery, an early downtown store. Concordia became a commerce center for the part of Cloud County south of the Republican River and grew rapidly during its first quarter-century. Many buildings like this sprang up in the downtown business blocks. Sidewalks were still boardwalks, and streets remained unpaved. (Courtesy of Cloud County Historical Society Museum.)

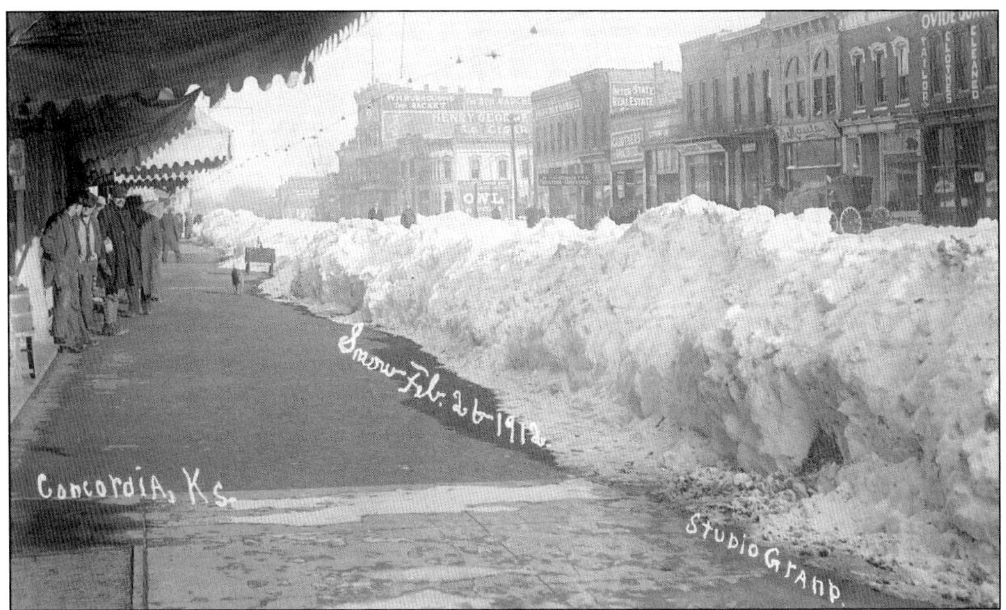

A Studio Grand photograph shows snow piled up on February 26, 1912, after an unusually heavy storm isolated residents, interrupting train travel for days. Sunny weather followed. In 1957, probate judge Finley Daugherty found a similar photograph taken from the Cloud County Bank doorway. The *Blade-Empire* published it, noting the event as one of the biggest snowstorms in Concordia's history. (Courtesy of Cloud County Historical Society Museum.)

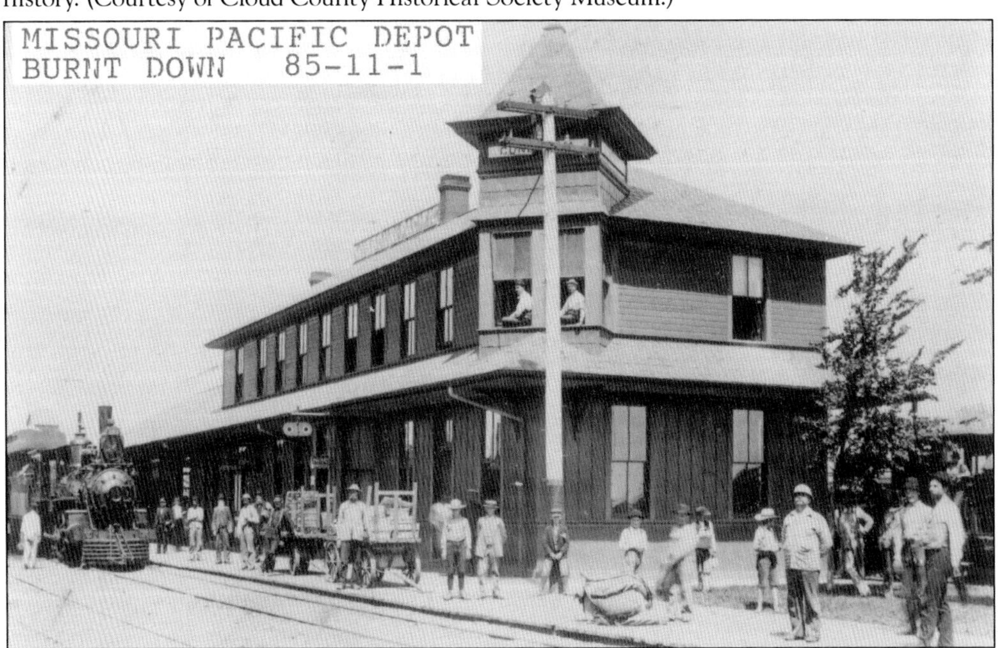

A train arrives at the Missouri Pacific Railroad Depot in Concordia in the early 1900s. This depot caught fire and burned to the ground April 10, 1913. It was replaced by another building on the same site. Missouri Pacific was one of four major railroads to have served Concordia. The others included the Union Pacific, Santa Fe, and Burlington railroads. (Courtesy of Cloud County Historical Socicty Museum.)

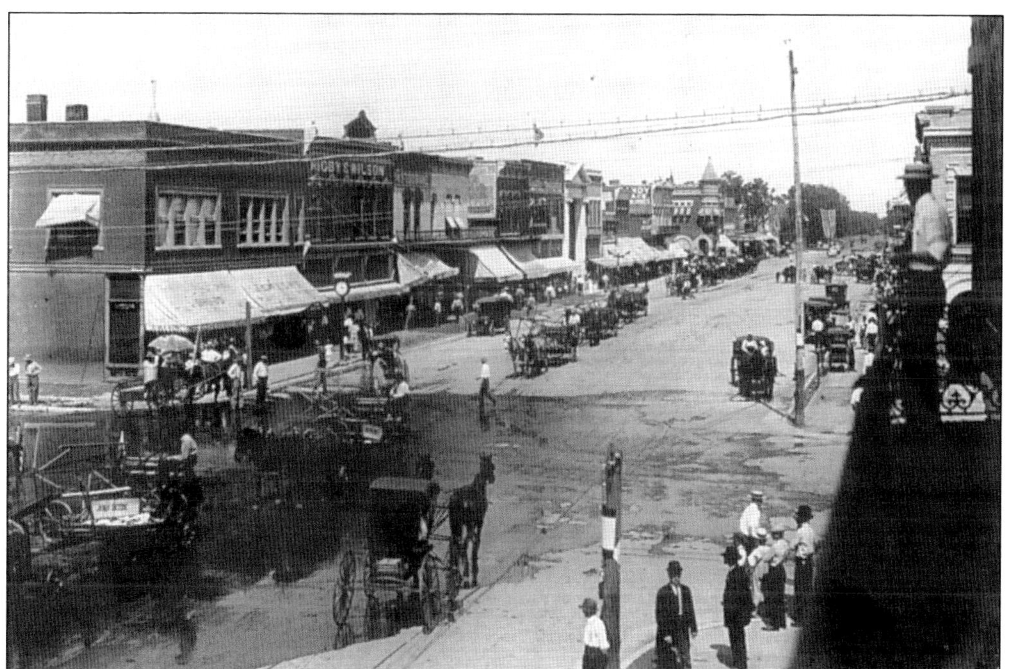

Delivery day for new John Deere farm implements was always important in Concordia because many farms surround the town. In the photograph above, teams of horses pull the new binders up the street to W.H. Burroughs's John Deere Implements store. Below, a crowd gathers in front of the store to see what is new. Several other businesses visible in the photograph include A. Linville Sash and Door Factory, Gill Coal Company, and Concordia Garage, also a Goodrich Tire dealer. (Above, courtesy of Richard Larson; below, courtesy of Cloud County Historical Society Museum.)

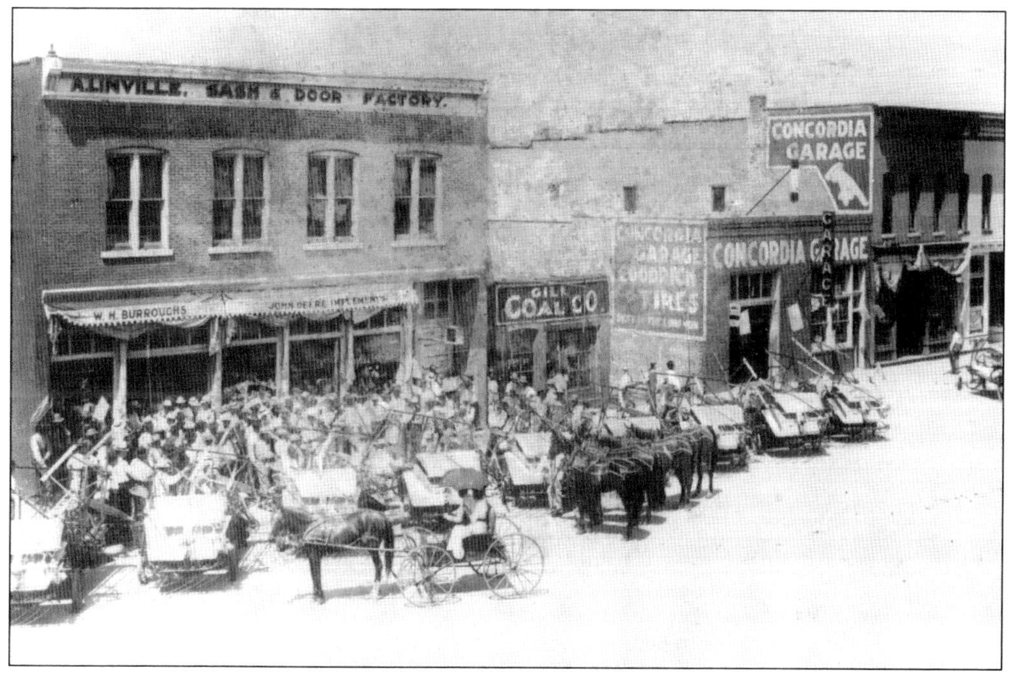

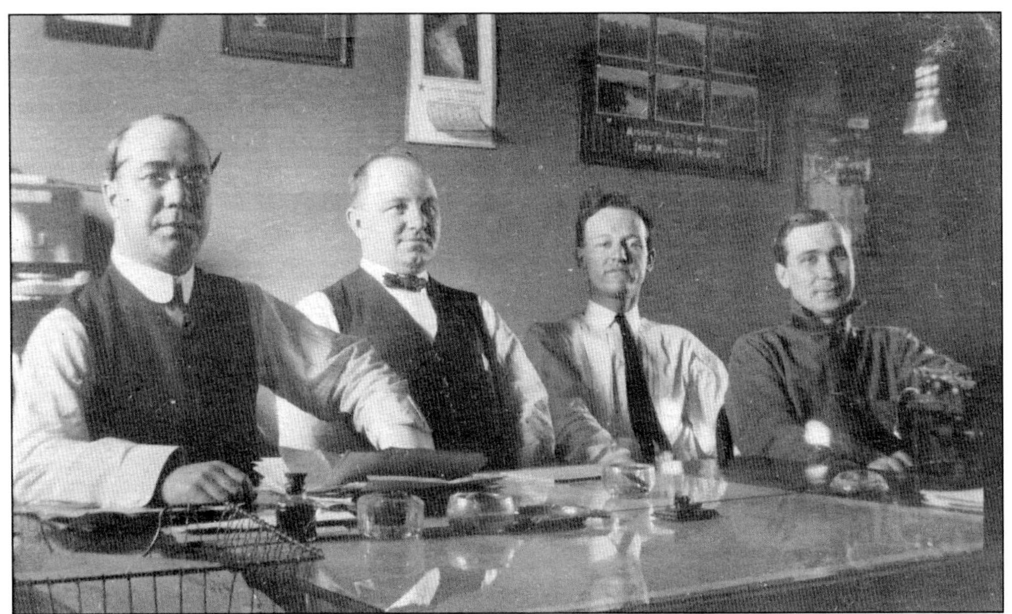

Four Missouri Pacific dispatchers pose in their office for a postcard photograph. They include H.M. Alexander, A.D. Peterson, Ernie Carouthers, and Robert Merriman. (Courtesy of Cloud County Historical Society Museum.)

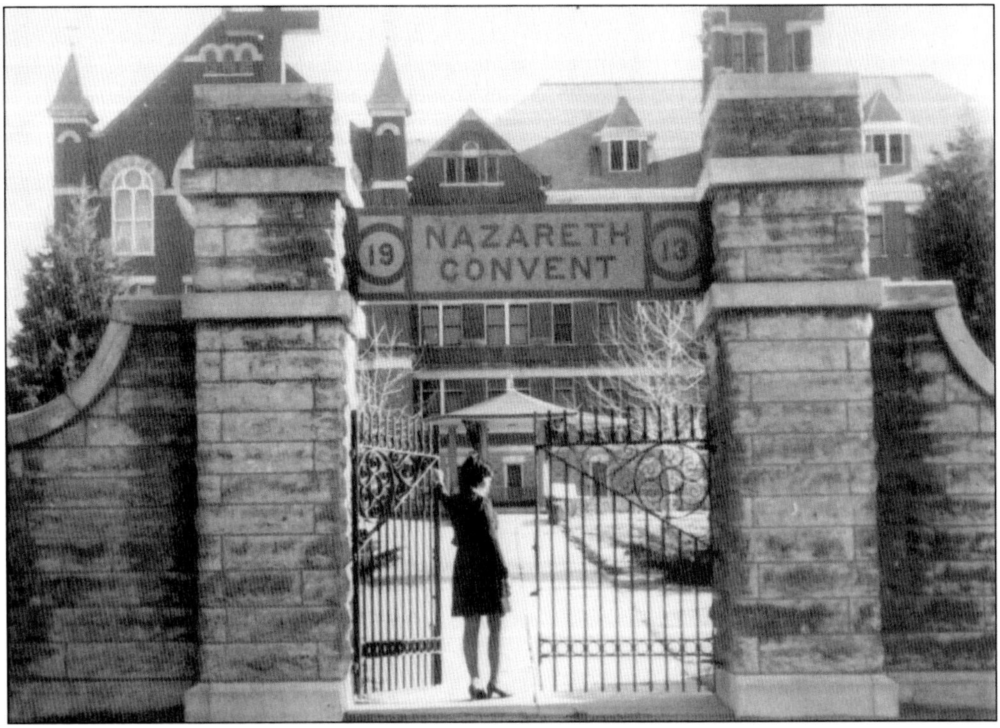

Nazareth Convent's front gate was completed in 1913. The stone and iron gate has become a local landmark along with the convent, which is now open to the public for tours. The identity of the young woman and date of the photograph are no longer known. (Courtesy of Sisters of St. Joseph Archives.)

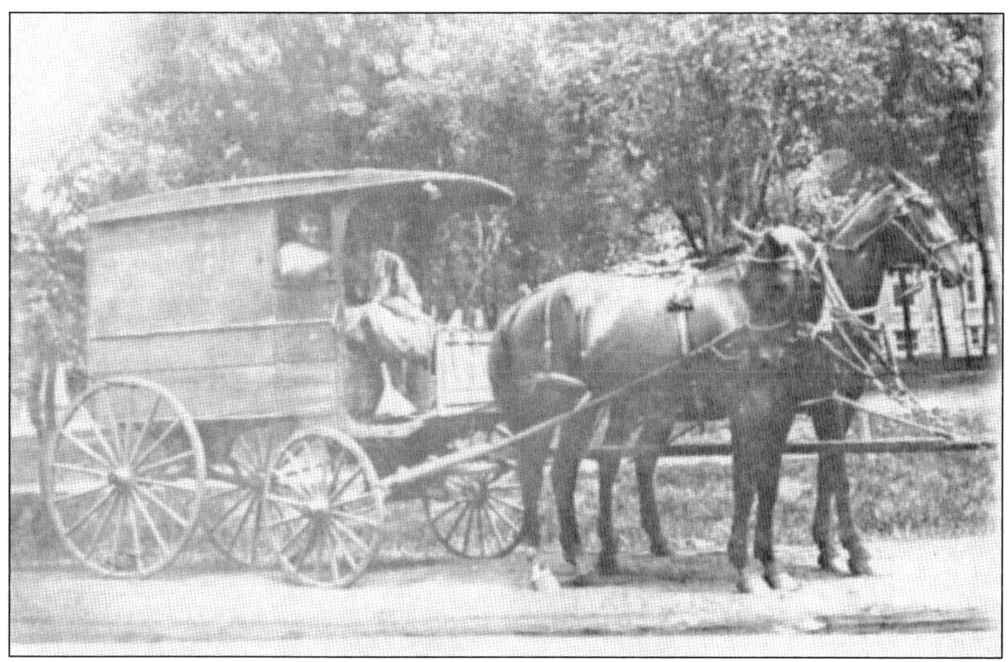

Harrison-Nelson Grocery offered delivery service in the early 20th century, starting with a horse-pulled wagon driven by Lynn "Scoots" Wilson. A cousin of Wilson, J.R. Hefner told a reporter for the *Blade-Empire* in 1971 that he remembered the wagon being replaced by a truck with solid rubber tires in about 1908. He recalled that it was one of the first motorized delivery vehicles in the community. The photograph below of the store was taken about 1915 at 216 West Sixth Street, when the telephone number was 176. Concordia has had many grocery stores and had 22 when Marinus Boogaart opened his first local store in 1933. One of them, Rod's Thriftway Grocery, is still located downtown. (Both courtesy of Cloud County Historical Society Museum.)

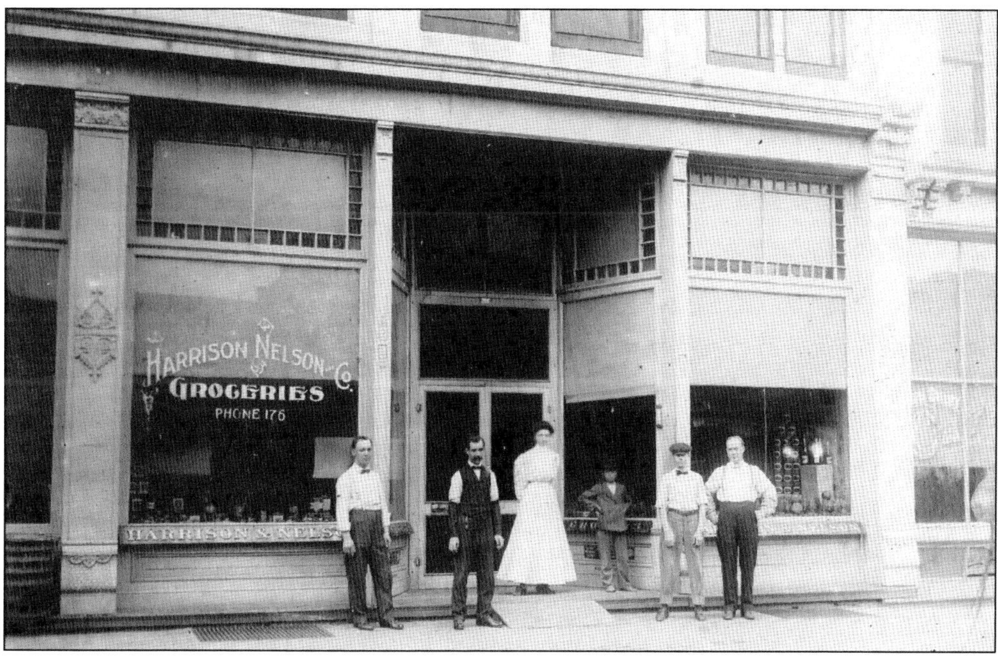

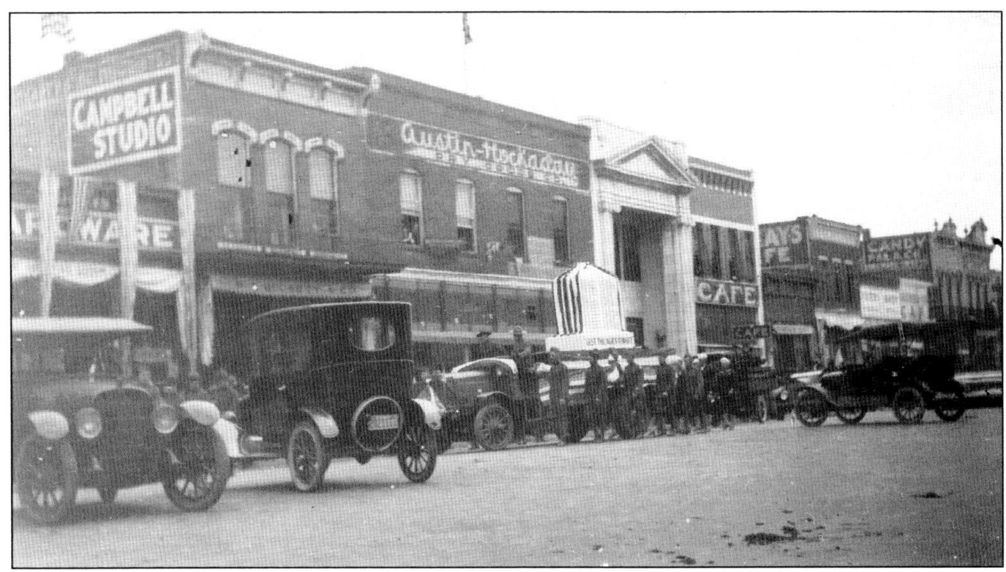

Soldiers surround a truck decorated with the slogan "Lest the Ages Forget" as it passes in front of W.A. McCarthy and Company and Austin-Hockaday Dry Goods Company during Concordia's first Armistice Day parade in 1919. Austin-Hockaday billed itself as "Concordia's First Department Store" and was one of the first chain stores in town. (Courtesy of Cloud County Historical Society Museum.)

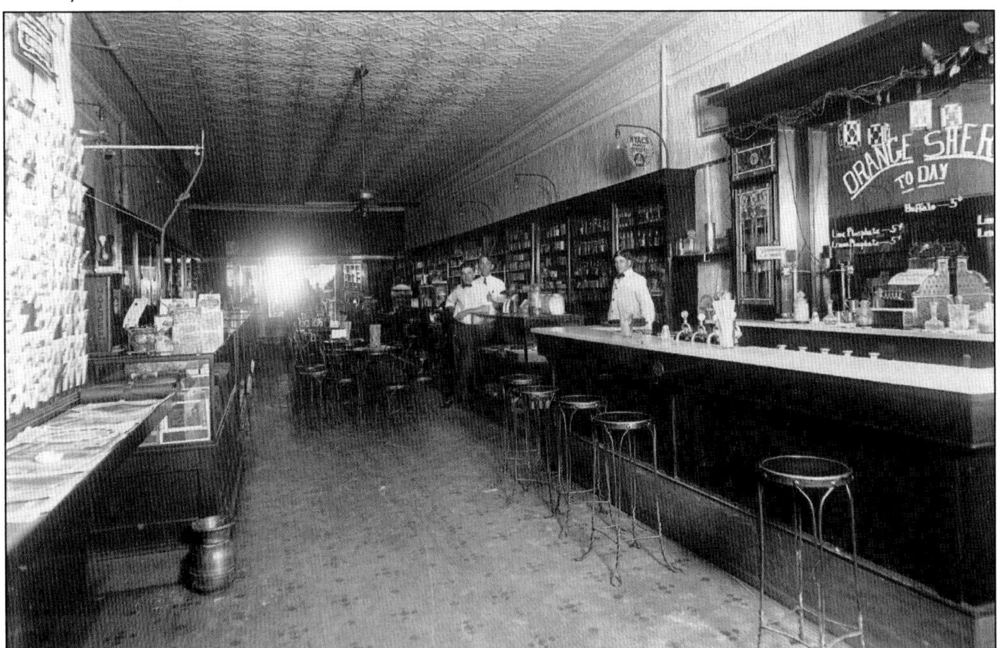

Neitzel's Drugstore was one of several Concordia establishments with soda fountains. Orange sherbet is the feature of the day. Phosphates cost 5¢. Another 5¢ item, a "buffalo," is probably some sort of local specialty. The store had an ornamental metal ceiling, popular in the late 19th and early 20th centuries. The employee farthest back in the picture may be Durl Laughlin. The Neitzels were early arrivals in Concordia and had one of the first buildings on Sixth Street. (Courtesy of Cloud County Historical Society Museum.)

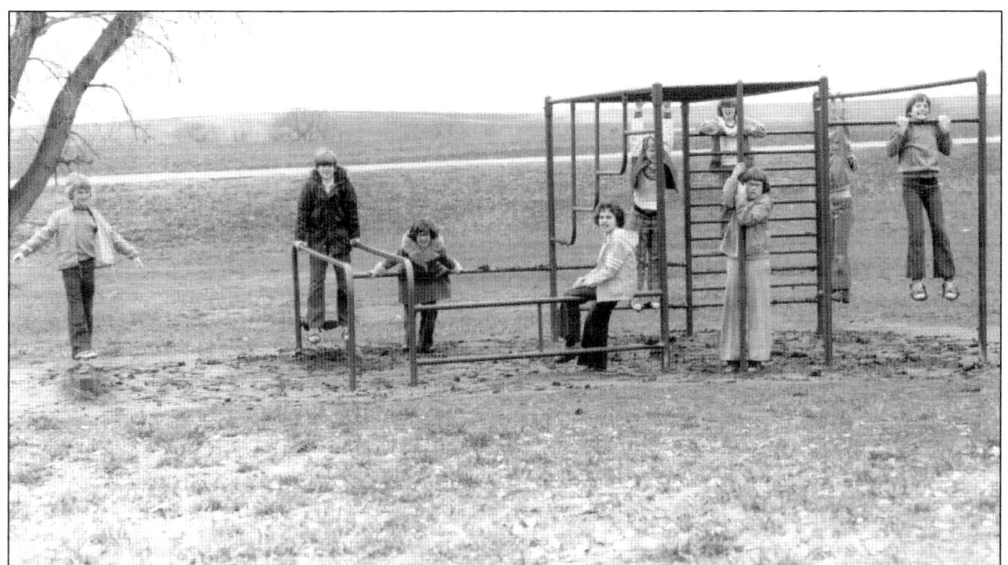

Delmer Harris Company opened in 1925 in the former Maddox block. Rehabilitation on the building, originally built for Banker's Loan and Trust, began shortly before publication of this book. The company stayed open until 1994 and belonged to the Harris family the entire time. Playground equipment became its main product. Here, a group of children try some out. (Courtesy of Cloud County Historical Society Museum.)

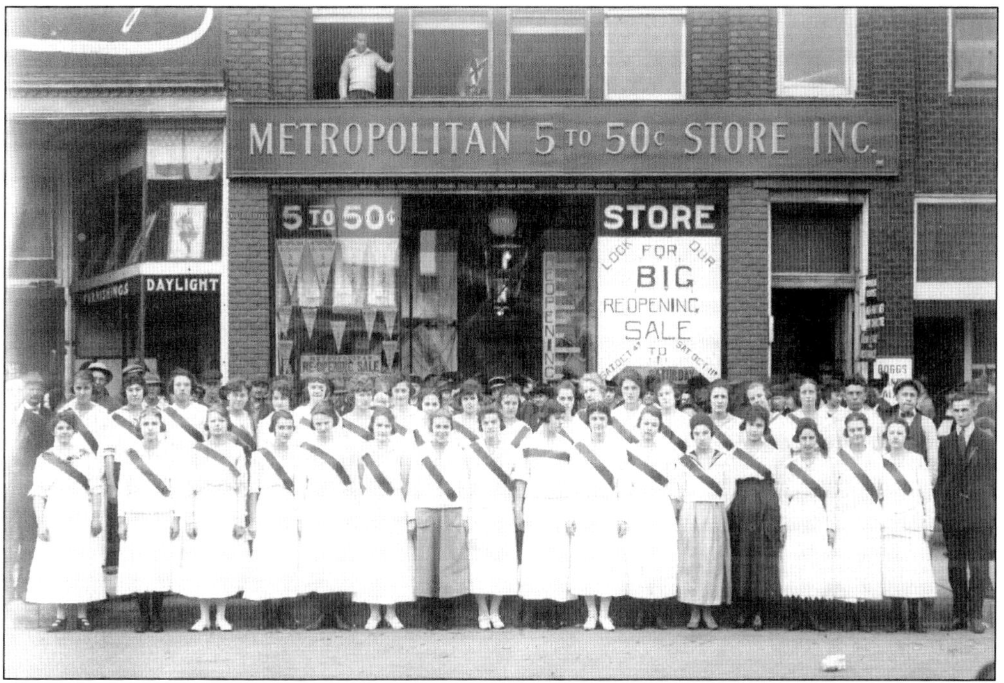

The Metropolitan 5 to 50¢ Store at 126 West Sixth Street had a weeklong reopening sale, commemorating the event with a photograph. The sale was October 4 through October 11, 1920. Two people watch from upstairs, where a dentist and a real estate and insurance business had offices. The entrance to Daylight Clothing Company is at left. (Courtesy of Cloud County Historical Society Museum.)

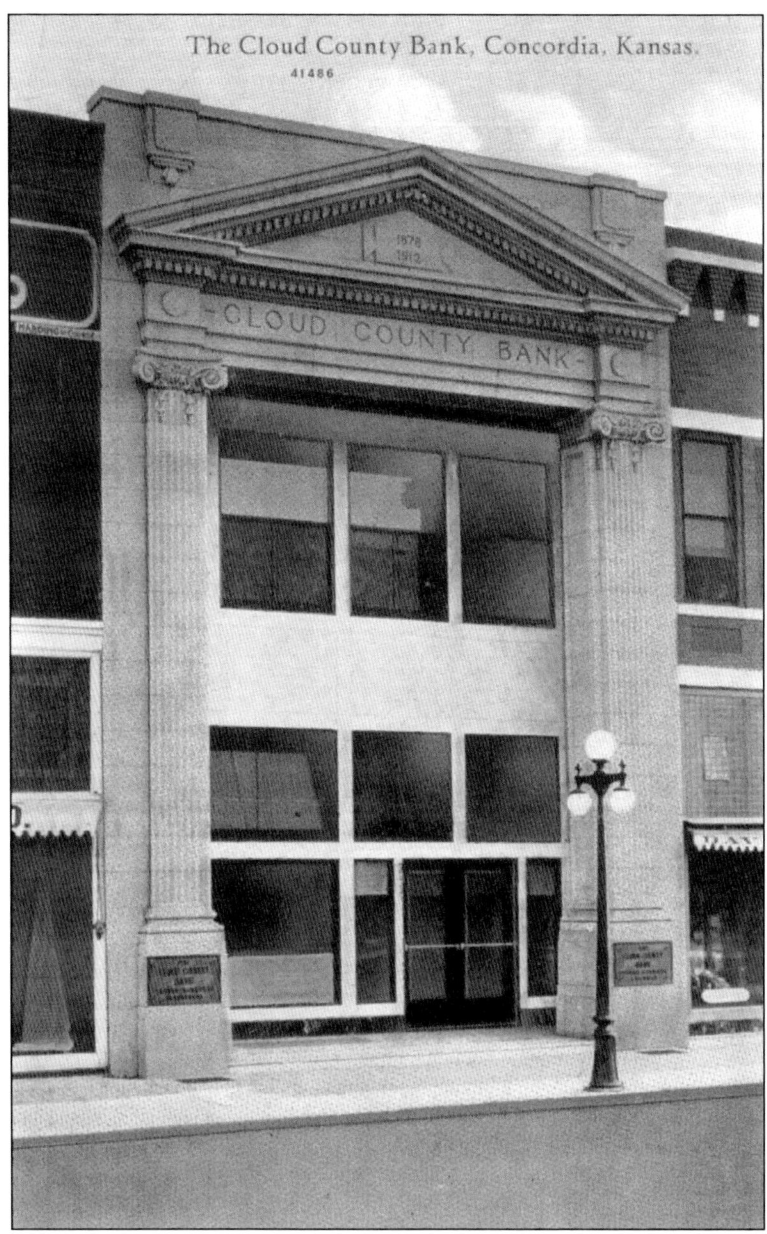

On July 26, 1932, six unmasked men believed to be connected to Alvin Carpis and Ma Barker robbed Cloud County Bank. Newspapers said their driver double-parked a Hudson sedan out front without arousing suspicion. One man directed an estimated 30 to 40 customers entering the bank to a back room and told them to lie on the floor. Bank vice president J.C. Peck was beaten around the head and ordered to open the safe. He was unable to open it, so a bookkeeper, Ida Cook, was called. The car horn signaled them before the safe was opened, but the criminals took $220,894 in bonds and securities and about $1,000 in property from boxes in the vault, as well as $13,738.15 in cash. The robbers took Cook, bookkeeper Marie Frederickson, and customer Nelda Appleby but released them at the north end of Cedar Street and apologized to them for using profanity. Months later, the bankers met with negotiators for the robbers and ransomed the bonds for $15,000. (Courtesy of Dena Bisnette.)

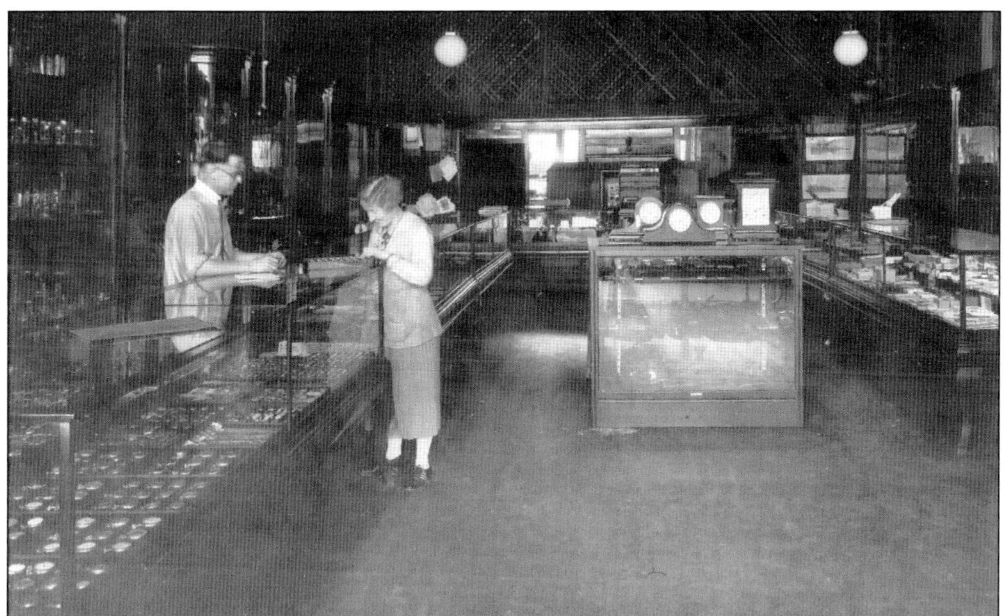

Ingersoll Jewelry at 133 West Sixth Street specialized in watches and clocks as well as fine jewelry. Here, a clerk shows a customer the contents of a tray from the watch display case. (Courtesy of Cloud County Historical Society.)

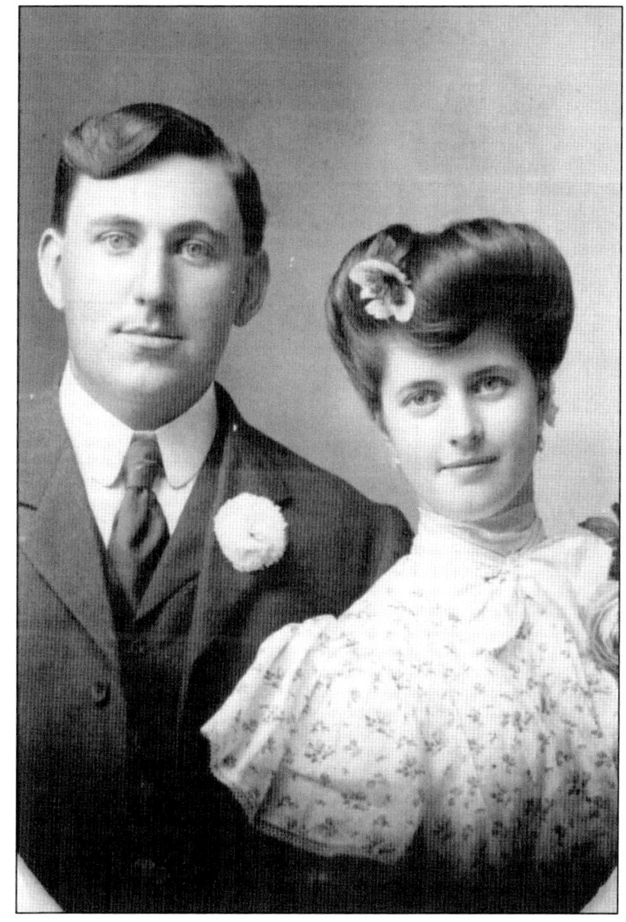

Marinus Boogaart, a Dutch immigrant's son, married Ida Lee Altman of Almena, Kansas, on May 14, 1907. Boogaart had run successful stores in four Kansas communities when he moved to Concordia. He wanted a chain of stores so he could buy directly from manufacturers and offer lower prices. After buying Concordia Mercantile Company, he was able to merchandise items under his own Bestyet label. (Courtesy of Cloud County Historical Society Museum.)

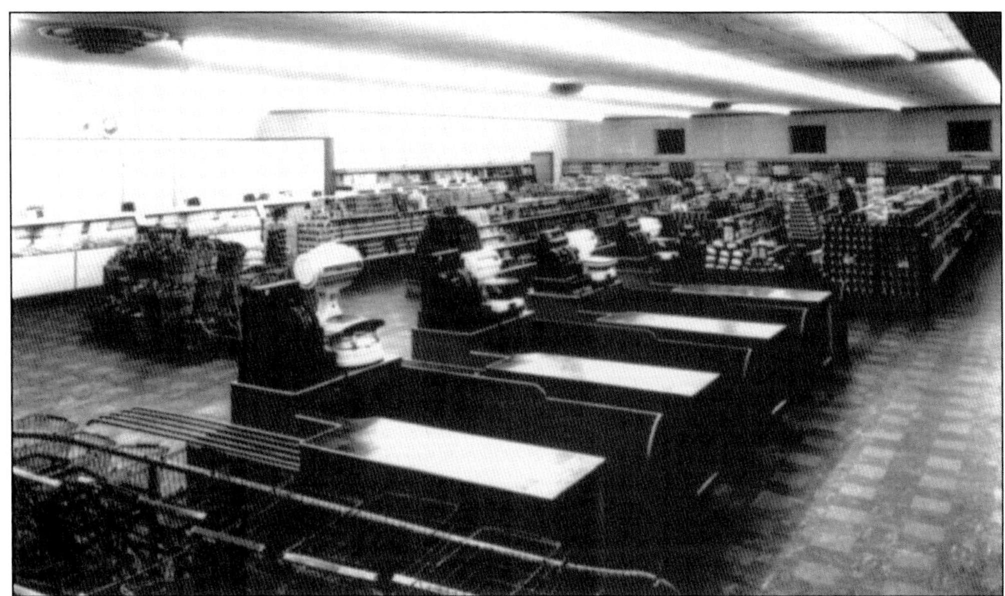

Boogaart opened his first grocery store in Concordia with his son Richard Boogaart and son-in-law J. Milton Sorem in 1933. The store at Fifth and Washington Streets, above, opened with improvised furniture made from orange crates and sold groceries, produce, some cheeses, and cured meats, but no fresh meat. Eventually, the business added locations as well as meat processing and warehouse facilities in Concordia. The store expanded and moved several times, and by 1991, Boogaart's two local groceries were consolidated into one 24,000-square-foot store at 1640 Lincoln Street. The store eventually merged with the Scrivner-Stephens chain in 1965 when Sorem retired. Boogaart had died in 1956 and his son had left the company in 1941 to establish chain grocery stores in Mexico. Not long after the merger, the Concordia Boogaart's closed. Shown below is the exterior of one of the Concordia stores. (Both courtesy of Cloud County Historical Society Museum.)

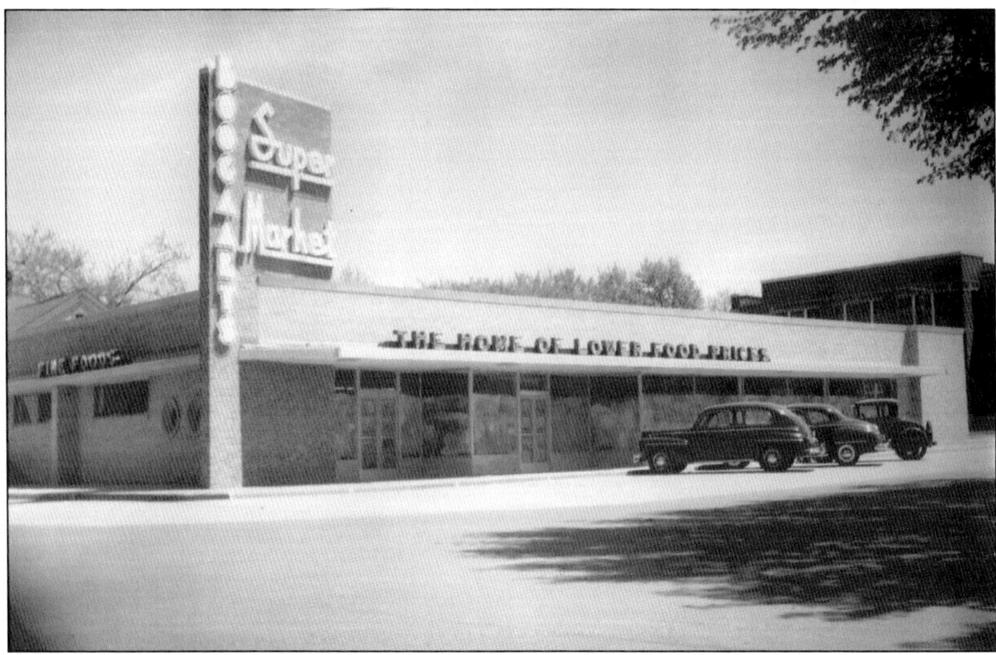

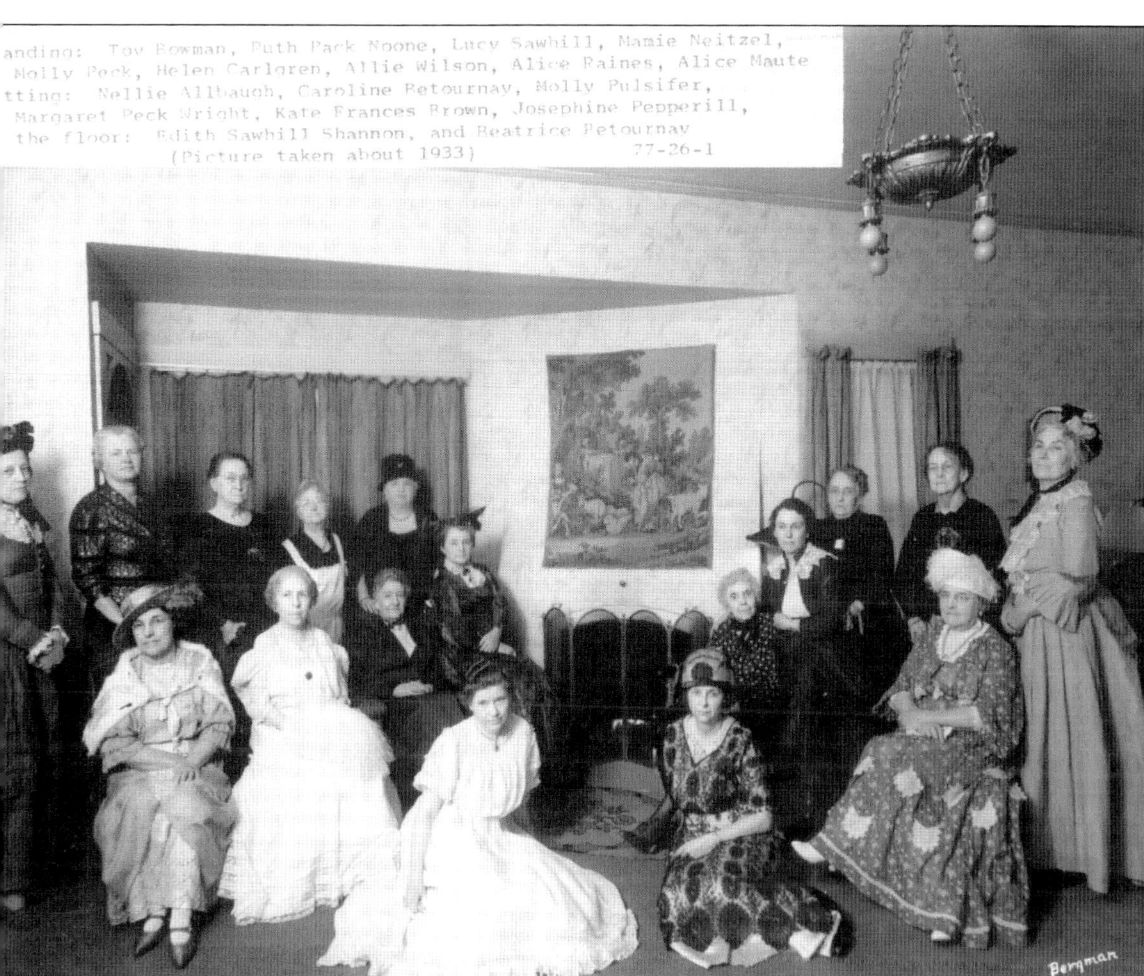

In 1933, Lloyd Bergman took this photograph of some of the wives, widows, and daughters of the most important men in Concordia in the first third of the 20th century. Their husbands and fathers were businessmen, educators, doctors, and lawyers. Their social position made these women the most powerful females in town. The specific reason for the photograph, possibly a charitable event committee or club meeting, was not recorded, but the women's dresses reflect fashions of different decades going back to 1870. The ladies include, from left to right, (sitting on the floor) Edith Sawhill Shannon and Beatrice Betournay; (sitting) Nellie Albaugh, Caroline Betournay, Molly Pulsifer, Margaret Peck Wright, Kate Frances Brown, and Josepine Pepperell; (standing) Tov Bowman, Ruth Pack Noone, Lucy Sawhill, Mamie Neitzel, Molly Peck, Helen Carlgren, Allie Wilson, Alice Raines, and Alice Maute. (Courtesy of Cloud County Historical Museum.)

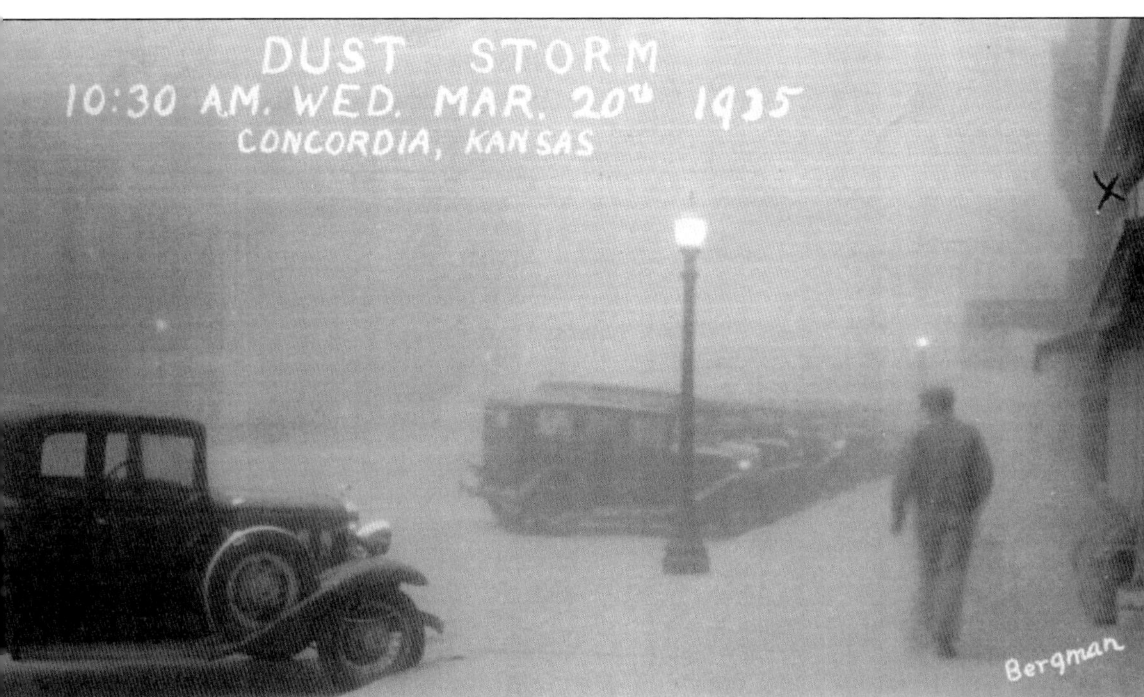

One of the worst times in the Midwest's history was the Dust Bowl era of the 1930s. A combination of farming practices that exposed loose topsoil to wind and several years of dry weather caused the problem, which was worst in Oklahoma, but the dust was blown far and wide. Getting caught outdoors too long could lead to a sometimes fatal condition called dust pneumonia, and people stuffed towels and other barriers into cracks around windows and doors to prevent dust from entering buildings. This dust storm hit on the morning of March 20, 1935, and local photographer Lloyd Bergman of Bergman Studio recorded this scene of a man hurrying south on Washington Street to seek shelter. Another dust storm hit Concordia on April 14 that year. (Courtesy of Cloud County Historical Society Museum.)

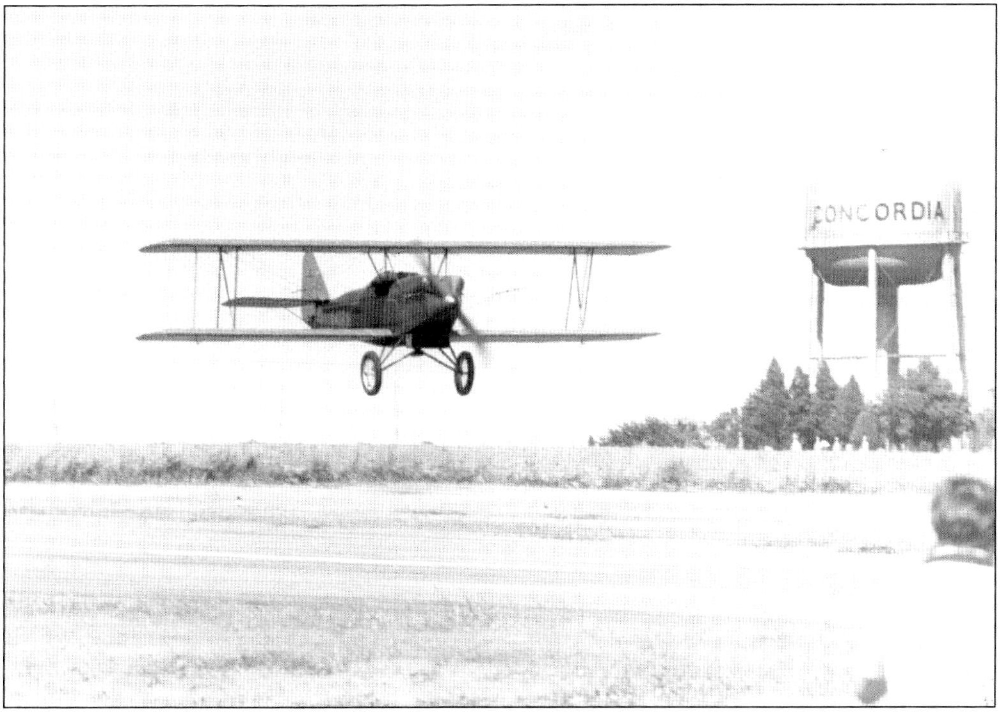

Charles Blosser's 1928 Lincoln Page biplane flies past the Concordia water tower. Blosser flew the plane during rescue efforts when the Republican River flooded in 1935. The pilot mounted an air horn on the plane. When he spotted stranded people, he used the horn to guide his brother Martin Blosser, who was following him in a motorboat. Martin Blosser then ferried the people to safety. Both plane and boat are on permanent display at Cloud County Historical Museum. Below, a Lloyd Bergman photograph shows the overflowing Republican River after a bridge washed out on Highway 81. The water rose so fast that 113 people, mostly in Nebraska, died. (Above, courtesy of Cloud County Historical Society Museum; below, courtesy of Dena Bisnette)

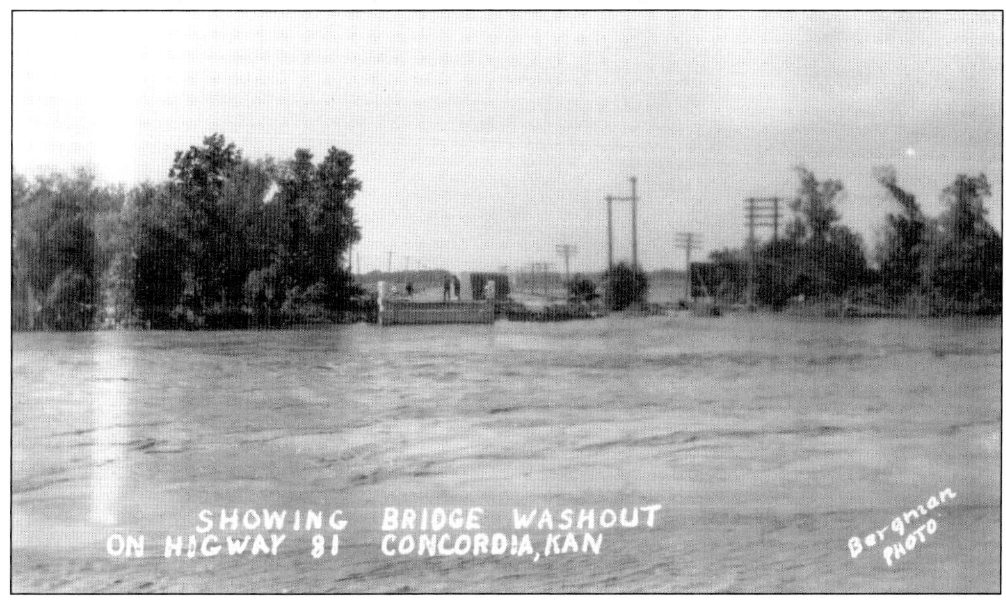

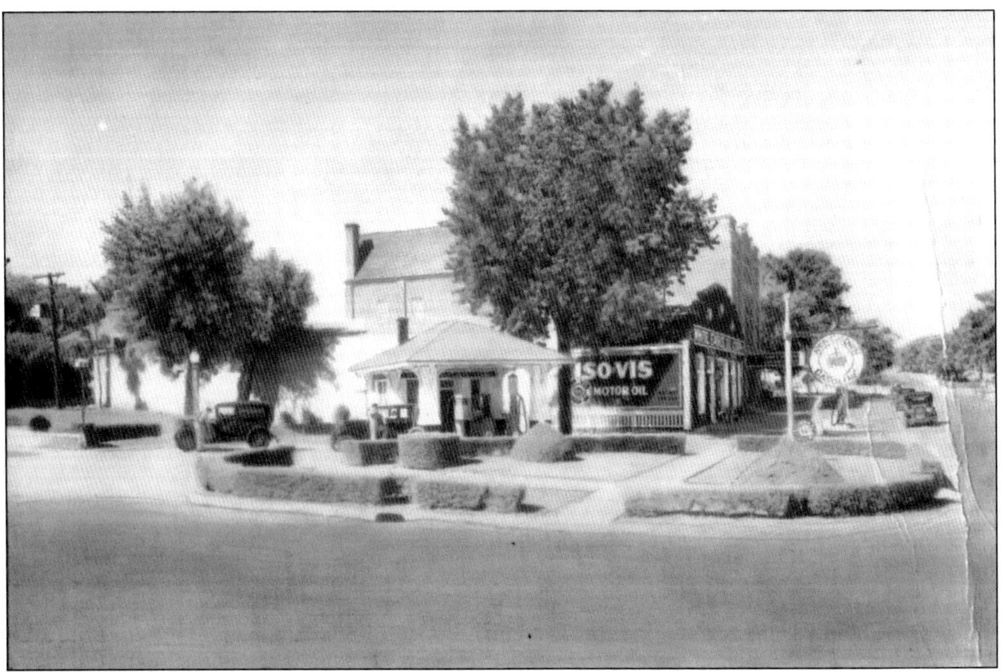

Among Charles Blosser's businesses was Blosser's Standard Oil at 301 West Sixth Street. Also visible is White Eagle Oil, next to the Brown Grand Theatre. The writing on the car at the far left identifies it as belonging to McDonald's Studio, which later became Bergman Studio. (Courtesy of Lori Halfhide.)

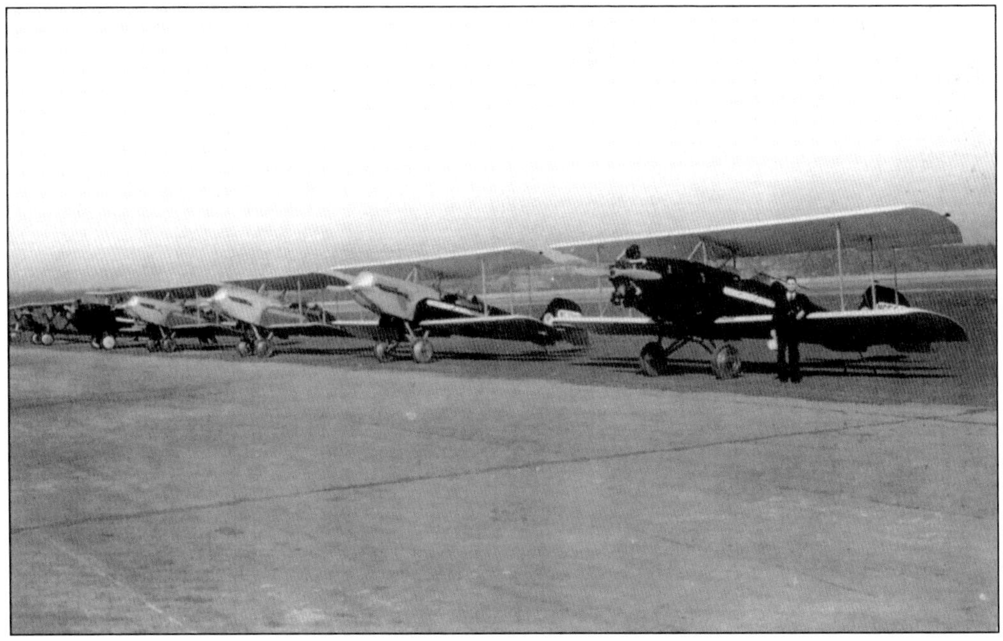

For years, one could buy an airplane without leaving Concordia. Charles Blosser poses beside a row of Lincoln-Page airplanes. The aircraft dealership was one of his many businesses. He also sold boats and had a Chevrolet and used-car dealership next to Everitt Hardware Store. (Courtesy of Cloud County Historical Society Museum.)

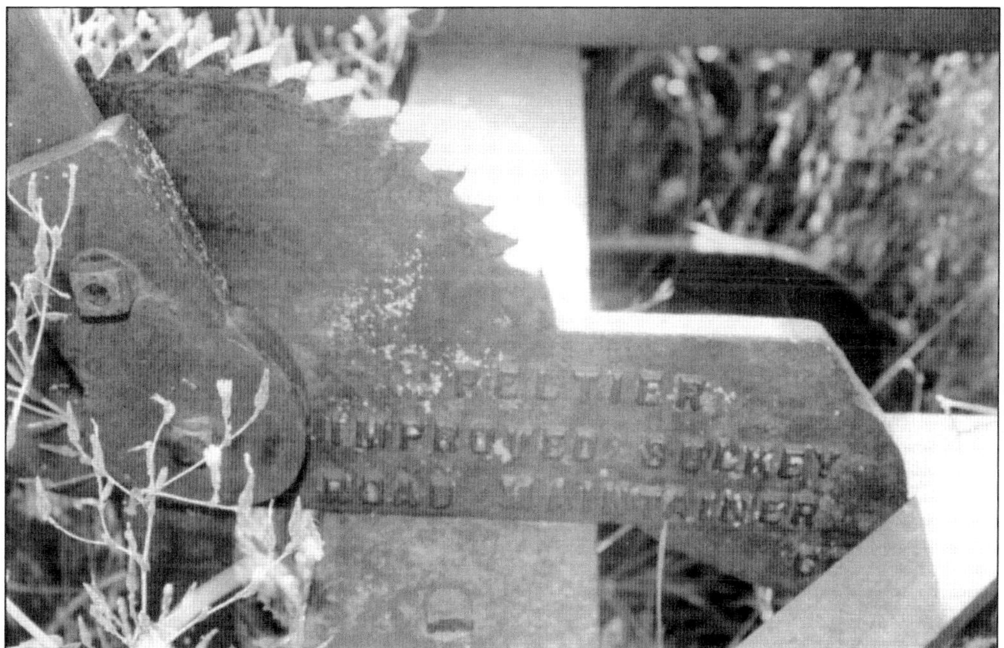

Peltier Foundry is still operating. In 1937, John and Frank Peltier bought Tieking Foundry. John H. Tieking established the foundry in 1915, and soon met Wilfred Peltier, a farmer who invented useful devices. The Peltiers manufacture metal items including roof trusses and building frames, some used locally. They also became known for their metal bridges. Shown above is the trademark on an early product, the Improved Sulkey Road Maintainer. Below is the entire piece of equipment, shown with horse and harness and ready to grade roads. (Both courtesy of Cloud County Historical Society Museum.)

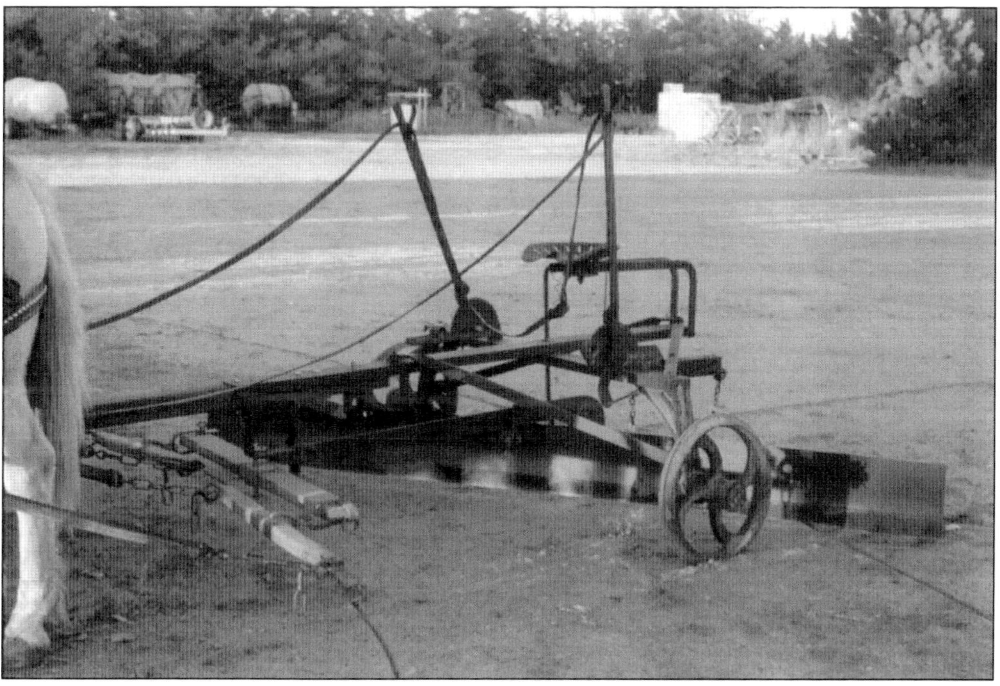

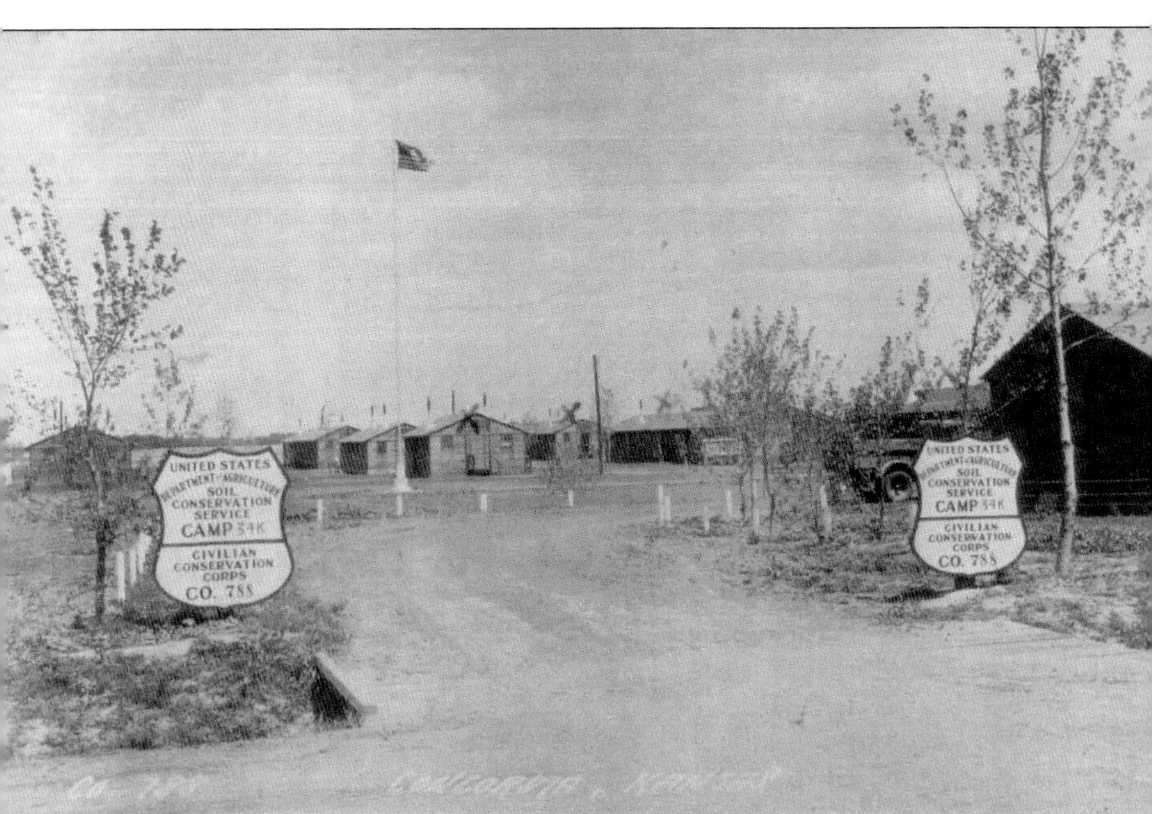

The CCC camp at the east end of Second Street was part of a Depression-era program set up to help young men ages 17 to 24 earn money to support their families. About 9.5 acres for the camp were leased for $16 per acre per year. Construction started in September 1939. The camp closed January 15, 1942, and seven of the buildings were moved to Camp Concordia, a Prisoner of War (POW) internment camp. There were about 200 participants when the CCC camp opened and 110 men in December 1941. They were paid $22 per month and were allowed to keep $5 to $8 while the rest was sent to their families. Work included planting trees and building terraces, ponds, and fences for local farmers. They enrolled for six months at a time and could stay two years or until they turned 24. (Courtesy of Cloud County Historical Society Museum.)

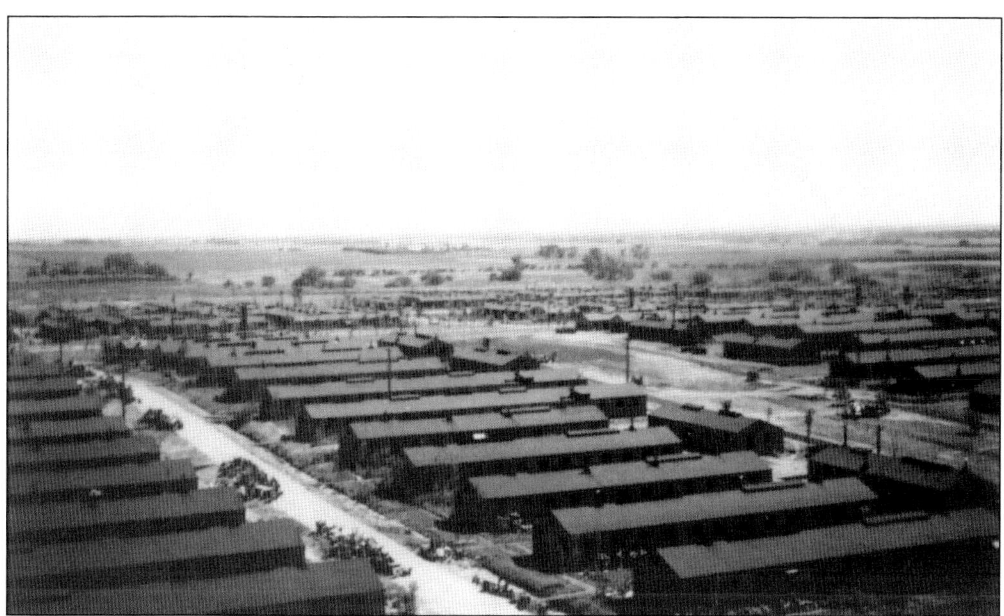

Camp Concordia was one of the POW internment camps where the US Army kept German officers and enlisted men from 1943 to 1945. Prisoners were brought into Concordia by train, because the camp was just a few miles from town. Most of the staff were regular Army personnel, but about 200 local residents were also employed there. The photograph above looks southeast over the camp and shows the prisoners' compound. Below, prisoners are eating a meal. Many of the Germans were stonemasons and other skilled workers and helped with local projects and tasks at the camp. (Above, courtesy of Cloud County Historical Society Museum; below, courtesy of POW Camp Concordia Museum.)

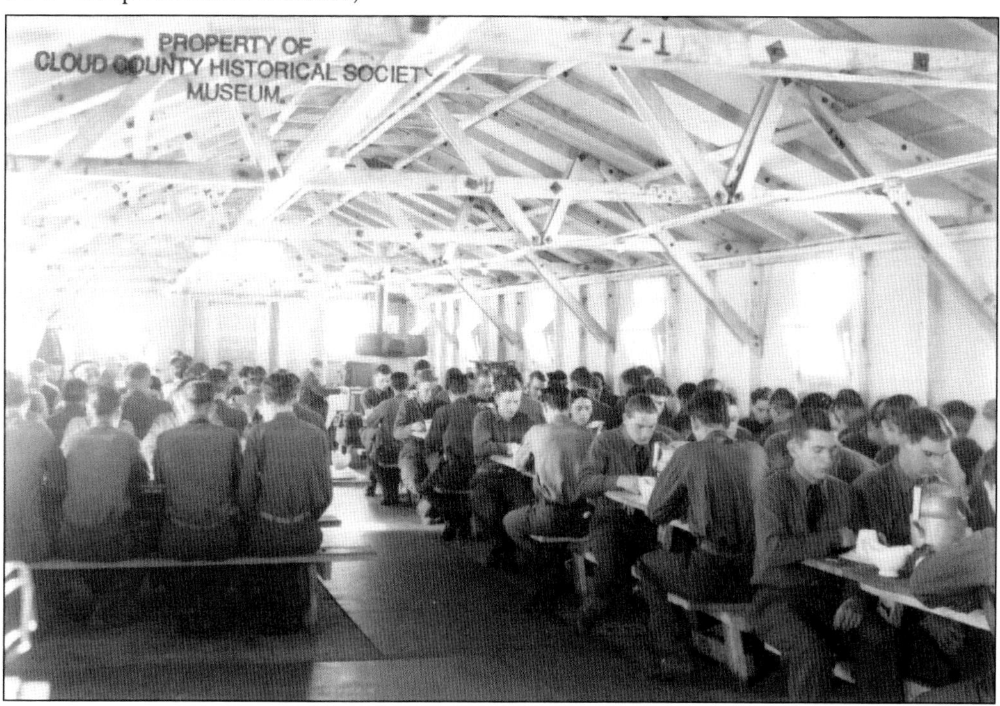

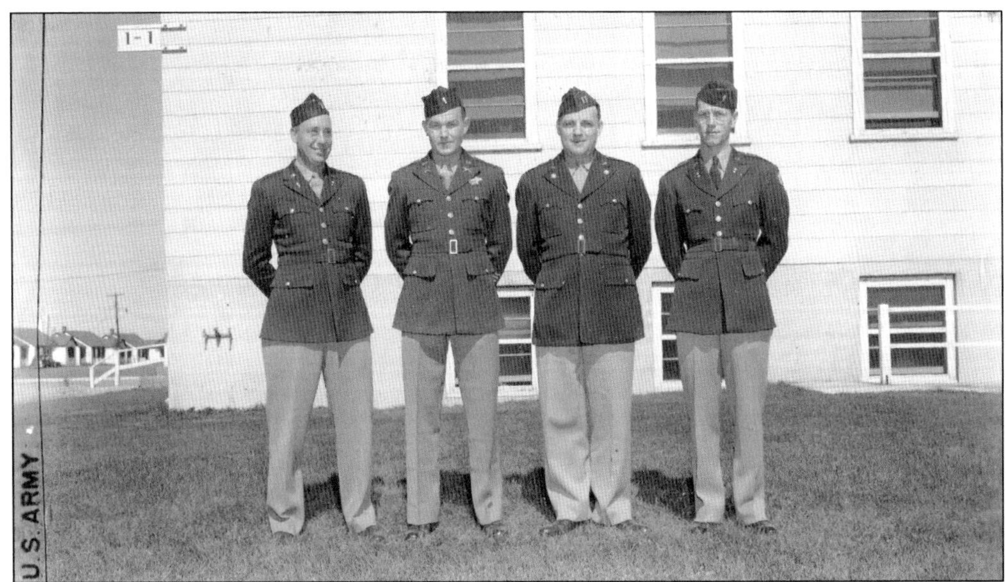

While Germans from Rommel's Division were being held in Camp Concordia, Lt. Merle Thomas, second from left, was a prisoner of war in Europe. Thomas was captured in Sicily while serving with Patton's infantry. After 17 months, he escaped and walked to Moscow, where Russians captured him. Released on D-Day, he walked to Istanbul to meet Allied forces. After the war, he opened Thomas Furniture downtown. (Courtesy of Robert A. Thomas.)

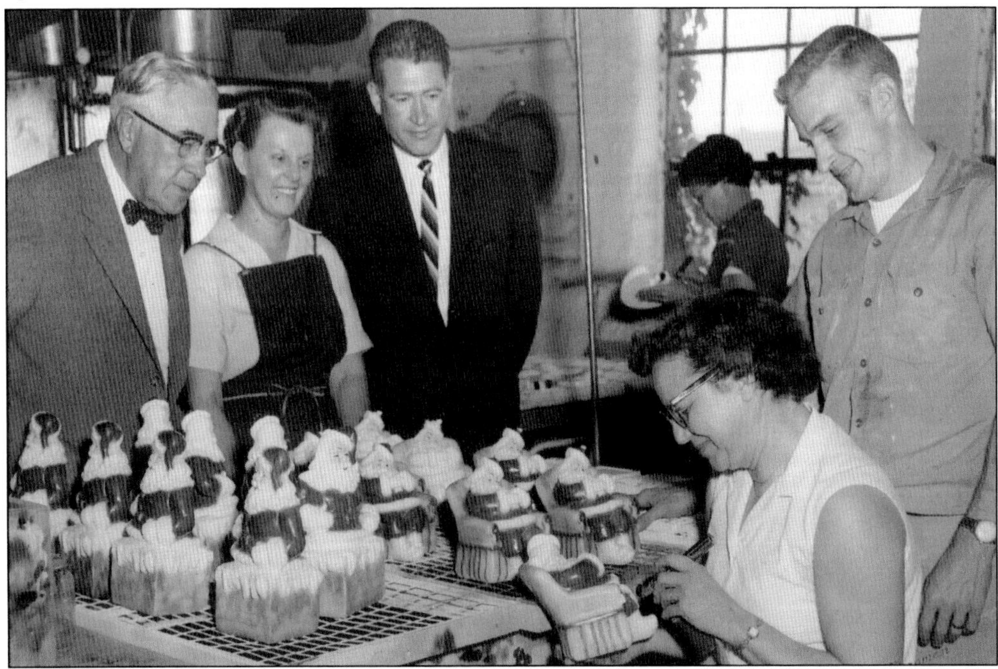
From left to right, Dr. Leo Haughey, Concordia Ceramics Sales owner Charlotte Wilcox, and John Peck of Cloud County Bank visit with Wilcox's customers during a grand opening. Dr. Haughey and Dr. E. Raymond Gelvin established Gelvin-Haughey Clinic, a medical specialists group, after World War II. The clinic helped make Concordia the medical center of North Central Kansas for over 30 years. (Courtesy of Cloud County Historical Society Museum.)

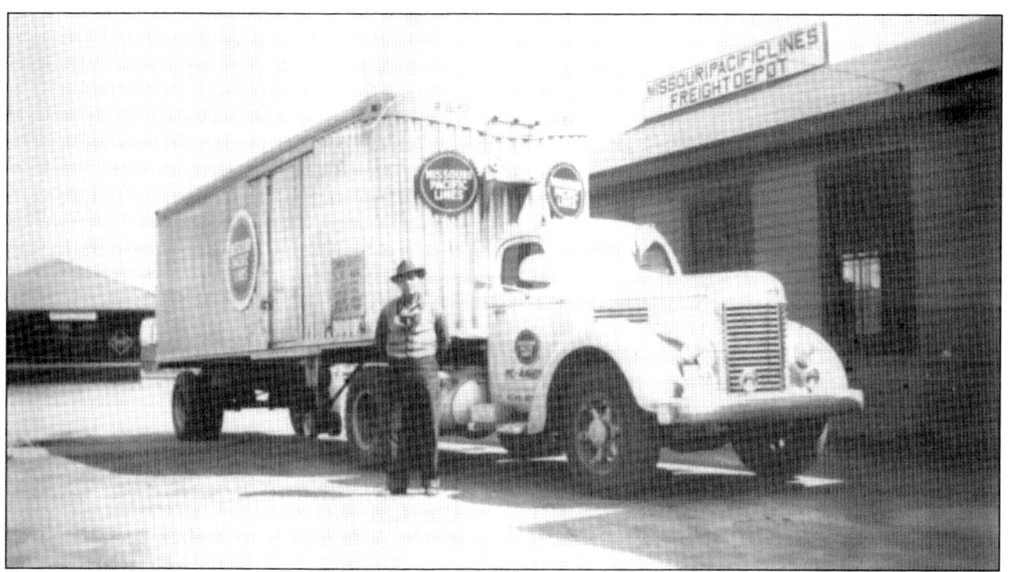

Boyd Dochow drove from Concordia to Downs and other nearby communities for Missouri-Pacific Freight Lines. His daughter-in-law, Marie Dochow, said this particular truck is one that he started driving in the 1940s. He is parked beside the Missouri-Pacific Lines freight depot. (Courtesy of Marie Dochow.)

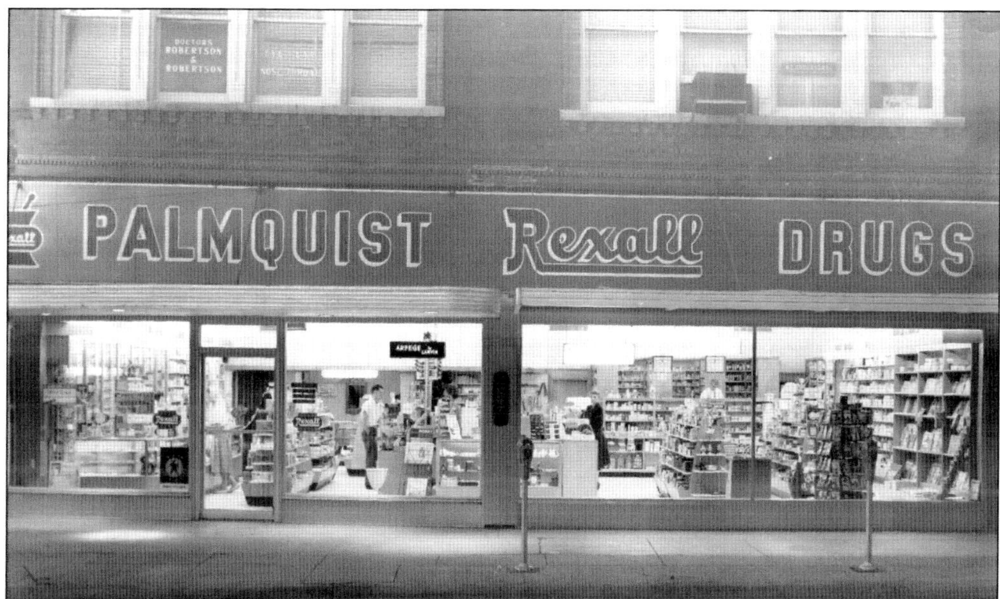

Palmquist Rexall drugs opened in 1945 at Sixth and Washington Streets in a storefront that had been occupied by a drugstore since 1900, when Layton and Neilson moved their drugstore from the next block. It had been Schmelling Drugs since 1930. Although the downtown store is closed now, the Palmquist family is still in the pharmacy business with Family Health Mart on Lincoln Street. (Courtesy of Cloud County Historical Society Museum.)

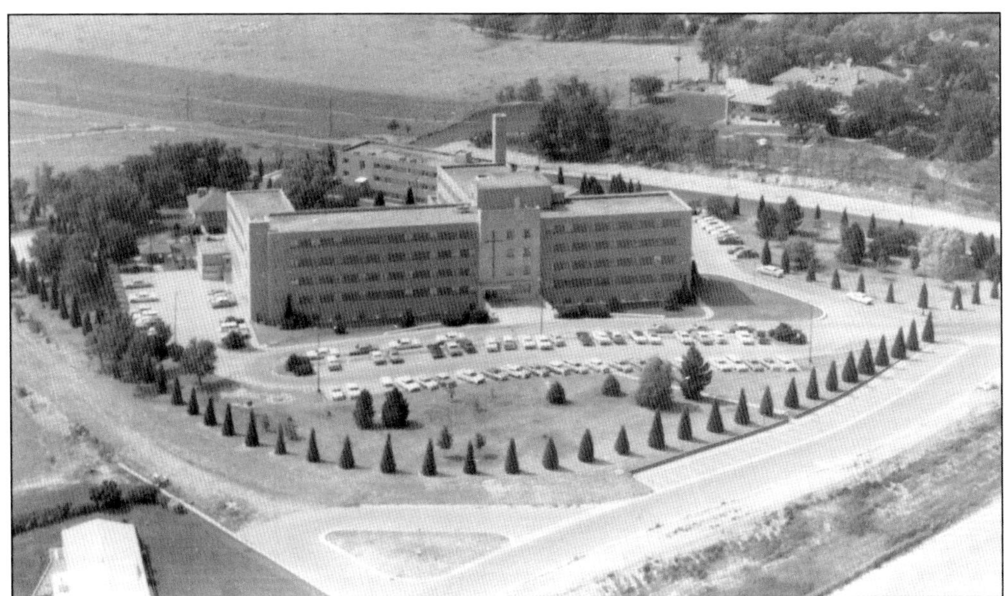

Construction on the new St. Joseph Hospital building on the west side of Concordia began August 16, 1949, and the new facility opened March 6, 1951. The hospital had 150 beds at that time. The old St. Joseph Hospital building stands on the site of the original home of the Sisters of St. Joseph. The sisters set up their original health care facility there after Nazareth Convent and Academy, now listed in the National Register of Historic Places, was built in 1903. Coauthor Dena Bisnette's grandmother Edith Bisnette worked at St. Joseph Hospital. (Courtesy of Cloud County Health Center.)

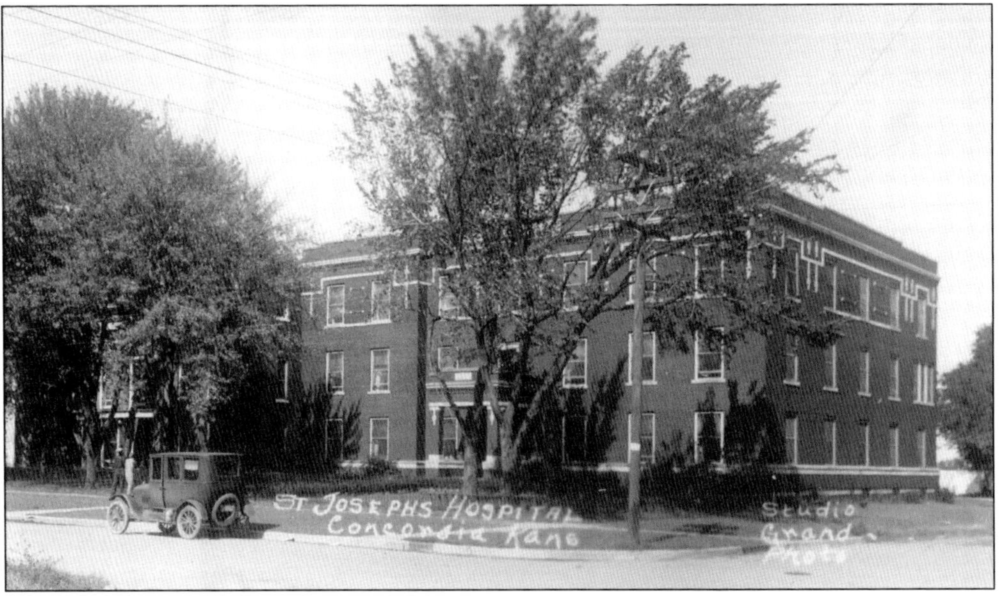

The old St. Joseph Hospital, photographed by Studio Grand, is now Manna House of Prayer. Established by the Sisters of St. Joseph in 1903 when Nazareth Convent and Academy was built, the old hospital was outgrown by the 1940s and was replaced in 1951 by the new hospital, now the core of Cloud County Medical Center. The sisters also started a school of nursing in 1919, which later moved to Marymount College in Salina. (Courtesy of Sisters of St. Joseph Archives.)

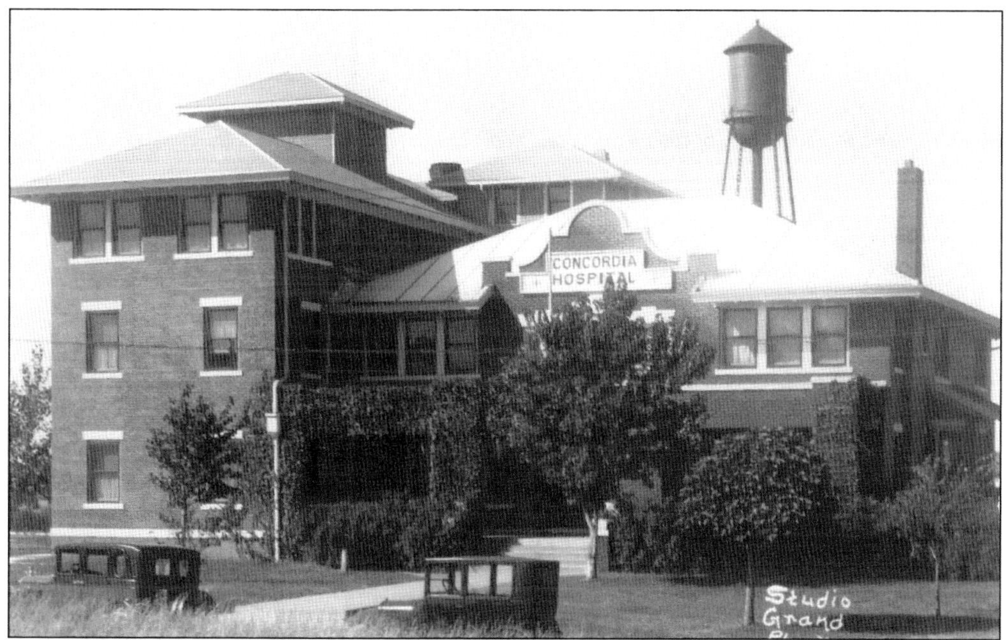

Concordia Hospital, sponsored by the Kansas Baptist Church, opened in 1920. The facility was located in the former home of J.W. Watts. When it closed in 1951, Concordia Hospital became the infirmary for the Baptist Sunset Home, formerly called the Swedish Home. Later, it became studio apartments before being torn down. (Courtesy of Cloud County Historical Society Museum.)

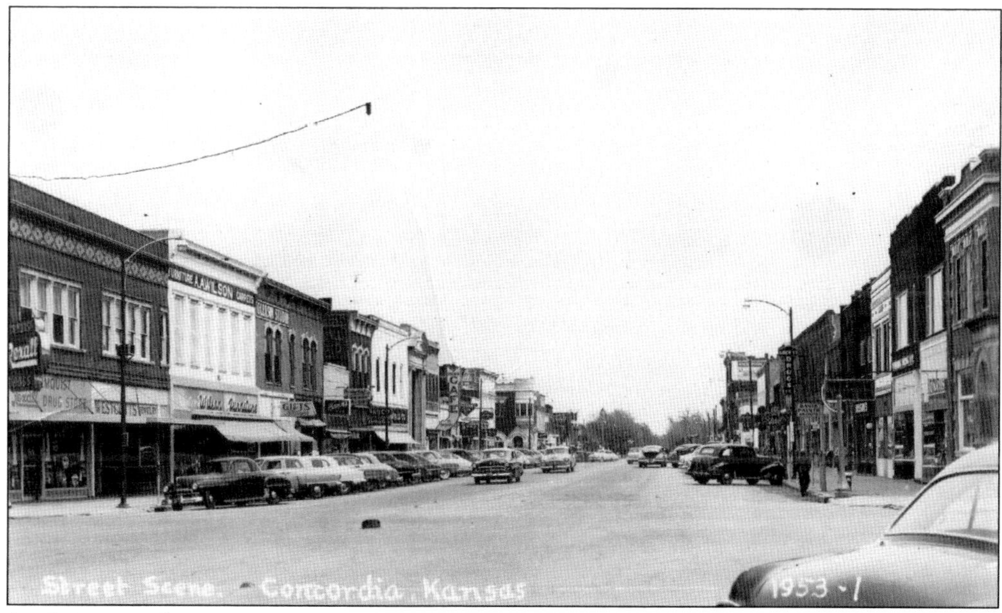

Sixth Street still serves as the main street of Concordia's downtown business district. This postcard shows how it looked in 1953. Visitors often comment that the street is wider than average. The original downtown streets were planned in the 1870s to provide room for stagecoaches to unload without holding up traffic. (Courtesy of Dena Bisnette.)

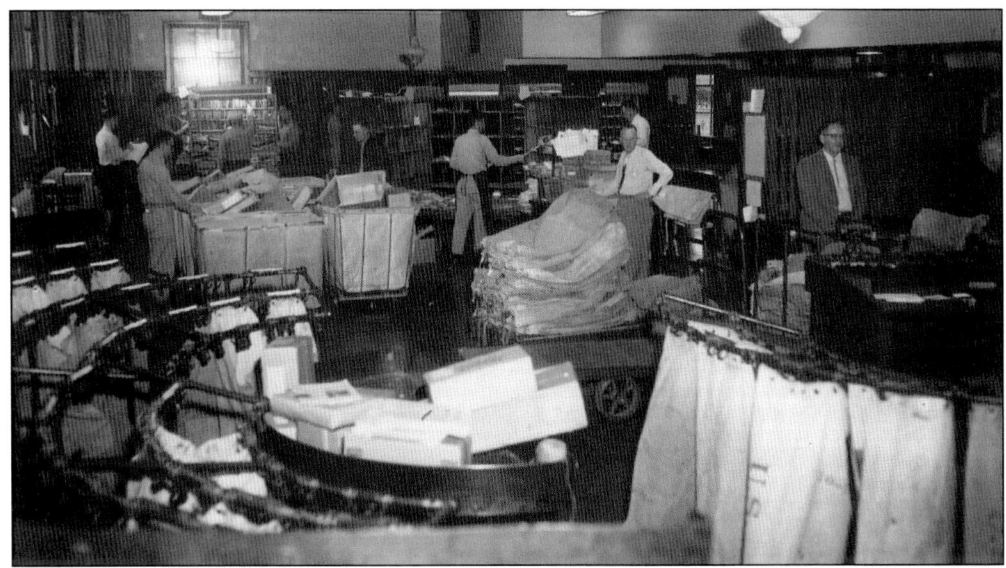

Above, workers at Concordia Post Office prepare mail and packages for their next destinations. From left to right are Don Campbell, Lyle Walker, Ed Luecke, Cecil Child, Axtell Humphrey, Glen Campbell, Shorty Blackburn, Oliver Delforge, Milburne Horkman, Harry Hanson, William "Buzz" Miller, Lyle Conley, and Joe Weaver. In 1954, the crew had a picture taken at the post office. This photograph (below) by Switzer Studio includes, from left to right, (first row) Oliver Delforge, Charles Burch, Ross Mackinnon, and Jim Loop; (second row) Postmaster Lyle Conley, Harry Hanson, Don Campbell, Lyle Walker, Shorty Blackburn, Leroy Breault, Axtel Humphrey, and Mel Horkman; (third row) John Christian, Buzz Miller, Cecil Child, Ed Luecke, Sid Knapp, and Ralph Rogers; (fourth row) Joe Weaver, Robert Chilcott, Lawrence Bailey, Glenn Campbell, Ray Culley, and Jack Perry. (Both courtesy of Cloud County Historical Society Museum)

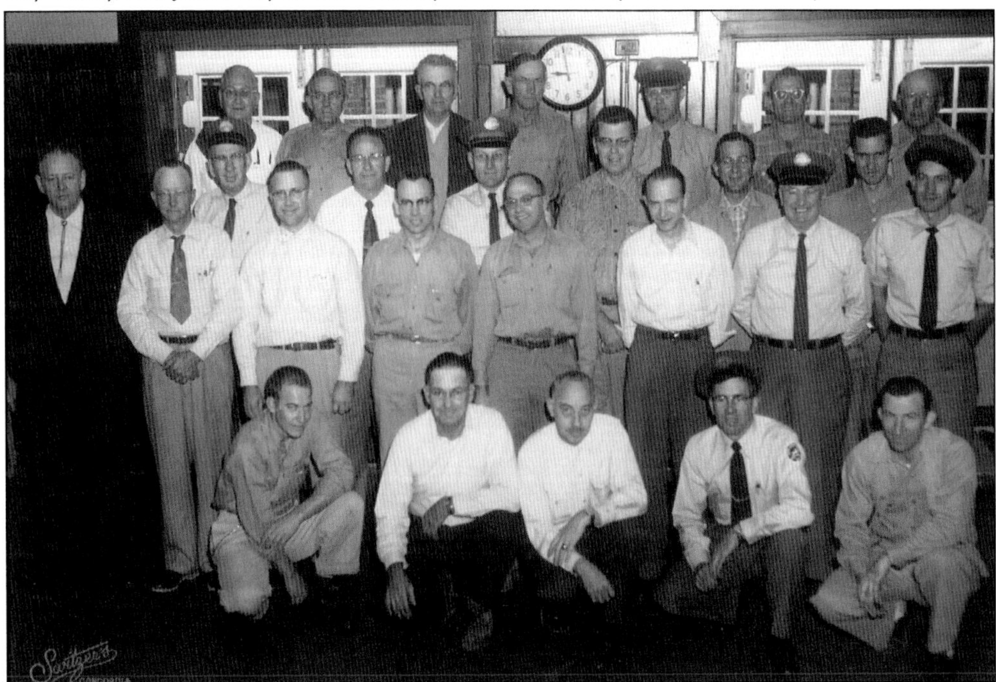

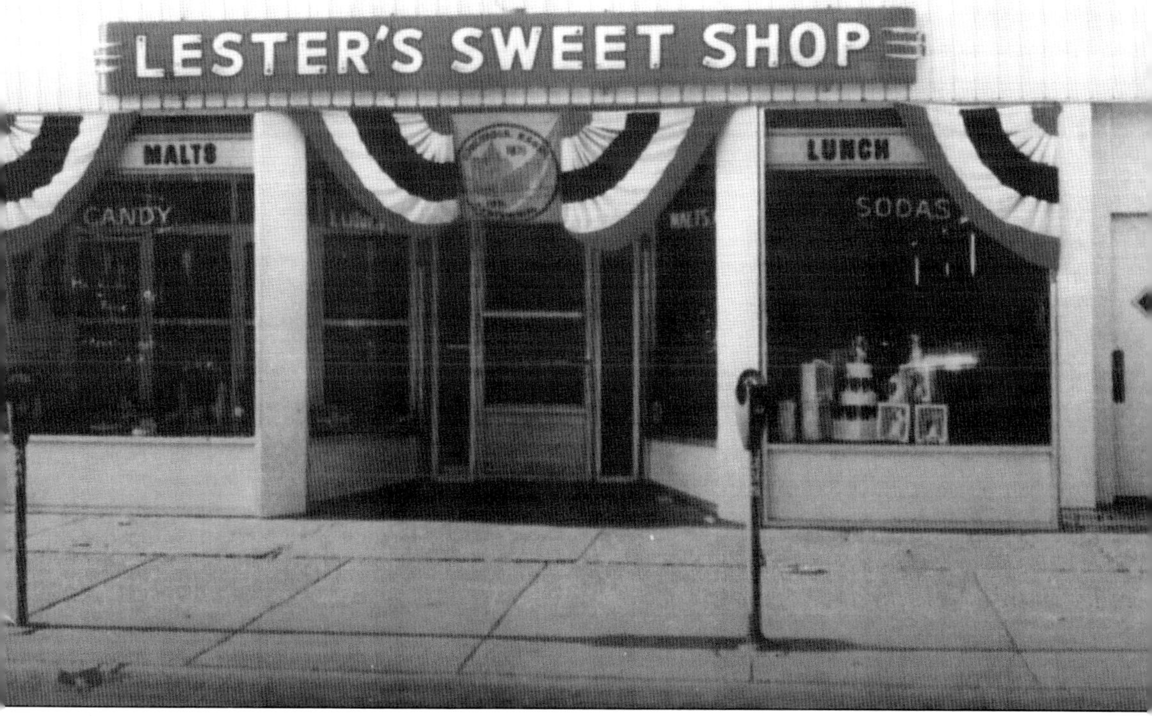

In the 1950s, the place to go after school and sporting events was Lester's Sweet Shop. Originally opened as Reichert's Candy Palace, it was sold to A.H. and Anna Barnhill, who operated it with a somewhat formal atmosphere. Candy maker Lester Davis and his wife, Wanetta, bought the shop in 1948 and installed a jukebox. When Davis became too ill to work, he turned it over to a friend, David Boll, who ran Burgers N Bones. One of Boll's employees, Kim Wiesner, became manager and operated the soda fountain and candy-making business with Wanetta Davis and Grace Henderson. In 1983, Fred and Clara Stegmaier leased Lester's and ran it for about 10 years, adding more diner food to the menu. Concordia native Brad Deal bought it in 1993. Lester's has closed, but the coin-operated horse ride that Davis bought in the 1960s is still operating in front of Trading Post Antiques. (Courtesy of Cloud County Historical Society Museum.)

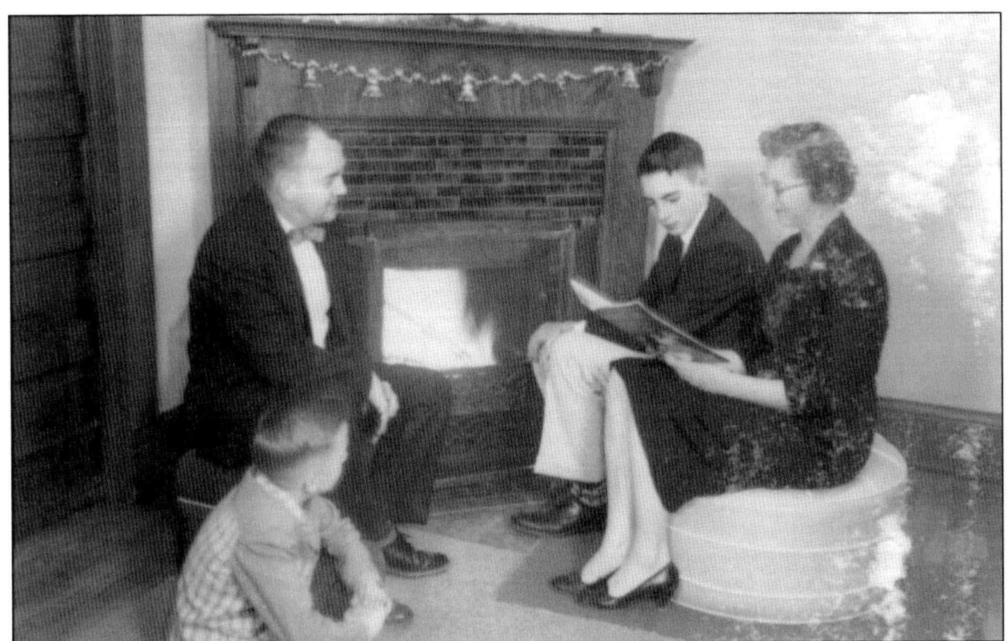

The fireplace in this photograph may look familiar to Concordians because so many photographs were taken in front of it. Wayne Switzer, left, operated a photograph studio out of this room in his home at 720 Cedar Street. With him are his sons, Charles, right; and Kenneth, left, and wife, Eleanor. Charles said this was taken in 1958. (Courtesy of Charles Switzer.)

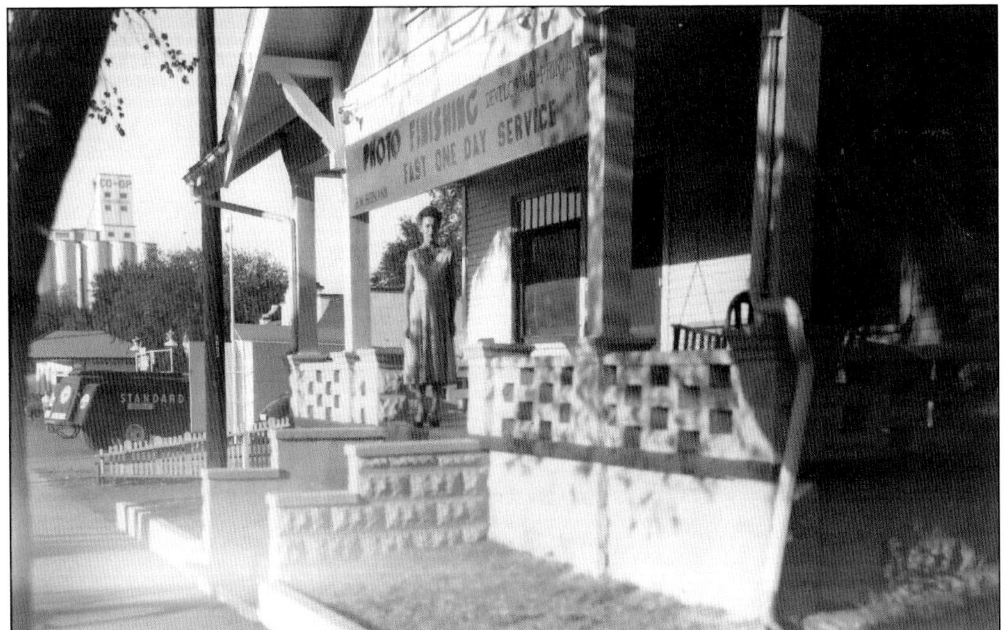

Barbara Riemann stands on the porch of B.M. Riemann Photo Studio on Lincoln Street in the early 1950s. Her husband, known as Marion, rented the lower floor from Frank Bombardier, a retired farmer who lived upstairs. Riemann also painted many houses in town. He moved to Washington, Kansas, to run a Sherwin-Williams store but returned because Barbara preferred Concordia. Upon their return, they rented the same house. (Courtesy of Cindy Riemann.)

Jim Buoy, funeral director, heads out for work at Smith Funeral Home on a cold morning in January 1957. Buoy was a newlywed at the time. Later, he owned Blachly and Buoy Funeral Home in Jamestown and Chaput-Buoy Funeral Home in Concordia, which he operated for many years before retiring. (Courtesy of Kim Buoy.)

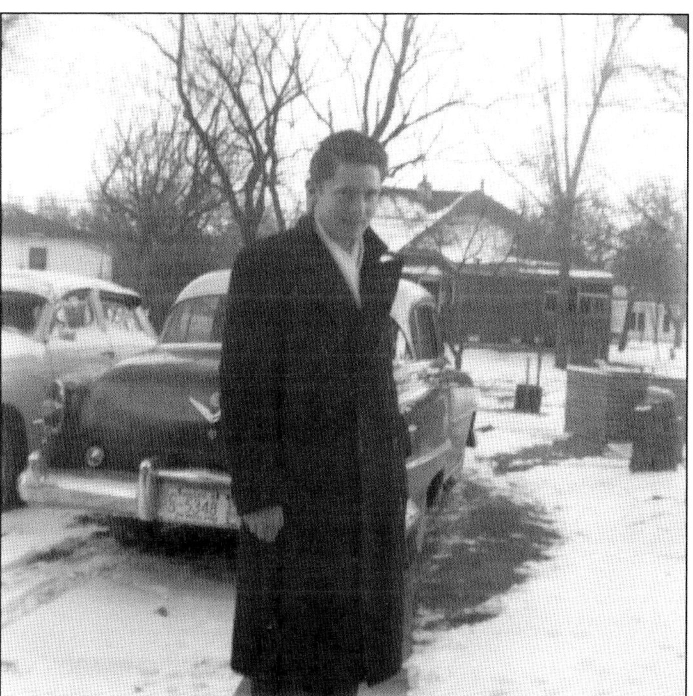

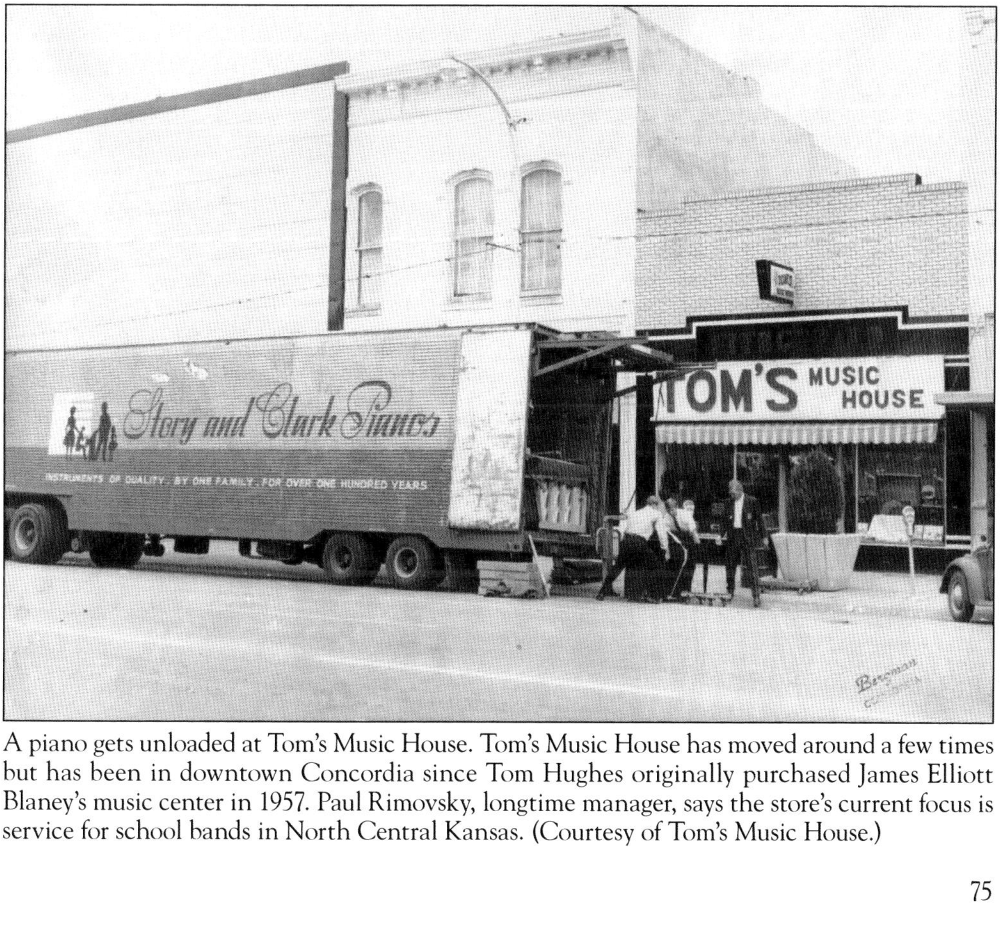

A piano gets unloaded at Tom's Music House. Tom's Music House has moved around a few times but has been in downtown Concordia since Tom Hughes originally purchased James Elliott Blaney's music center in 1957. Paul Rimovsky, longtime manager, says the store's current focus is service for school bands in North Central Kansas. (Courtesy of Tom's Music House.)

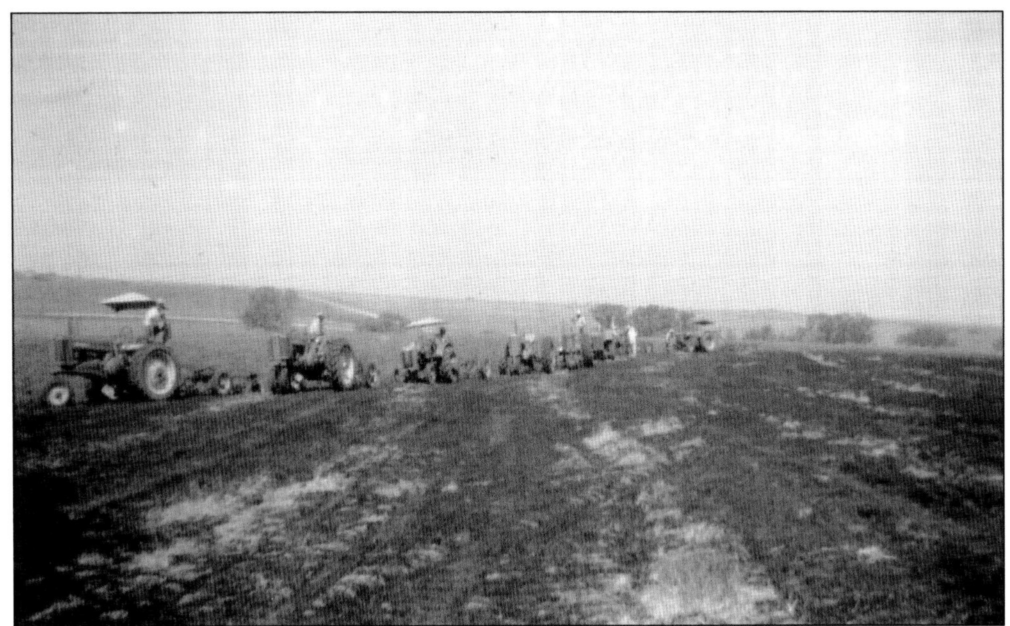

Concordia is mostly surrounded by farmland, and farmers stick together. This photograph from summer 1958 was taken on a farm belonging to Bill Hofflinger, who had died not long before this picture was taken. Neighboring farmers brought their tractors to help Bob Hofflinger and Bill Hofflinger's widow, Esther L. Hofflinger, with plowing. The Hofflinger farm was a few miles south of town. (Courtesy of Kurt Kocher.)

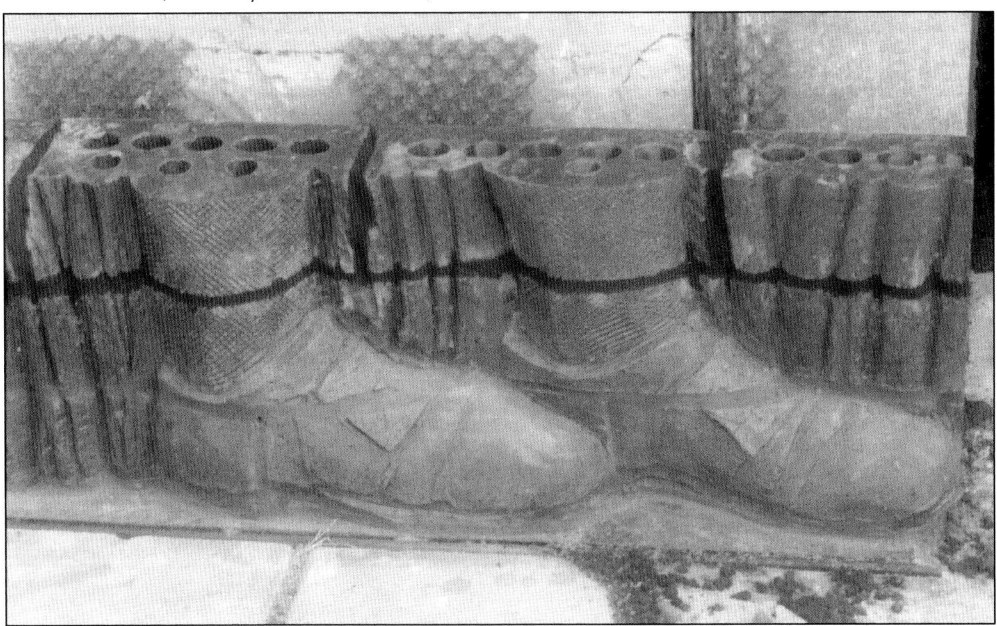

Charles S. Cook opened Cloud Ceramics in 1946, which continues to provide bricks for schools and other public buildings, mostly in the eastern United States. The company still mines the same local clay deposit as in 1946. Cloud Ceramics made these green bricks for Concordia's Whole Wall Mural. Artists carved the bricks by hand and sent them back to the company for firing. (Courtesy of Cloud County Historical Society Museum.)

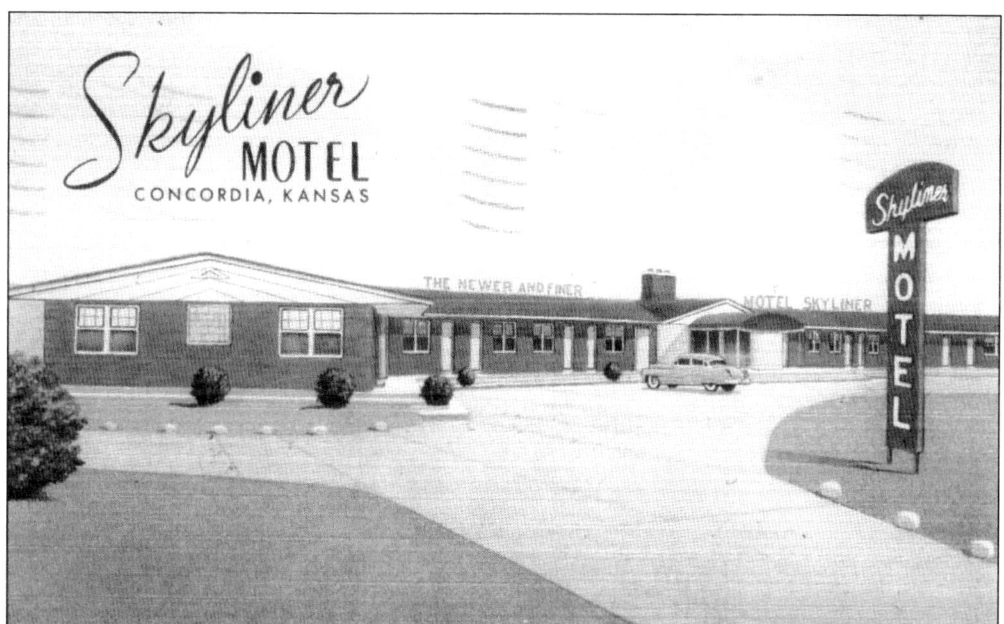

Above, a postcard depicts the Skyliner Hotel, owned by Charles Blosser. The 34-room motel boasted the latest amenities of the early 1950s, including wall-to-wall carpeting, colored tile baths, and radios and telephones in every room. It had forced-air heat and air-conditioning and a café nearby and was conveniently located just south of Concordia on US Highway 81, near Blosser Airport. Below, firefighters prepare to spray water on the motel as fire breaks through the roof of the building the night it burned down in 1989. (Above, courtesy of Lori Halfhide; below, courtesy of Dallas Nading.)

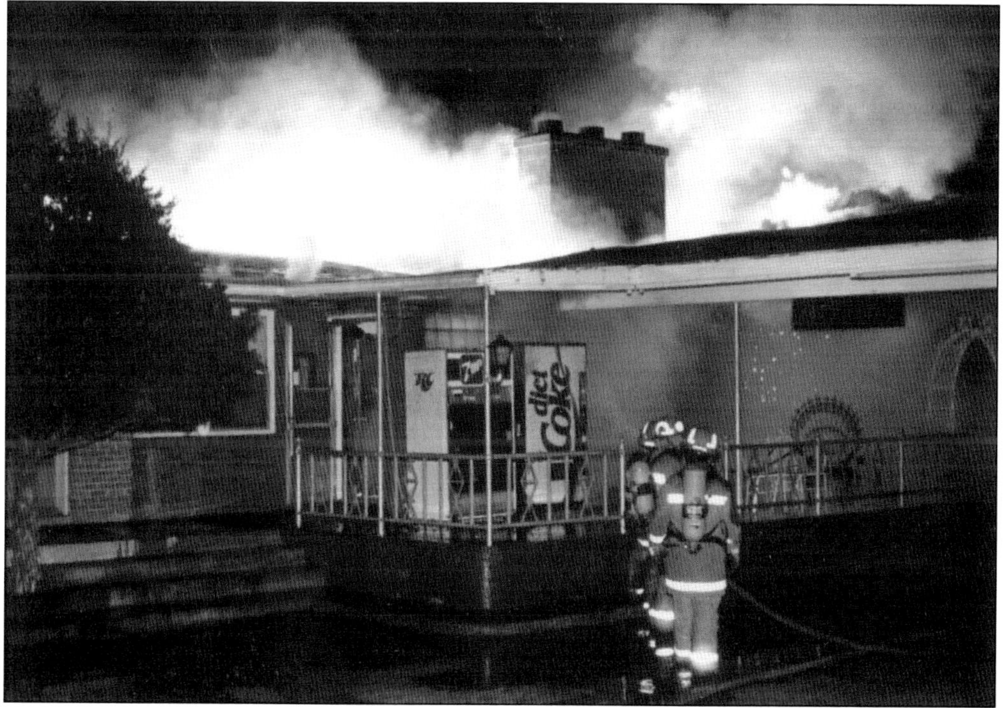

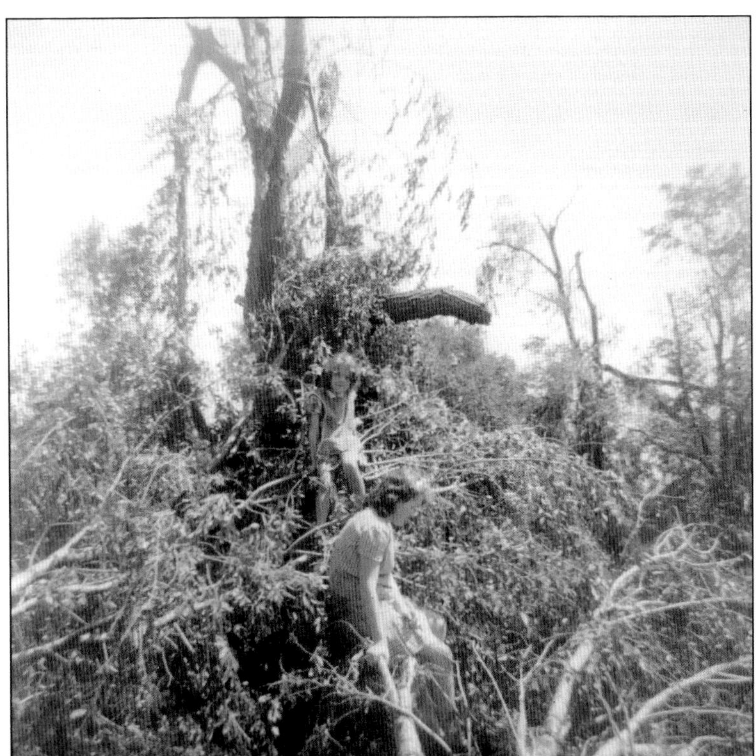

Annette and Mardell Snavely inspect damage in their yard after a tornado hit part of Concordia in 1967. The storm hit southwest of town first, killing one person, and then moved into Concordia where it knocked down trees and did extensive property damage. (Courtesy of Mardell Snavely.)

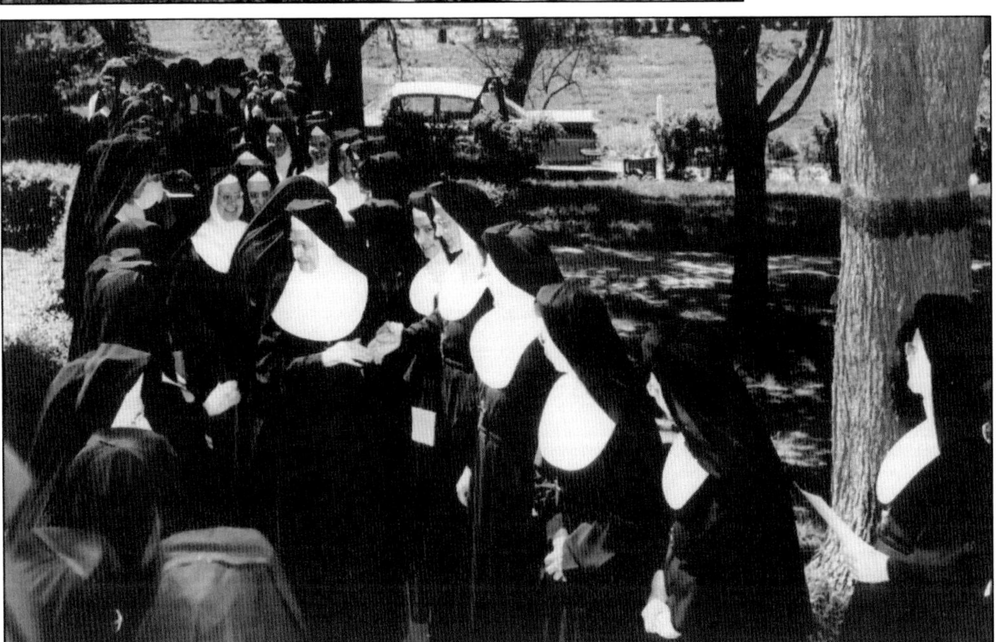

Sisters of St. Joseph gather on the grounds of Nazareth Convent and Academy in 1962, where they held a ceremony for several sisters leaving on a trip to Brazil. The Sisters of St. Joseph have a tradition of travel. They originally came to the Midwest to establish schools and started one in Newton, Kansas, in 1883 before opening their academy in Concordia. (Courtesy of Sister of St. Joseph Archives.)

Three

Concordia Celebrates 100 Years

Concordia started its second century with a centennial celebration in 1971 that included everything anyone would expect and then some. After more than a year of planning and fundraising events, the party lasted for two weeks.

There were special newspaper editions of both the *Kansan* and the *Blade-Empire* with contests for the most interesting old photograph. Every store in town had a sale. There was an old-fashioned day, as well as a beard-and-moustache-growing contest for men. Not one but two parades highlighted the celebration, as did a historical pageant with a cast and crew of about 100 people. Two books about the town were published. Cloud County Bank displayed the entries in a centennial painting contest. Centennial belles were selected, and all over town there were displays and demonstrations, including a threshing bee and a tractor pull. There was an interdenominational religious service on Sunday. Every organization contributed help, and many residents volunteered to make it the best centennial possible. Although some events actually started a few days earlier, the *Blade-Empire* reported that the whole thing officially kicked off Friday, August 6, at the bandshell in city park, with Sen. Frank Carlson himself serving as centennial committee president. There were speeches by the mayor and heads of the centennial committee, then a box dinner auction, and, just as there had been at Concordia's very first celebration, dancing.

Once the party was over, Concordians were ready to start their town's second century.

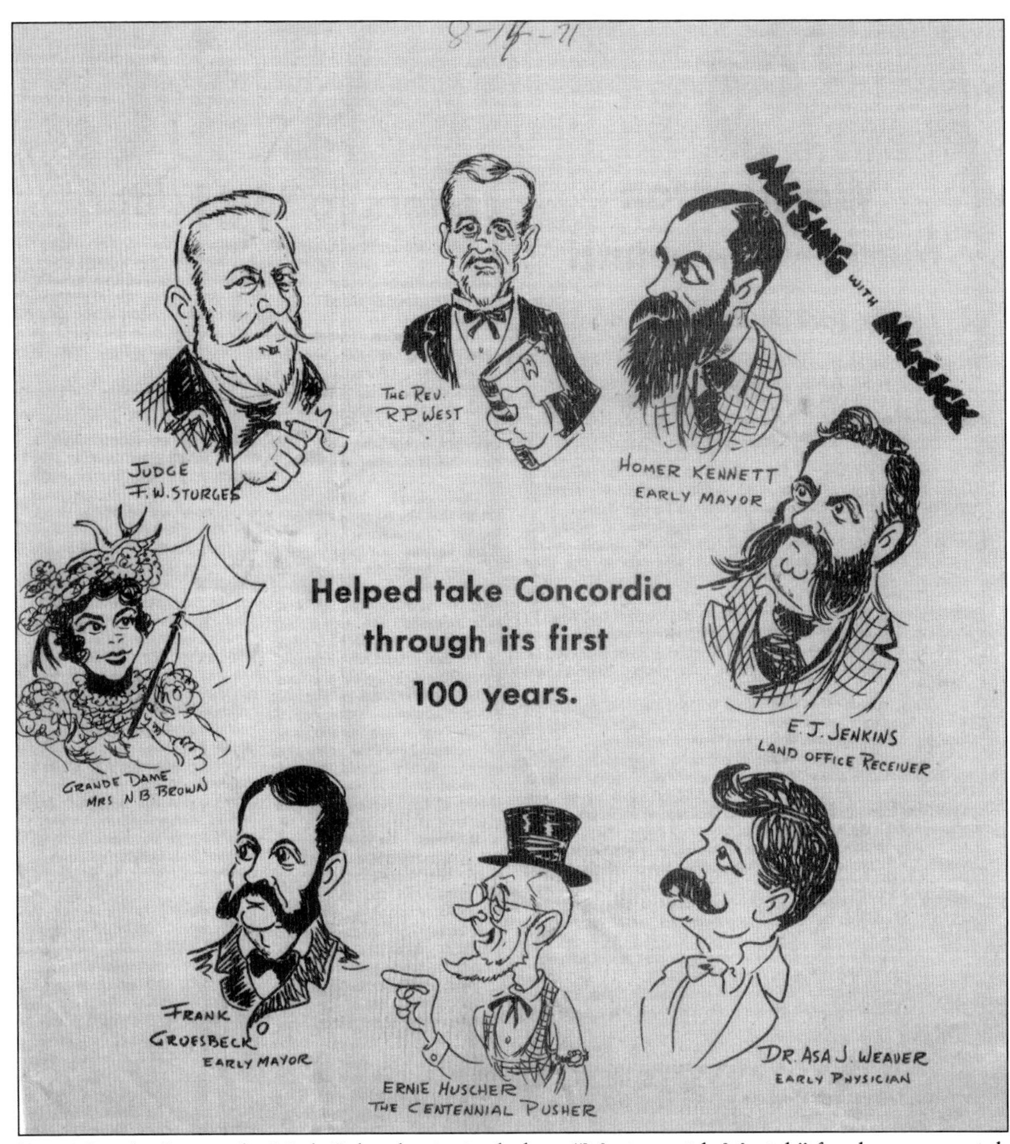

Don Musick, Concordia High School principal, drew "Musing with Musick" for the centennial. This cartoon celebrates some of Concordia's pioneers in honor of the centennial, and sneaks in one of the celebration chairmen, Ernie Huscher, whom Musick called "The Centennial Pusher." Clockwise from the top, they are Rev. R.P. West, the Methodist circuit rider who preached the first religious service in Concordia; Homer Kennett, an early mayor; E.J. Jenkins, land office receiver; Dr. Asa J. Weaver, who ran one of the first hospitals in Concordia; Huscher, sporting a beard in honor of the centennial; Frank Groesback, another early mayor; grand dame Mrs. N.B. Brown, widow of Napoleon Bonaparte Brown and one of the most important women in early Concordia society; and Judge F.W. Sturges, who, in addition to being an important early jurist, was journalist Marion Ellet's grandfather. (Courtesy of Cloud County Historical Society Museum.)

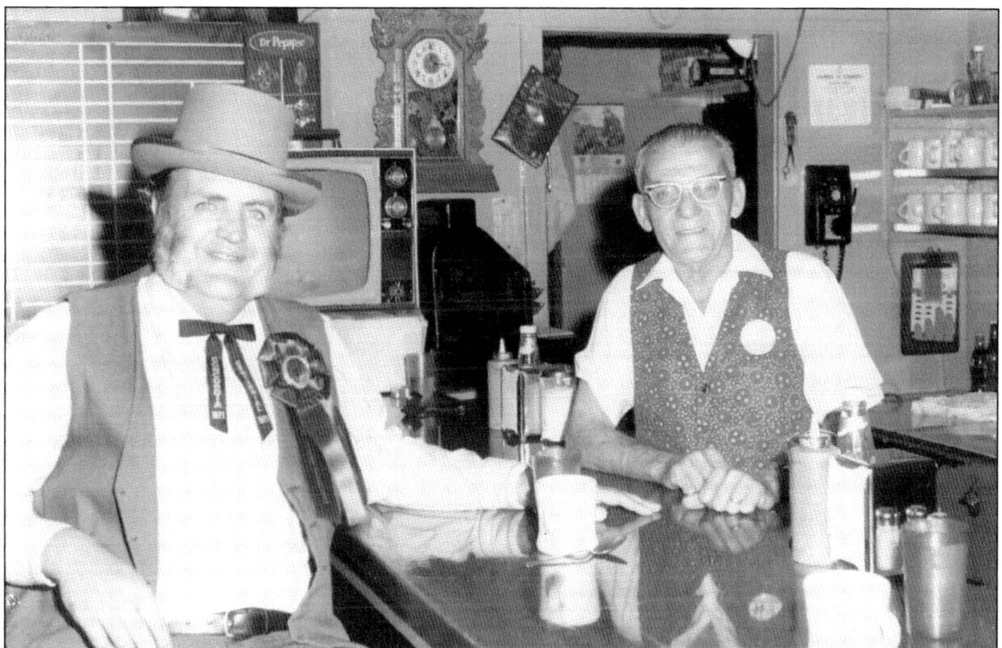

George Chaput, left, drops by West Side Inn for a cup of coffee and a visit with café owner Harlan "Woody" Woods. Both are decked out for the occasion. Chaput sports a top hat, bow tie, and vest, along with a ribbon designating him as assisting with one of the events. Woods gets into the spirit with a vest and a centennial button. (Courtesy of Sue Vignery.)

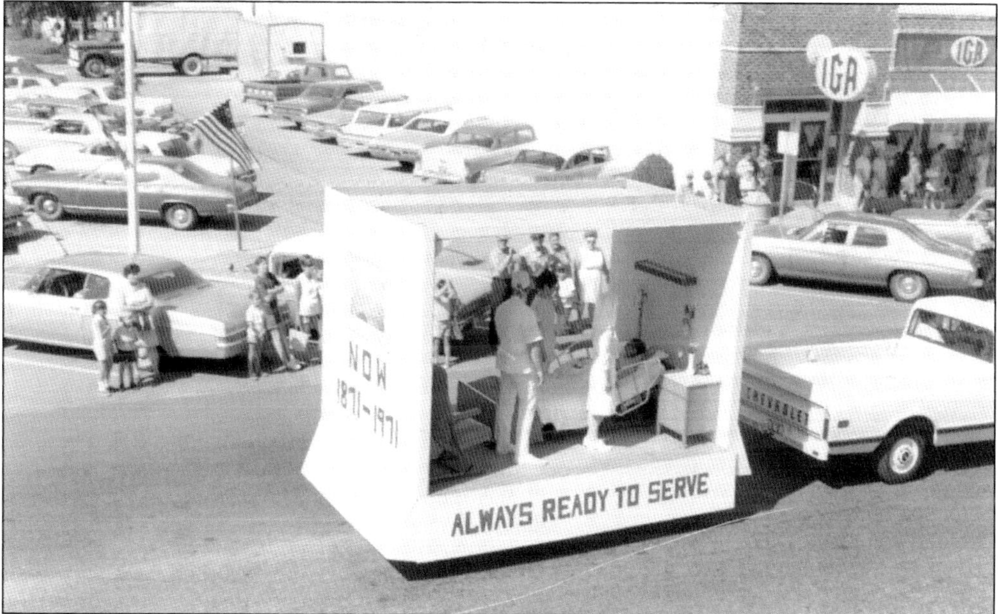

Spectators watch as one of several floats representing St. Joseph Hospital passes the parking lot of the IGA store during the Concordia Centennial Parade. The hospital, now called Cloud County Health Center, sponsored more than one float in the parade and was among many businesses that entered. A second parade was held for younger participants in the centennial celebration. (Courtesy of Cloud County Health Center.)

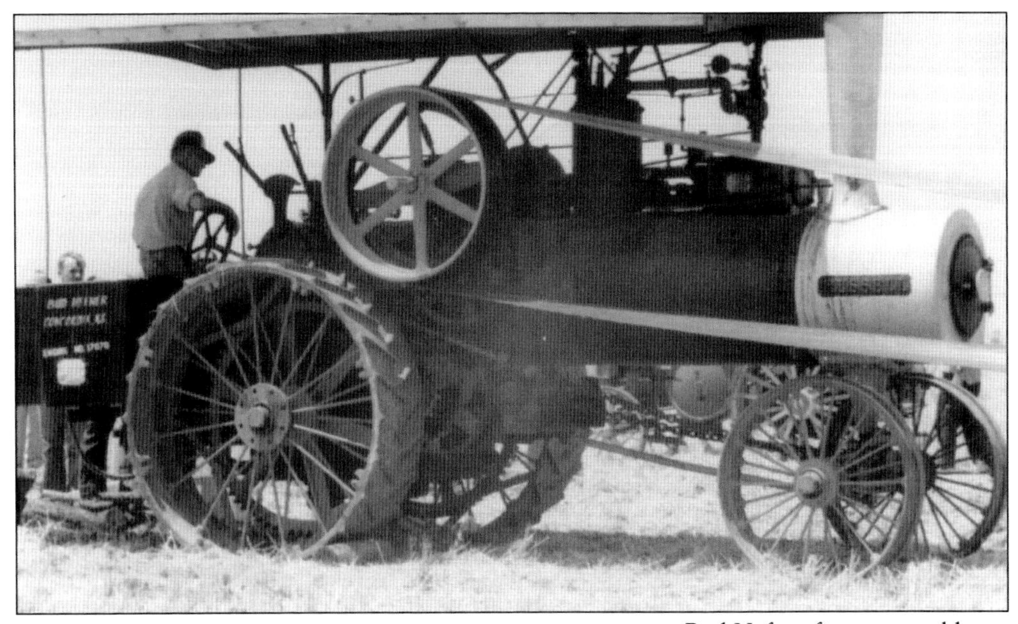

Bud Hefner fires up an old steam-powered tractor for a threshing demonstration in the early 1980s. The tractor was more than 60 years old at the time. A similar demonstration took place during the Concordia Centennial in 1971. Four acres of wheat were harvested for the event. (Courtesy of Dallas Nading.)

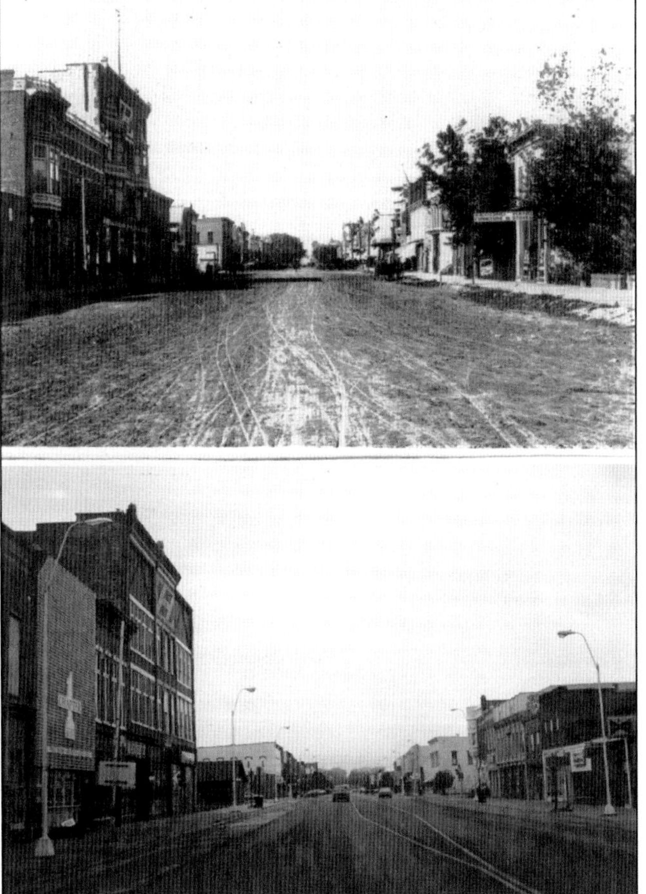

This "then and now" postcard of Concordia as seen from 622 Sixth Street was published in 1994, twenty-three years after the centennial. The then photograph was taken in 1894, and the now photograph was taken 100 years later. (Courtesy of Margo Hosie.)

Four

Concordia Goes to Church and School

Religion was important to the early settlers of Concordia and so was education. Churches came first, and congregations formed nearly as quickly as the town sprang up. Schools did not lag too far behind. The pioneers of Concordia wanted their town to be a civilized, cultured center of trade, and they knew it would take churches to do it.

Each of the different ethnic groups that settled in Concordia brought their own religion and made their own contributions. Some of them started schools and hospitals. Many of the founders were Methodists, and Janet Pease Emery, in her book *It Takes People to Make a Town*, noted that a Methodist circuit-riding preacher, Romulus Pintus Westlake, also called Rev. R.P. West, provided Concordia's very first religious service in mid-January 1871 to about 20 people in the recently completed land office building. From that humble start, she noted, Concordia acquired 12 churches that were still around when the town celebrated its 100th birthday in 1971.

There are more now, and those shown in this chapter are merely a random sampling. Time has apparently only increased faith in God, at least in Concordia.

There have been a number of schools as well. Some, like Notre Dame High School, were run by churches. But public schools were available shortly after the town was founded. The elementary schools were named after presidents, like Lincoln, Garfield, Washington, and McKinley, but Concordia High School has always been Concordia High School. There was a normal and business college in town once; now, there is Cloud County Community College.

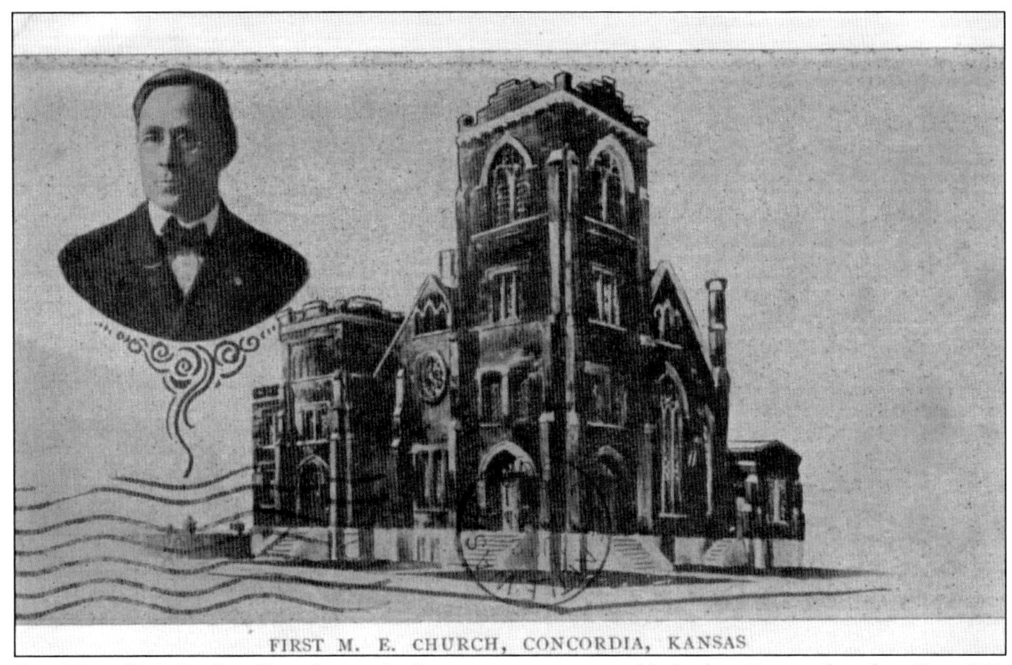

First United Methodist Church was the first congregation established in Concordia when Rev. R.P. West preached in the land office in 1871. The church received its official charter in 1873 as First Methodist Episcopal Church, shown on the postcard above in an artist's drawing before it was built. The back of the postcard (below) provides details on cost. The first church building was built at Seventh Street and Broadway in 1878 but was replaced in 1908 with a new building at the same site when the original suffered severe structural damage. The church is presently located at Eleventh Street and Highland Drive in a building completed in 1966. When the new church was completed, members held a march from the old church to the new one. (Both courtesy of Dena Bisnette.)

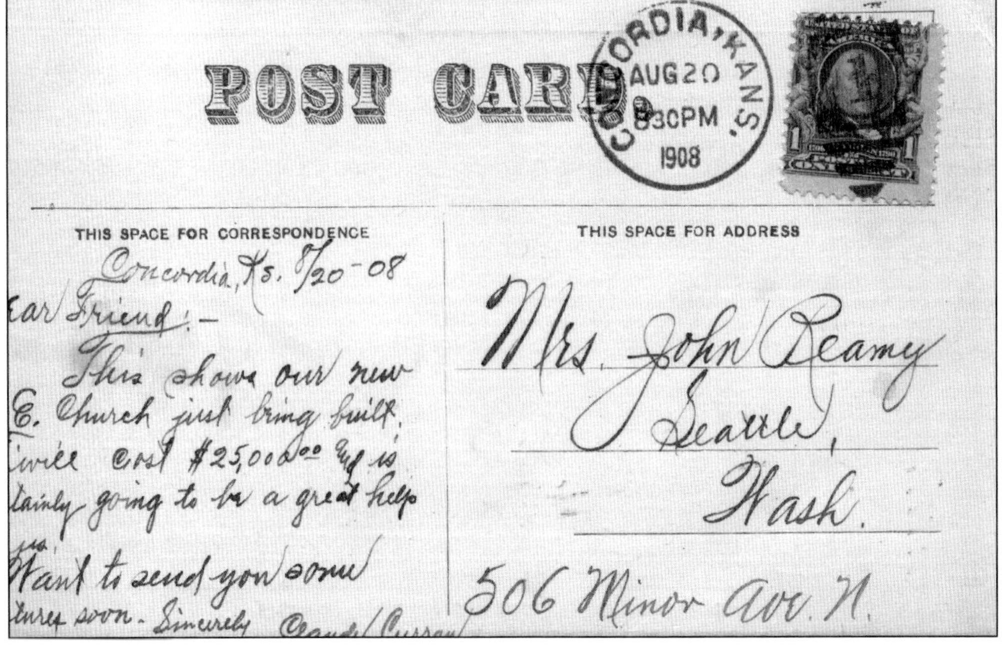

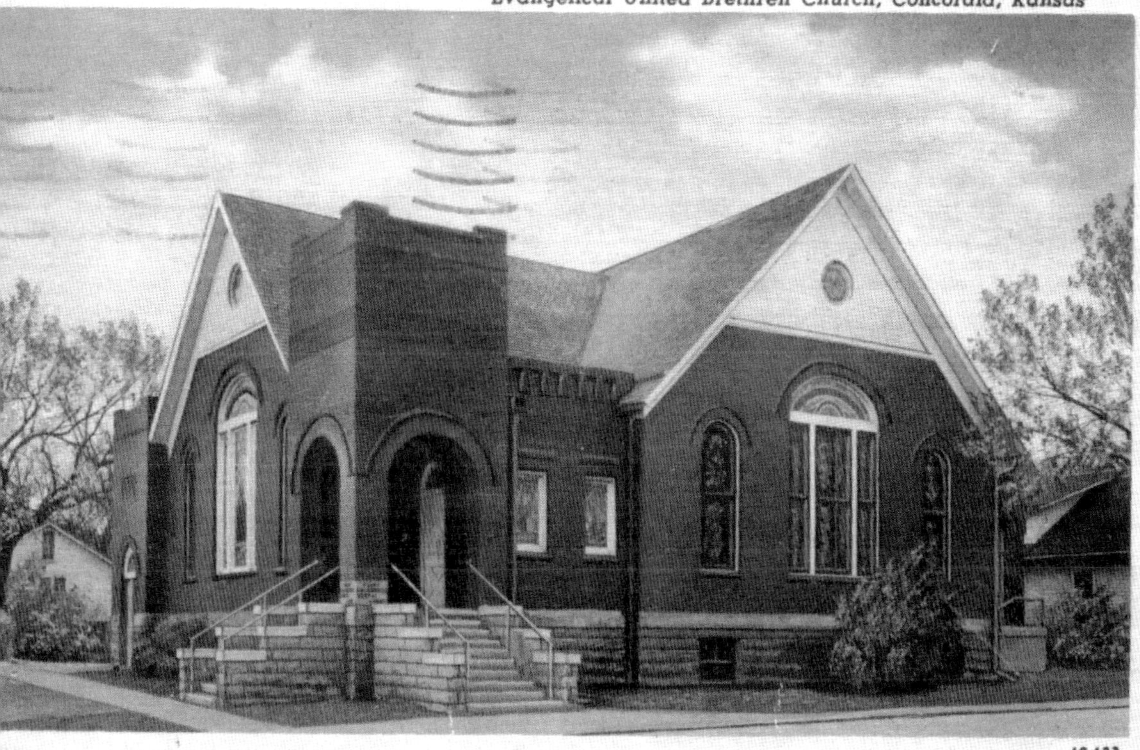

Started in 1886, the United Brethren Church originally shared space on the corner of Ninth and State Streets with the Swedish Baptist Church and then met in rented halls until the membership grew enough to build a frame church in 1887 north of McKinley School. The members soon decided to move closer to the main population of Concordia and started building a new church in 1892 at Eighth and Lincoln Streets. The old building was torn down in 1893, and the materials were used in the new church. They built this brick church in 1911, tearing down the existing building for material and again meeting in a tent in the interim. In 1946, the church became Evangelical United Brethren Church when the two denominations merged. In 1968, it became Trinity United Methodist Church after a merger with that denomination. The 1911 building has been enlarged and remodeled over the years, and its bell tower has been removed, but it is still in use. (Courtesy of Cloud County Historical Society Museum.)

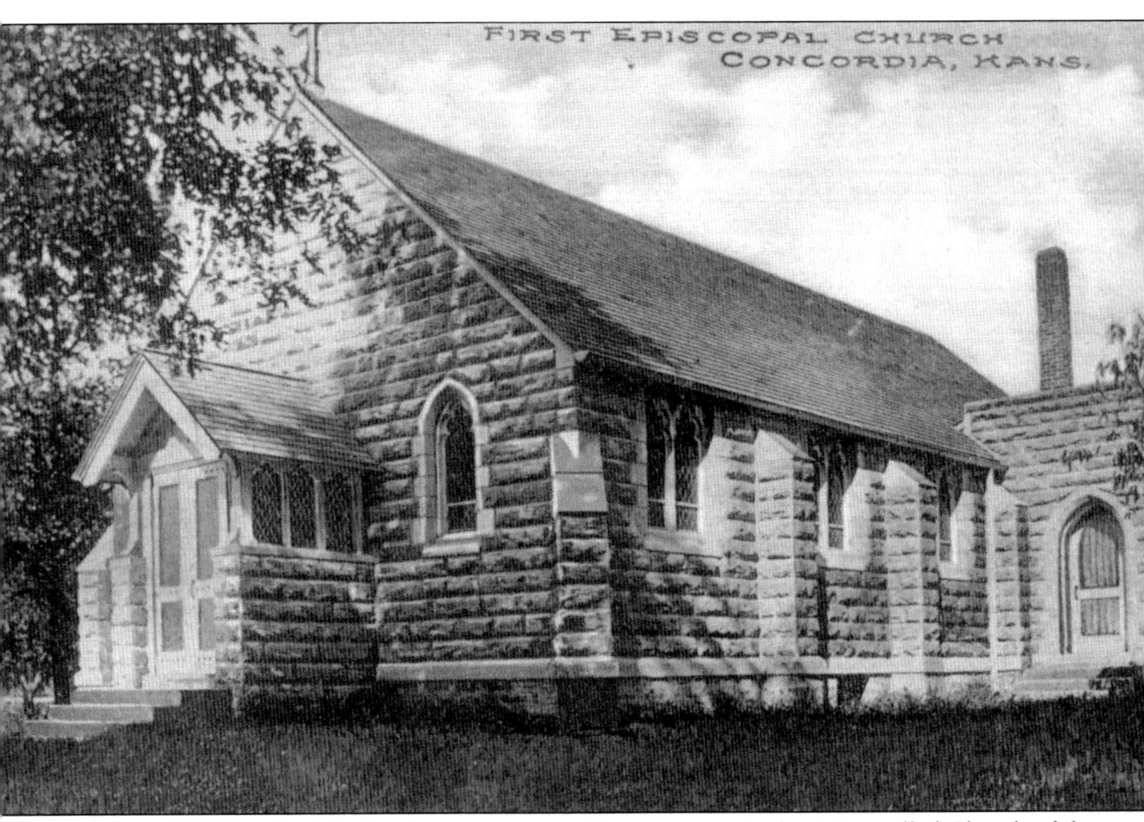

Episcopal Church of the Epiphany was originally an unorganized mission called Church of the Crucified, which started when a priest from Clay Center held Concordia's first Episcopal service on November 10, 1887. Services were intermittent until the 1880s, when a priest from Belleville came to town on a regular basis. By the 1890s, the church met in the YMCA downtown and had gone through two name changes, including Calvary Church and Church of the Resurrection. Church of the Epiphany acquired its present name in 1904. Members met in the Eureka Parlours above a store just east of the Kansan Building. In 1907, the first pastor, Fr. William N. Colton, laid the cornerstone of the present building on Eighth Street. Fr. Wilfred Hotaling, who served as pastor for 31 years, bought a dismantled altar carved of French limestone and previously used by two churches from New York City. Reassembly was completed in 1974. The church also features American-made stained-glass windows from Hauser Art Company, which tell the story of Christ's life. (Courtesy of Dena Bisnette.)

Our Lady of Perpetual Help Catholic Church looked like this in 1928 when it was the cathedral for the Roman Catholic Diocese of Concordia, a designation the church kept from 1887 until the diocese moved to Salina in 1945. The building is listed in the National Register of Historic Places and incorporated local materials, including post rock and Cloud County shell rock into its construction when it was erected in 1879. The church replaced the original wooden church. The inside has been renovated several times, and a new parish hall was attached to the church in 1996. The photograph below shows the parish plant as it looked in 1886, including the school. (Right, courtesy of Dena Bisnette; below, courtesy of Our Lady of Perpetual Help Catholic Church.)

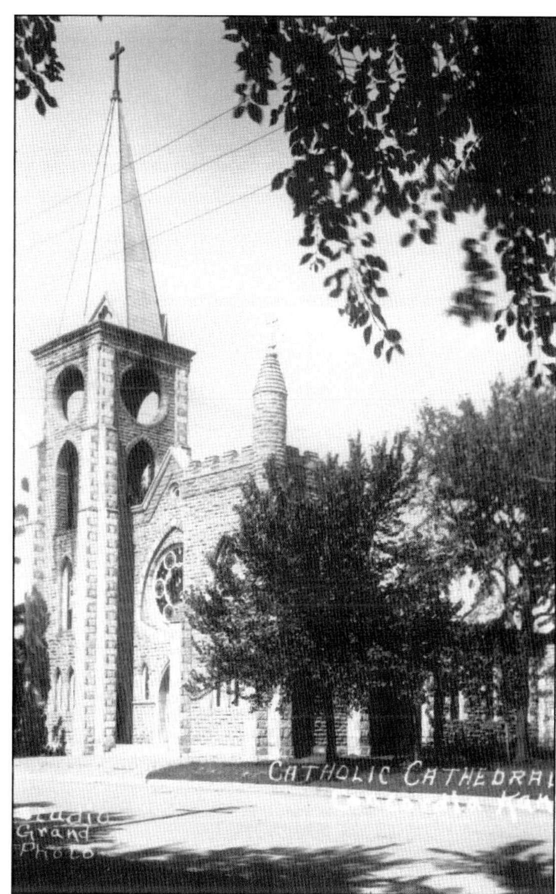

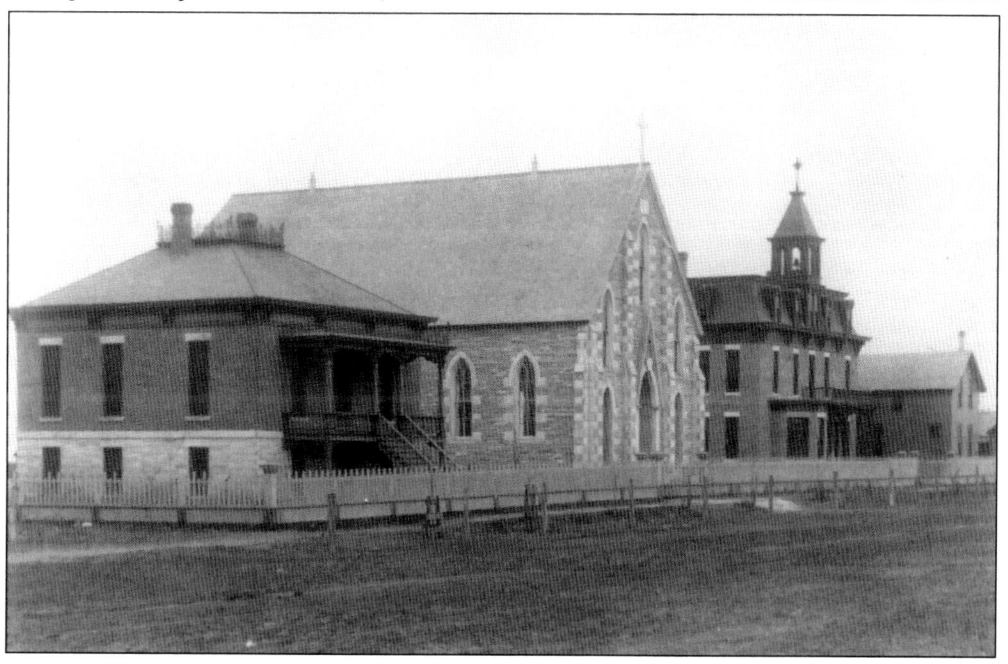

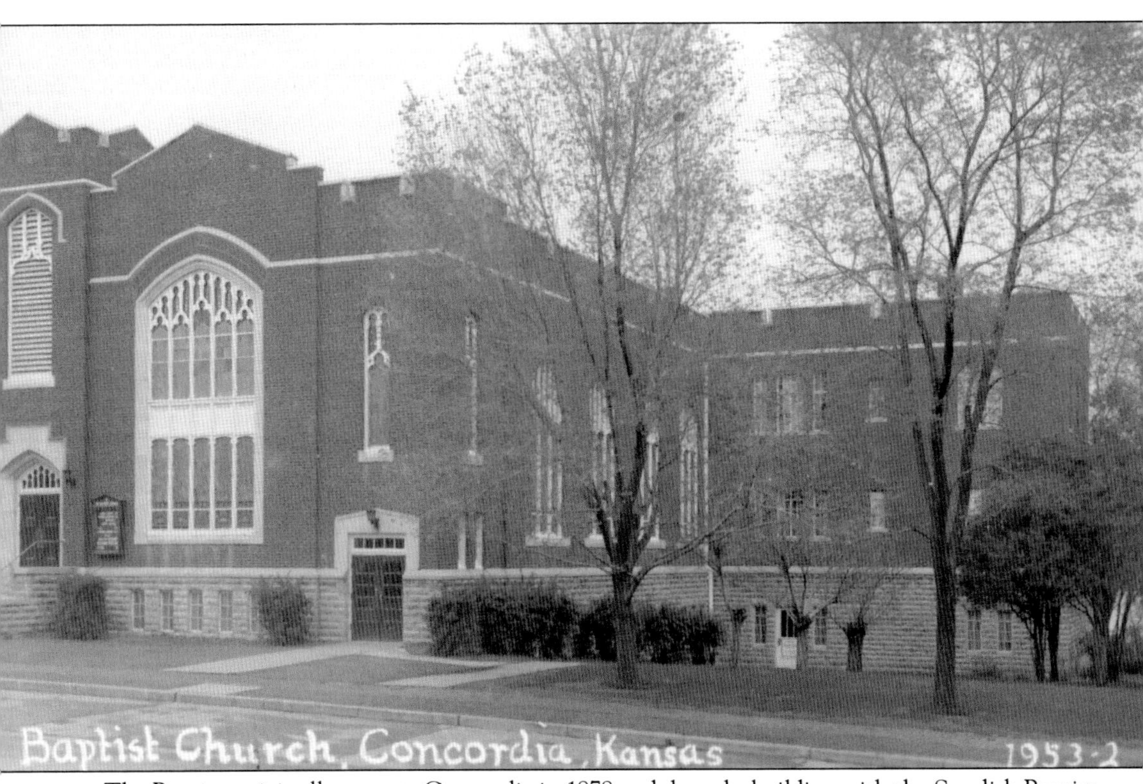

The Baptists originally came to Concordia in 1878 and shared a building with the Swedish Baptist Church at first but then built First Baptist Church at Seventh and Washington Streets in 1888. Later, they sold that building to Wesleyan Methodist Church in 1926, two years after a merger with the Swedish Baptists. The Swedish church, started in Concordia in 1878, had conducted its services in Swedish until the language died out locally. Their stone church, built in 1900, was torn down, and the stone was used in the foundation of the new Baptist Church at Seventh and Cedar Streets, where the Swedish church had stood. This photograph is from 1953, before the educational wing was added in 1956. (Courtesy of Cloud County Historical Society Museum.)

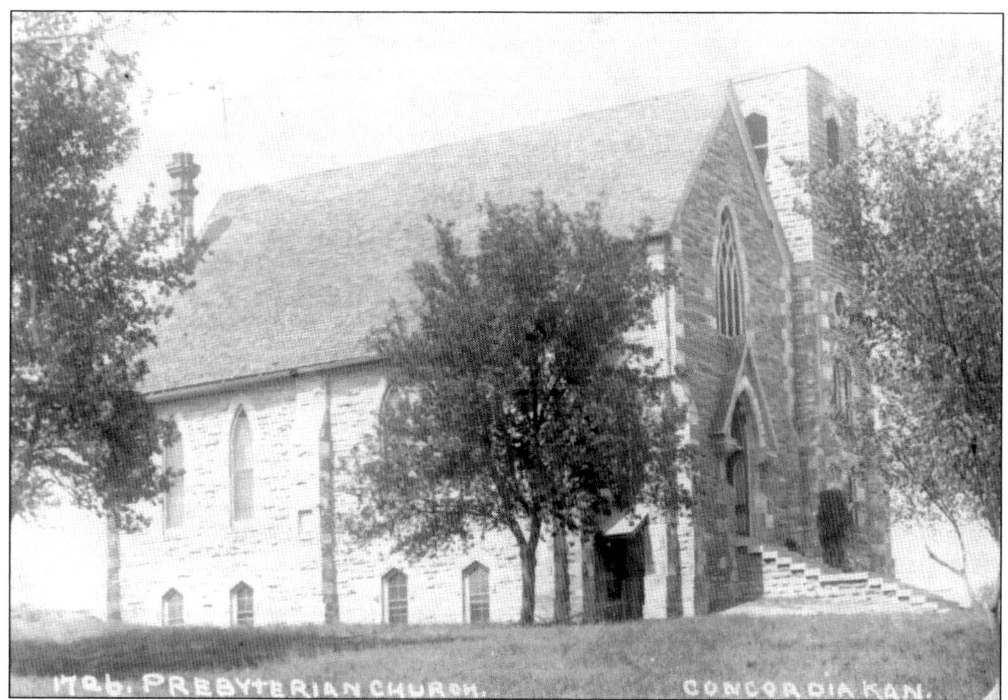

Presbyterians were also early arrivals in Concordia, organizing in 1871. Their first church was built in 1874, and members worshipped in this stone building, shown in 1907, until construction of their new Greek Revival building in 1915, pictured below. The old stone church on Seventh Street, which had been the first church constructed in Concordia, was demolished. Additions have since been made to the 1915 building. One year after the Presbyterians organized, in 1872, the Church of Christ arrived in Concordia, and built its first church three years later. (Both courtesy of Dena Bisnette.)

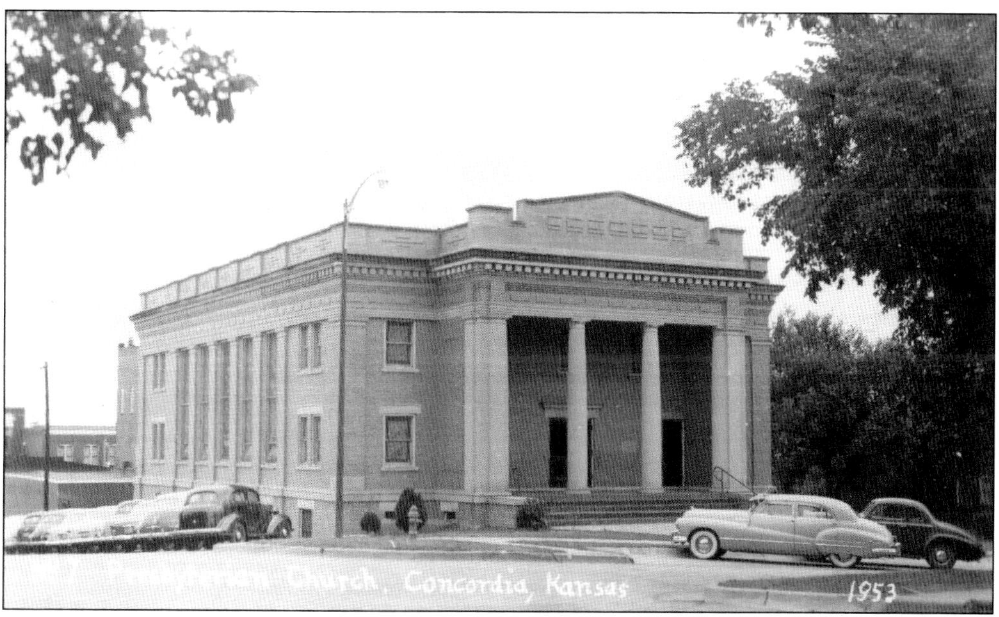

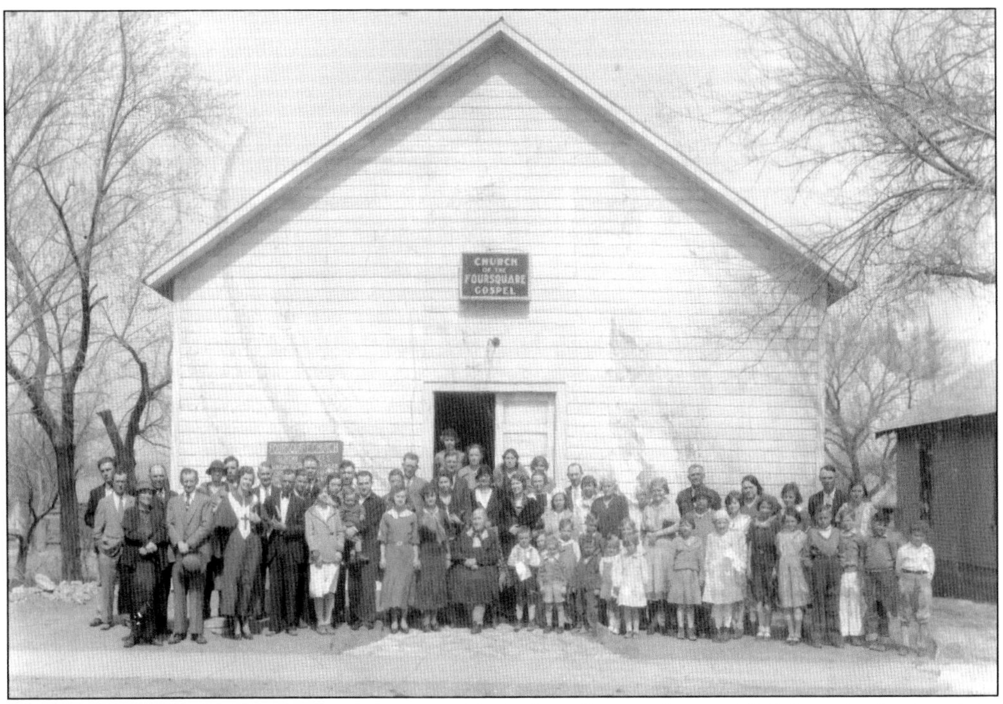

Church of the Foursquare Gospel was established in Concordia in 1934, but the little white church building in which services were originally held was older and had been used by other congregations before. The church now meets downtown. (Courtesy of Cloud County Historical Society Museum.)

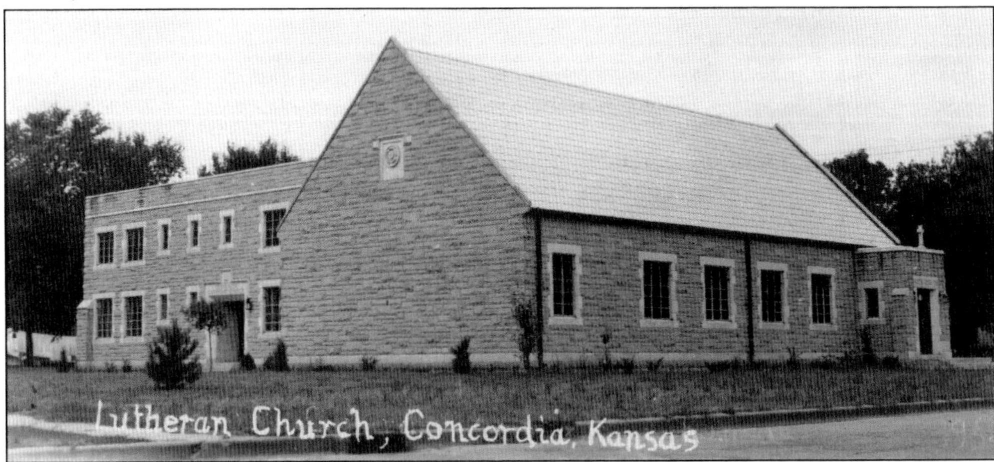

Concordia Lutheran Church conducted its first service in city hall in 1940 and formally organized in April 1943. Six years later, the native limestone church and an educational facility at Eighth and Olive Streets were dedicated. A theater at Camp Concordia, the World War II POW camp outside of town, was dismantled to provide the benches, windows, a boiler, and wood for the church. Members of the congregation helped move the dismantled theater. The 1949 construction plans, however, also called for construction of a sanctuary. About 40 years later, when the needs of the congregation had outgrown the existing facility, the sanctuary was finally built. Use of volunteer labor for the project saved enough money to build a balcony and add extra seating. (Courtesy of Cloud County Historical Society Museum.)

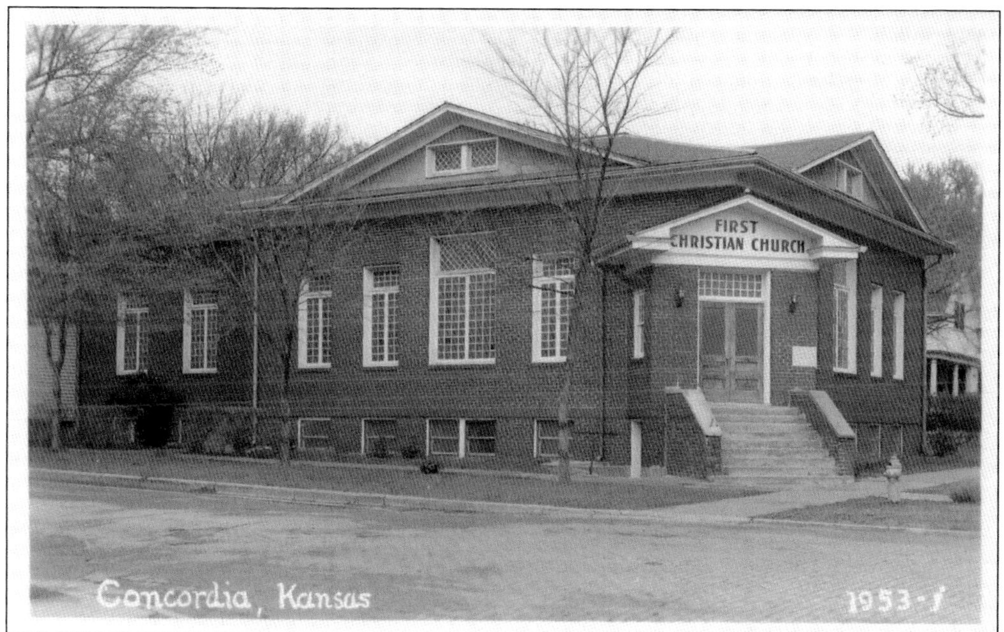

First Christian Church organized in Concordia in 1900. The congregation purchased the original Swedish Baptist Church when that congregation moved to its new building in 1900. In 1924, they built this church at Sixth and Cedar Streets. Additions to the building were completed in 1968. (Courtesy of Cloud County Historical Society Museum.)

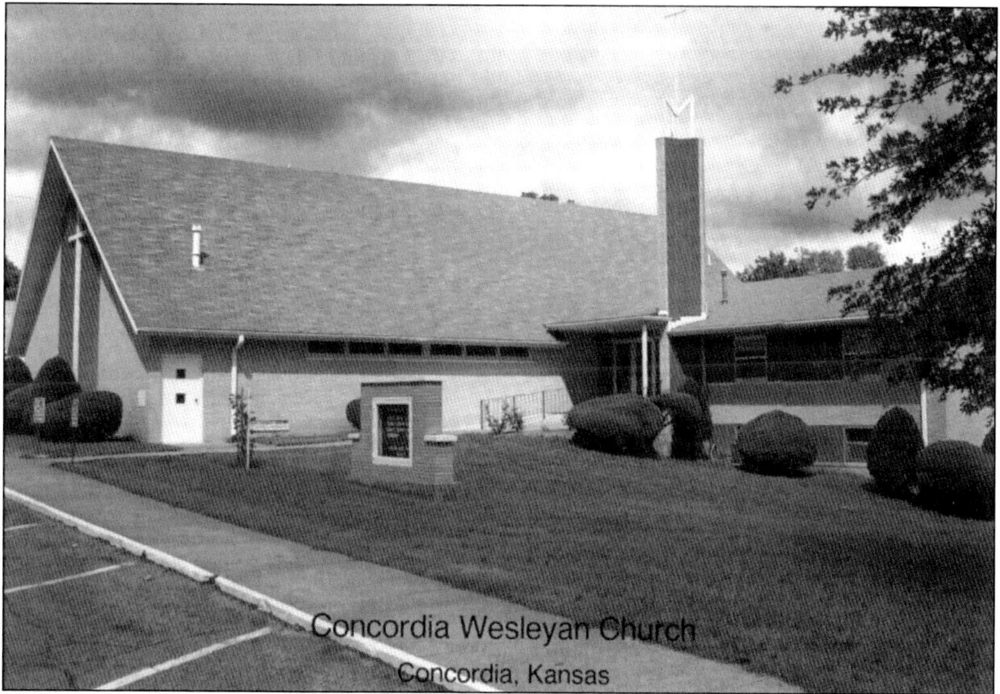

Wesleyan Methodist Church met in the old First Baptist Church Building until constructing a new brick building at Sixteenth and Cedar Streets. The congregation was organized in 1924. (Courtesy of Dena Bisnette.)

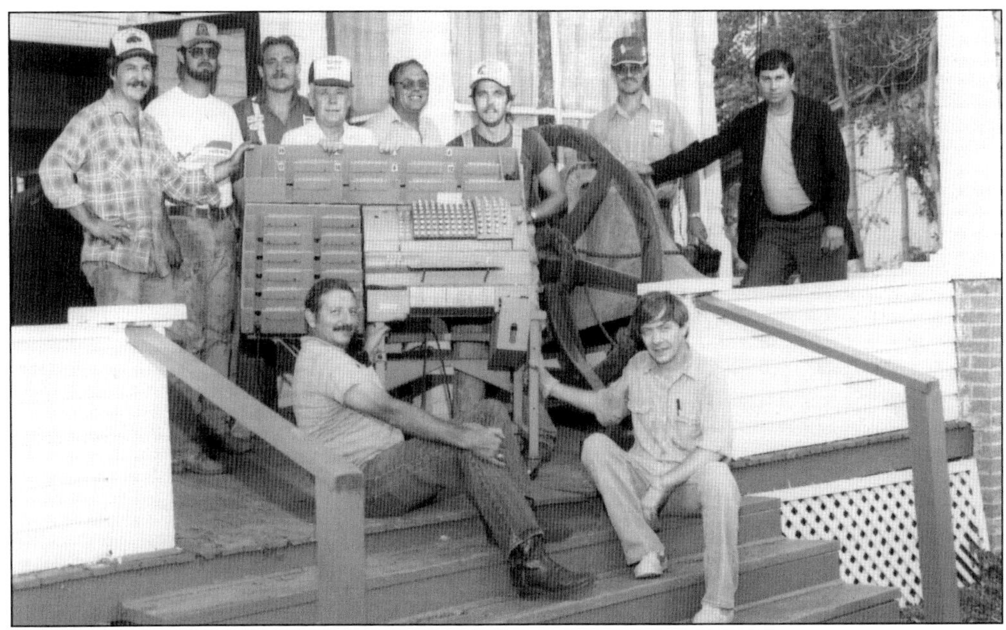

Workers prepared to move the bell from Trinity United Methodist Church to Cloud County Historical Society Museum in 1985. The bell was donated after the bell tower was removed from the building during renovations. Pictured are Lowell Thomas, Kurt Kocher, Doug Hower, unidentified, Dean Holbert, Roger Demanette, Joe Strecker, Leigh Davenport, and two unidentified. (Courtesy of Cloud County Historical Society Museum.)

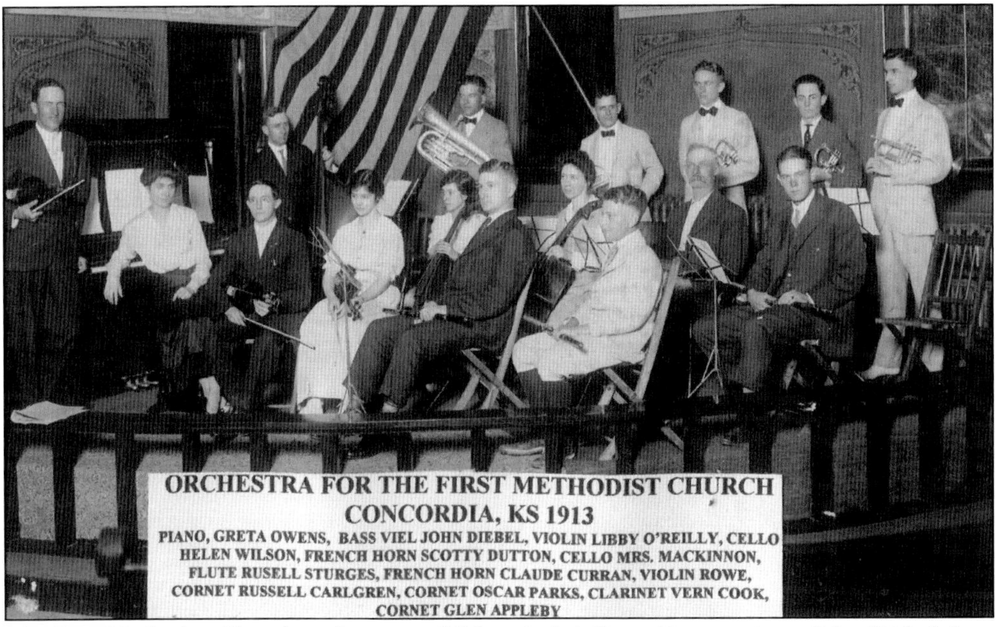

The First Methodist Church orchestra in 1913 included Greta Owens, piano; John Diebel, bass violin; Libby O'Rielly, violin; Helen Wilson, cello; Scotty Dutton, French horn; Mrs. Mackinnon, cello; Russell Sturges, flute; Claude Curran, French horn; Russell Carlgren, cornet; Oscar Parks, cornet; Vern Cook, clarinet; Glen Appleby, cornet; and four unidentified musicians. (Courtesy of Cloud County Historical Society Museum.)

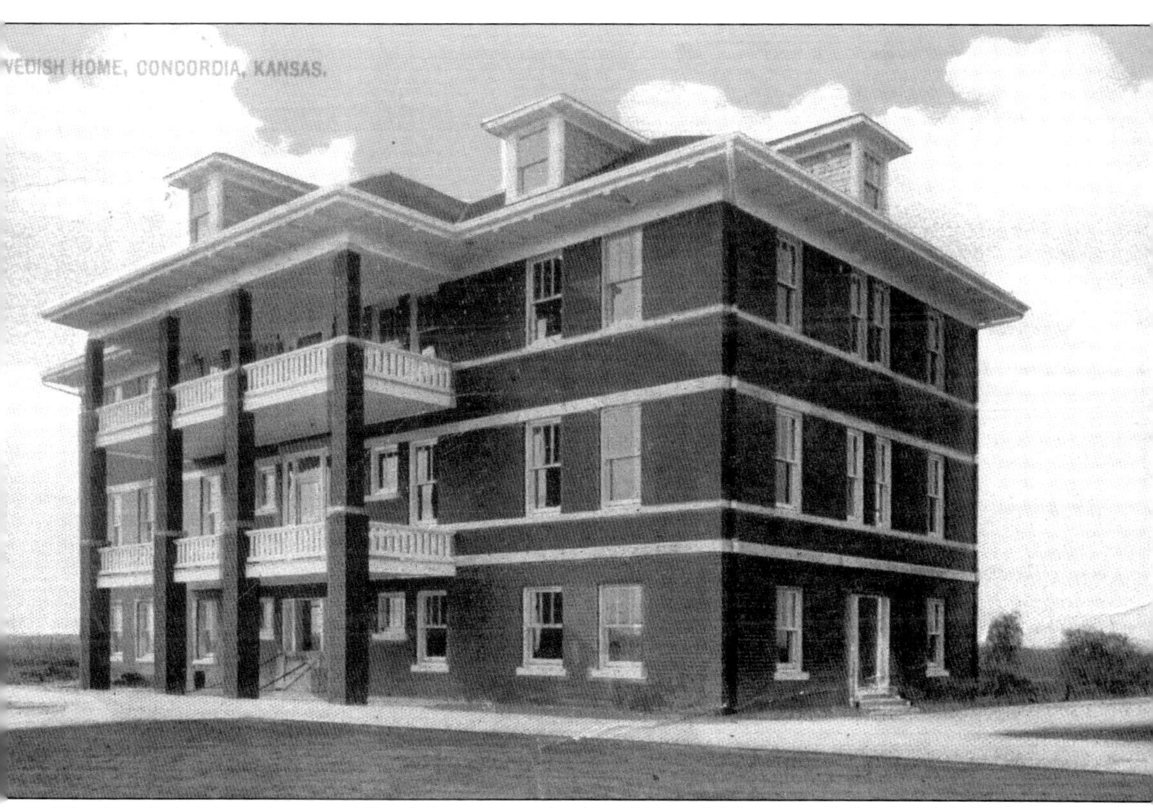

The Swedish migration into Cloud County resulted in the establishment of the Swedish Baptist Church in Concordia, where services and Sunday school were conducted in the Swedish language. In 1878, the congregation built a frame building that was sold to the Christian Church in 1900 after the Swedish Baptists built a new stone church building on Seventh Street. Eventually, local use of the language died out, and the church merged with First Baptist Church. They also built the Swedish Home, which became Sunset Home for the Aged. (Courtesy of Cloud County Historical Society Museum.)

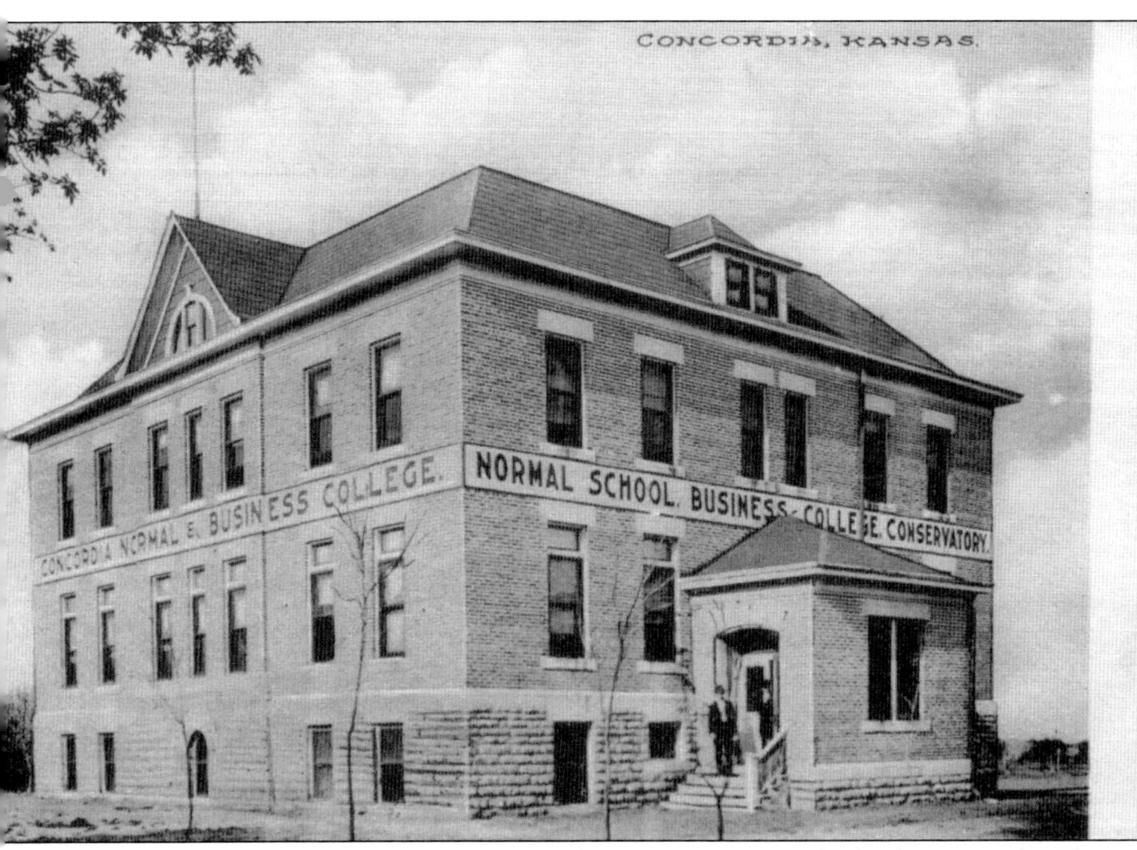

In 1874, the governor approved the opening of a Kansas State Normal School at Concordia. The school opened on March 5, 1874, with B.F. Robinson as principal and J.S. Shearer as assistant. Its mission was to prepare high school graduates for the teaching profession, and it was given funding by the state legislature for its first and only year. Several attempts to establish some kind of college in Concordia failed or were short-lived until the establishment of Concordia Normal and Business College, shown here. The building was on Matthews Street, looking west down Seventh Street, and the college thrived for about 20 years and closed in 1933. The building was razed in 1962. Prior to that, it housed a Catholic high school and Cloud County Welfare Department. (Courtesy of Dena Bisnette.)

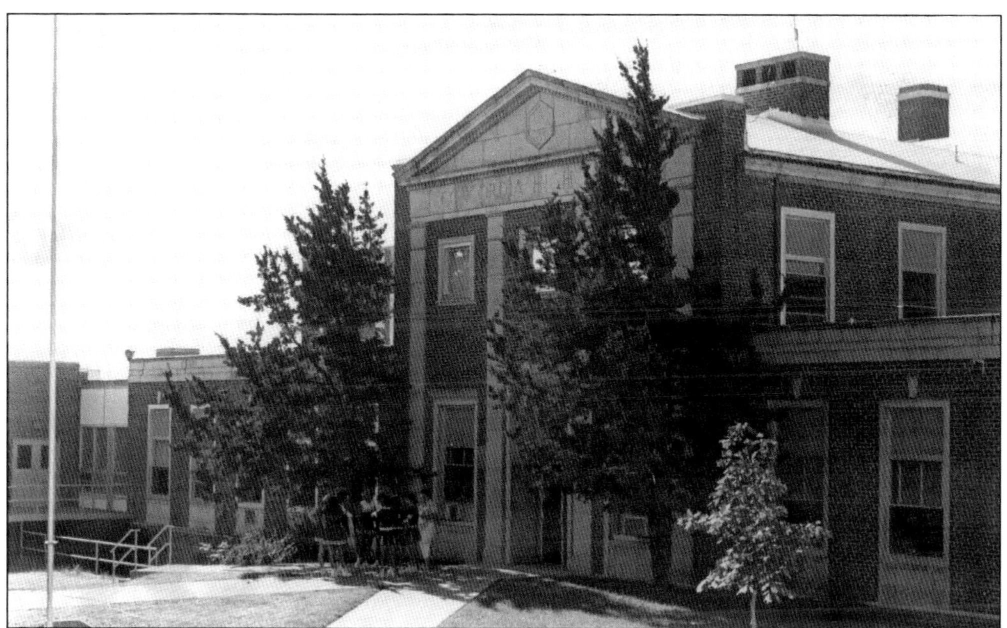

Concordia High School has been holding classes since the 1880s, and the original building was replaced early in the 20th century by a new one at Tenth and Cedar Streets, where the modern high school is. The school has never had any name other than Concordia High School. (Courtesy of Cloud County Historical Society Museum.)

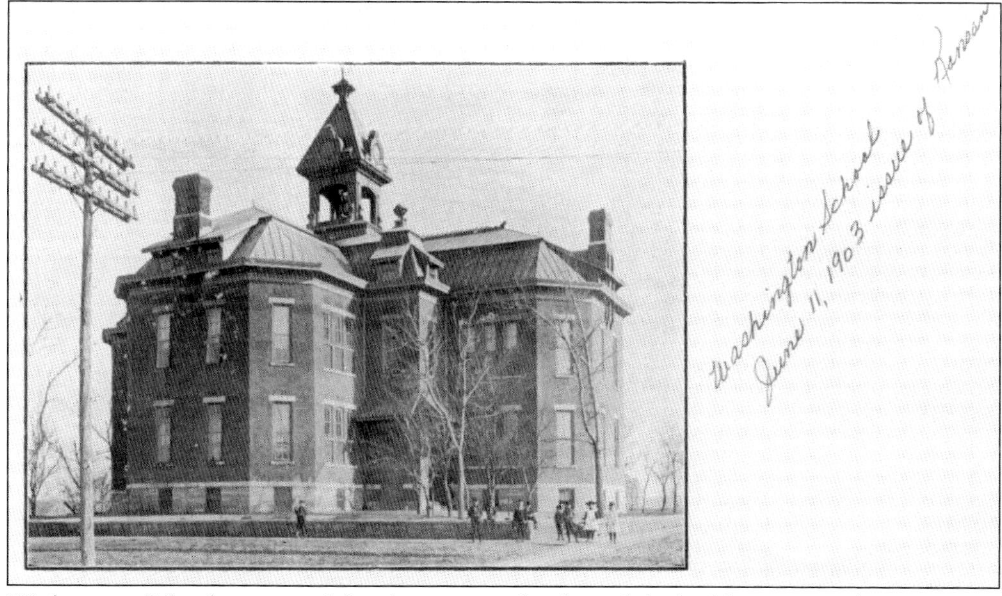

Washington School was one of the elementary schools, and the building was used as a Masonic hall for a few years after the school closed. The building was used by a number of different tenants after a more modern school was constructed. (Courtesy of Cloud County Historical Society Museum.)

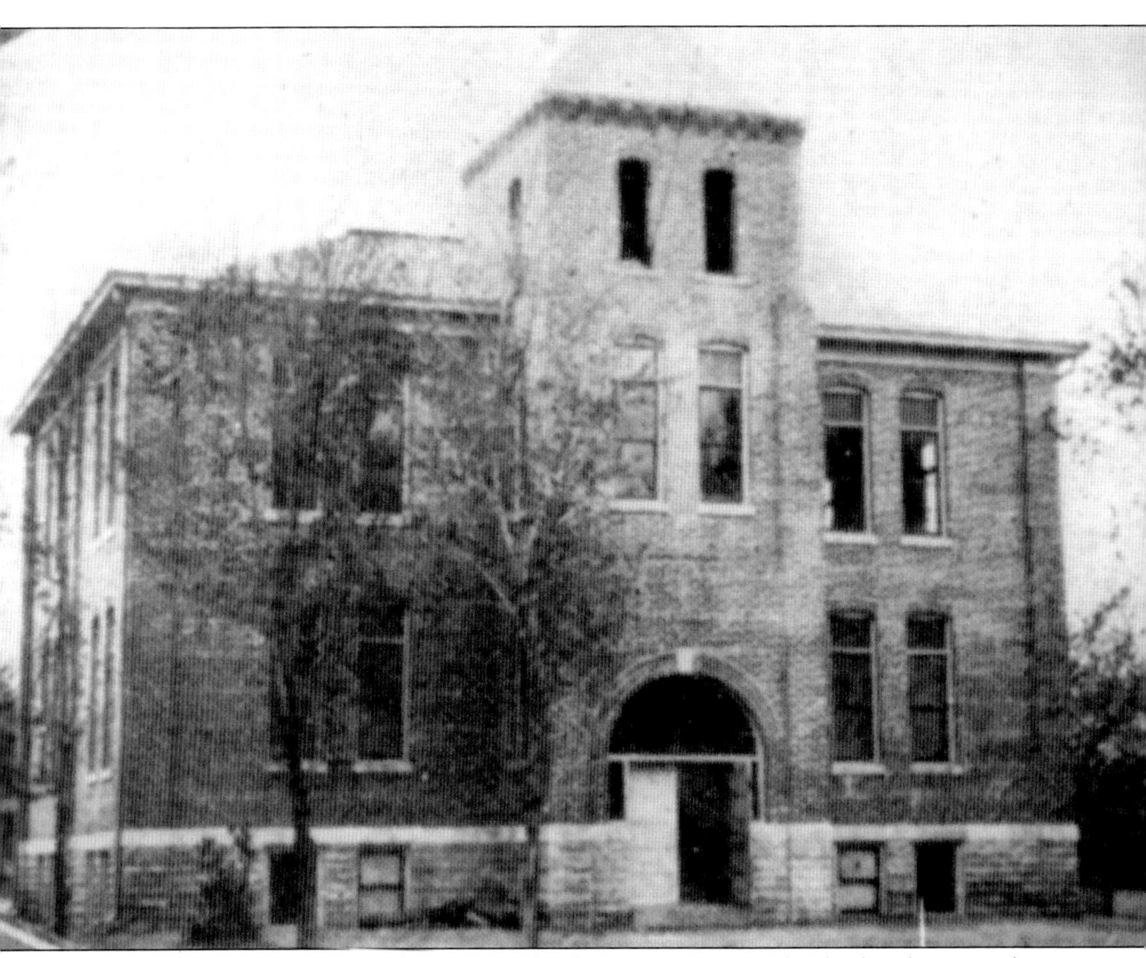

Our Lady of Perpetual Help Elementary School was just one example of a church-operated private school in Concordia. There were also two Catholic high schools, the older of which met in the old Concordia Business and Normal College building. That school was replaced in 1962 by Notre Dame High School, which closed in 1971. Among the early religious schools was Nazareth Academy, established by the Sisters of St. Joseph. The last academy class in Concordia graduated in 1922. (Courtesy of Our Lady of Perpetual Help Catholic Church.)

Five

Concordia Is on Parade and Having Fun

People in Concordia have always enjoyed a good celebration and a bit of fun. Despite attempts to make Concordia a quiet place with a more somber (and sober) attitude, including an "anti-cuss league," a visit from Carrie Nation (long after her ax-swinging phase), and Prohibition, the town's residents have always liked amusements, ranging from circuses, parades, fairs, and festivals to movies, concerts, and dances. In fact, one of the first things that happened in the land office in 1871—after business, of course—was a dance.

Some annual events, like the fall festival that originated as a market day in the 1800s, now coincide with several class reunions and draw former residents back to visit. Concordia also hosts the Cloud County Fair.

A number of civic clubs and lodges have called Concordia home during its history. Civic clubs included Lions, Kiwanis, Rotary, Optimists, and Business and Professional Women. Lodges have included Elks, Moose, Masons, Odd Fellows, Eastern Star, Rebeccas, Knights of Columbus, and more. Other clubs were established to further cultural interests or for specific projects, like establishing the town's first library, and have come and gone along with their reasons for being. There are also veterans' organizations, including Veterans of Foreign Wars and American Legion posts.

The sporting life has not been forgotten, and there are opportunities, in school and out, for both youths and adults. Concordia has a country club that dates back to 1919 and is now operated by the American Legion, a public pool, parks, ball fields, and more.

Like any town, Concordia had downtown movie theaters like the Strand and the Apollo, something now missing in many smaller Midwestern towns. Even the Brown Grand Opera House went through a phase when it was a movie theater. Today, Concordia has the Majestic, next to the Elks Building.

The bandshell in city park was a casualty of time, but the light-hearted spirit it personified is alive and well in Concordia.

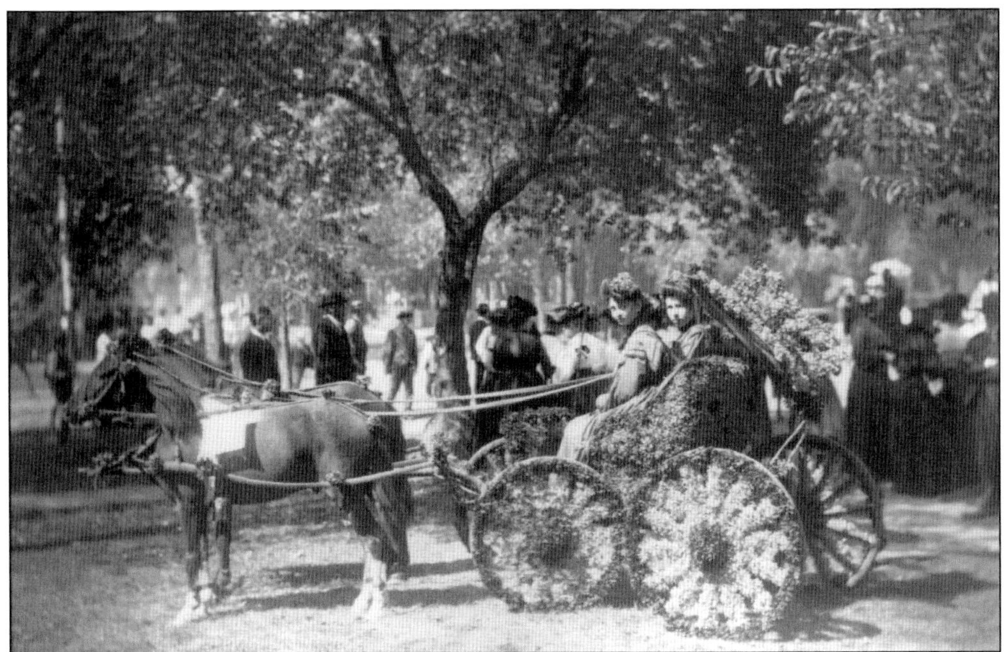

C.A. Betournay's daughters pose in their decorated carriage before a parade. Flowers were considered appropriate decoration for both young ladies and carriages in the late 19th and early 20th century. The girls are wearing flowers in their hair. (Courtesy of Cloud County Historical Society Museum.)

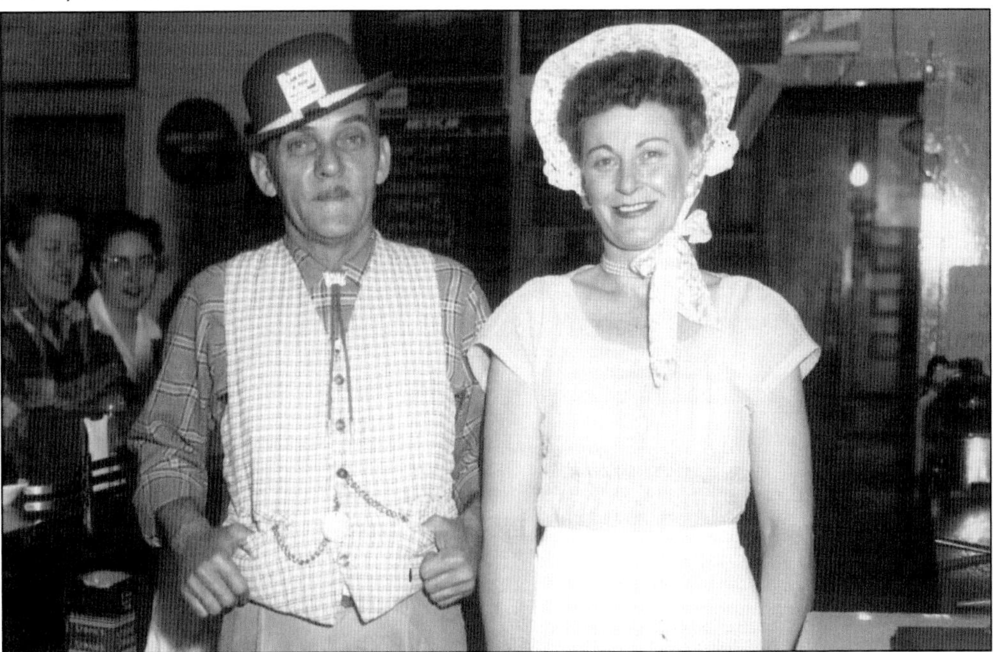

West Side Inn celebrates during the Frontier Days Rodeo in 1957. Dressed for the occasion are Nadine LeClair and Agnes Odette. Behind them are café owners Harlan "Woody" Woods and Helen Woods. Frontier Days was an annual event in Concordia. The café was across from the Majestic Theatre. (Courtesy of Sue Vignery.)

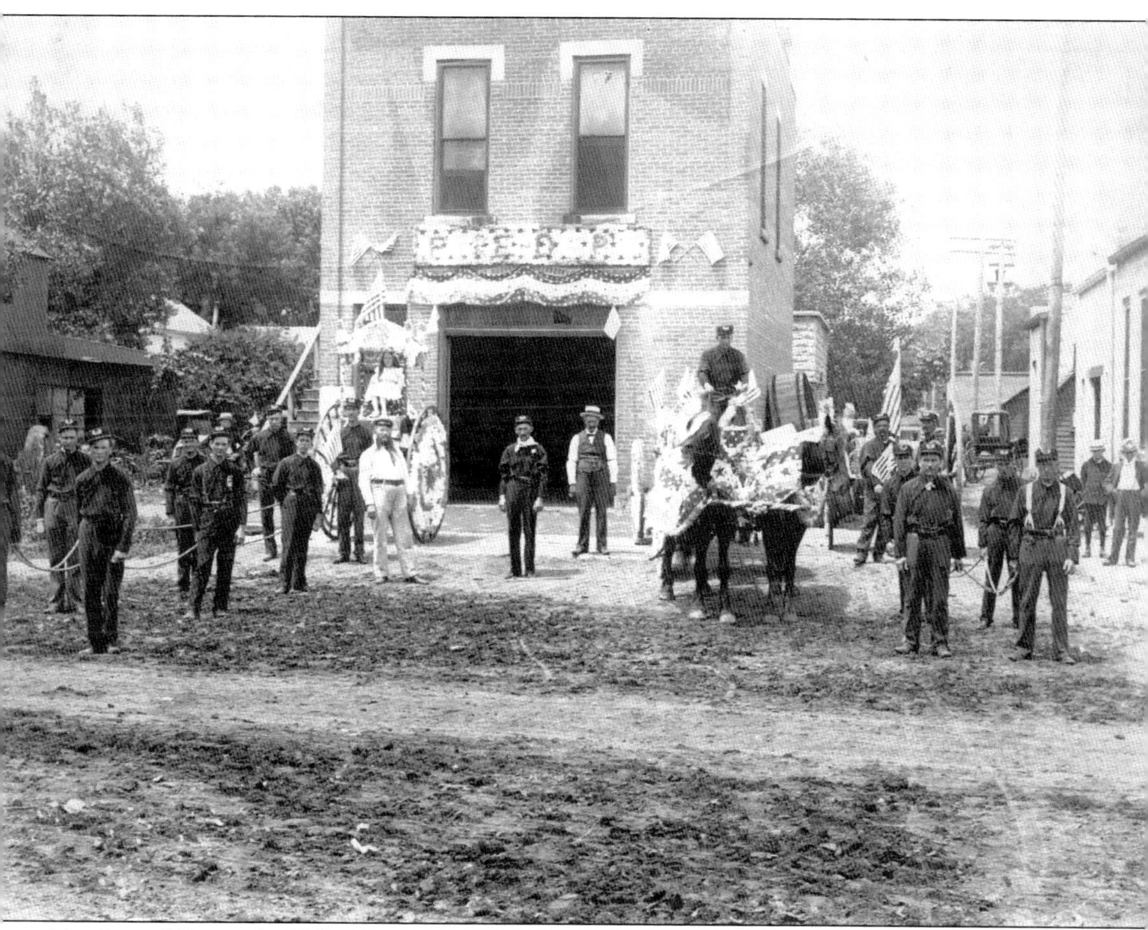

Members of Concordia Volunteer Fire Department pose with horses and decorated wagons as they prepare for a c. 1900s Fourth of July parade. The volunteer fire department was organized in 1898. Prior to that, the town had a volunteer bucket brigade. Prairie fires were a problem for only a short time after the town was built, and posed less danger after farmers moved in and cultivated the land around Concordia. The building behind them was the city jail. A few names are written on the bottom of the photograph and include G. Francouer, Moseley, Hinkel, W.T. Short, J. Wilkie, A. Renard, and Luke Brown. (Courtesy of Cloud County Historical Society Museum.)

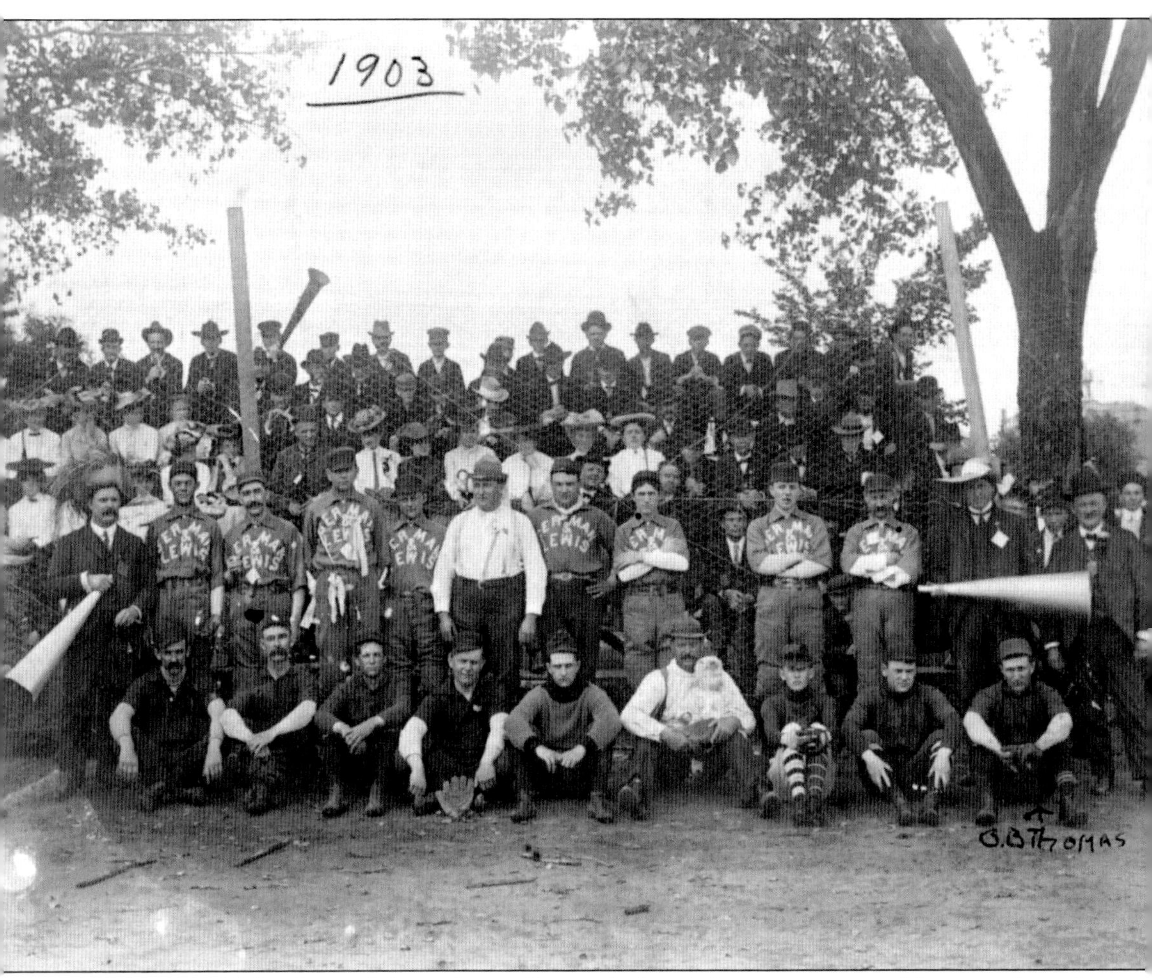

When a 1903 flood stranded travelers in Concordia hotels because trains could not get through, someone thought it would be a good excuse for a charity baseball game to benefit flood victims in Topeka. The two teams consisted of "stranded commercial travelers" of Colson's Café and Baron's House, and a photographer with King Photo took the players' picture on game day, June 4, 1903. (Courtesy of Cloud County Historical Society Museum.)

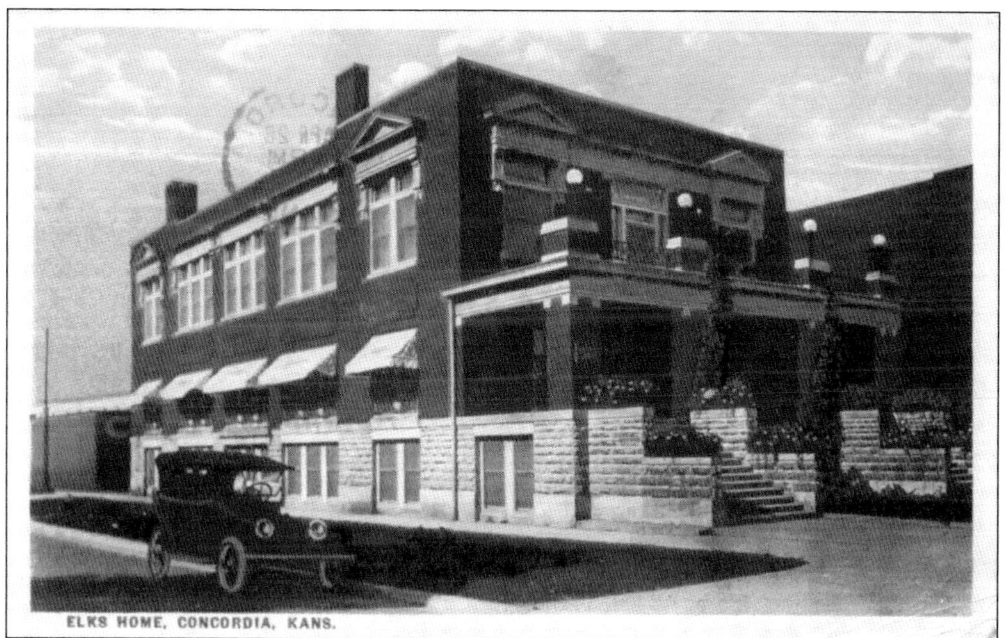

Concordia had several lodges, including Loyal Order of the Moose, International Order of Odd Fellows; Optimists, Masons, and Benevolent and Protective Order of Elks. Time has taken them from Concordia, but their halls remain. Above, the Elks building, shown in a postcard, is now used for other purposes. The bronze elk statue that stood in front was moved to Pleasant Hill Cemetery. Below, members and guests wait for a dance to begin at the Elks ballroom in 1906. Several ladies display dance cards; the lady fourth from left has hers tucked into her belt. A gentleman who wished to dance with a lady signed her card, and then she danced with the men in the order they had signed. (Above, courtesy of Dena Bisnette; below, courtesy of Cloud County Historical Society Museum.)

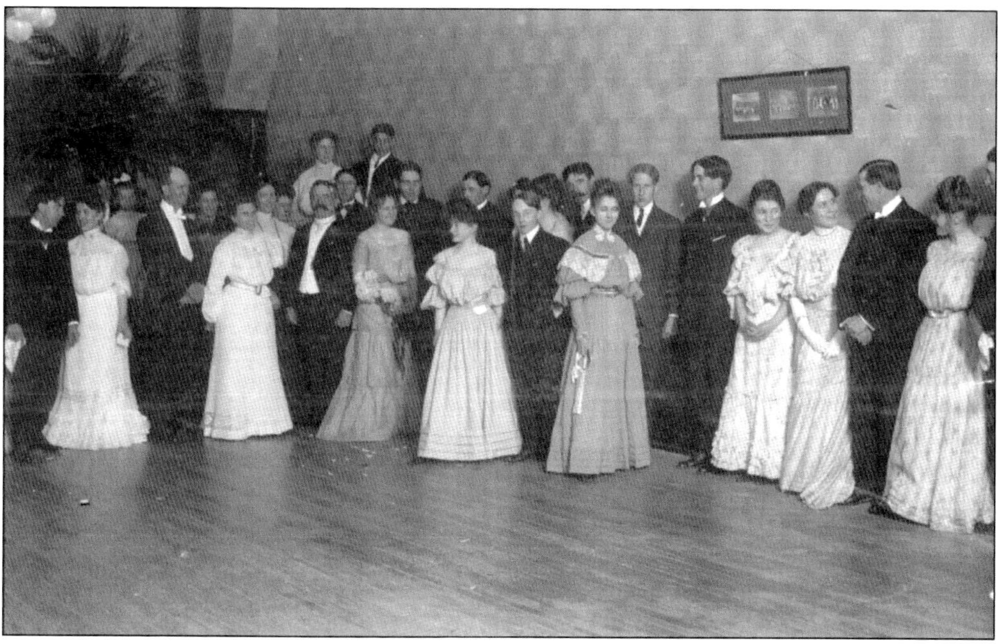

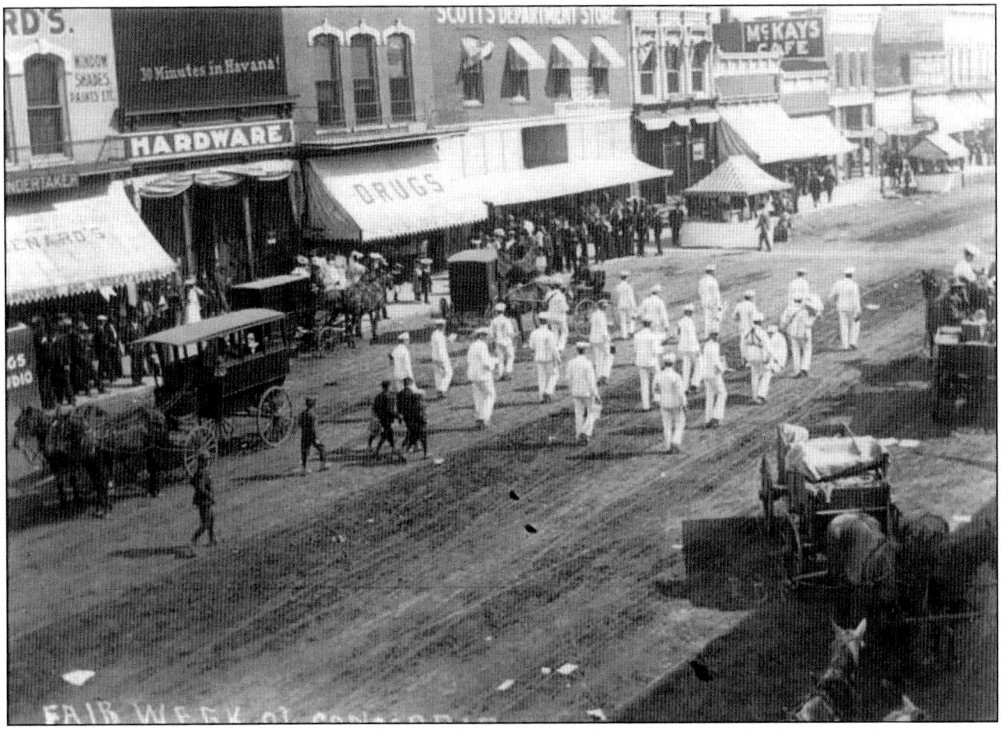

Fair week at Concordia has always been a big event and attracts people from nearby towns as well as local residents. The first Cloud County Fair was held in Concordia in 1873. The first fair association was organized in 1883. It folded after several years, but others followed. Here, a marching band passes down Sixth Street in the early 1900s. (Courtesy of Charles B. Johnson.)

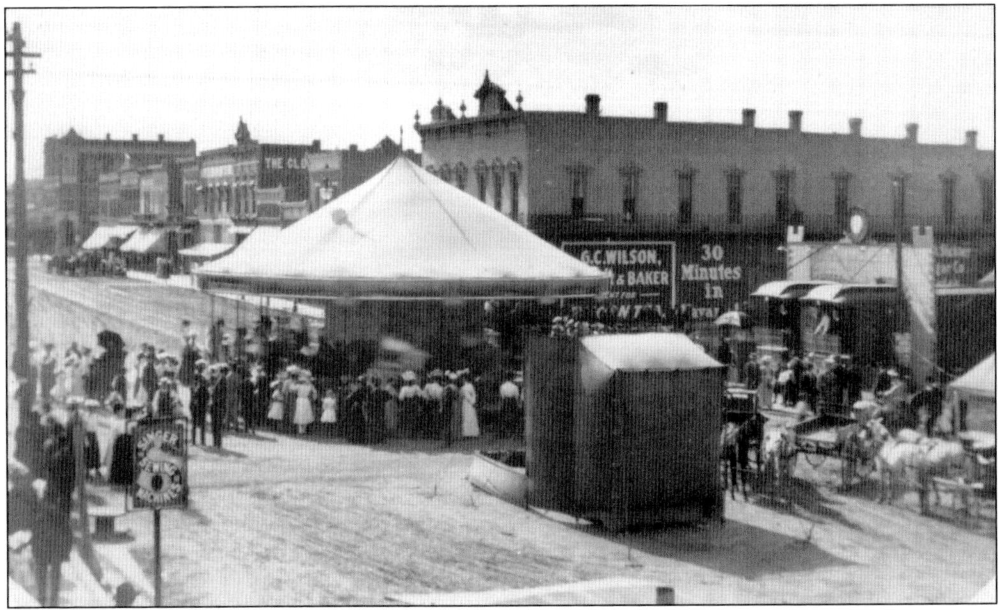

This photograph looks west on Sixth Street during a fair in 1911. A carousel has been set up in the street and children crowd around it as they wait for a chance to ride. An advertisement painted on one of the buildings at left identifies it as G.C. Wilson's bakery. (Courtesy of Charles Switzer.)

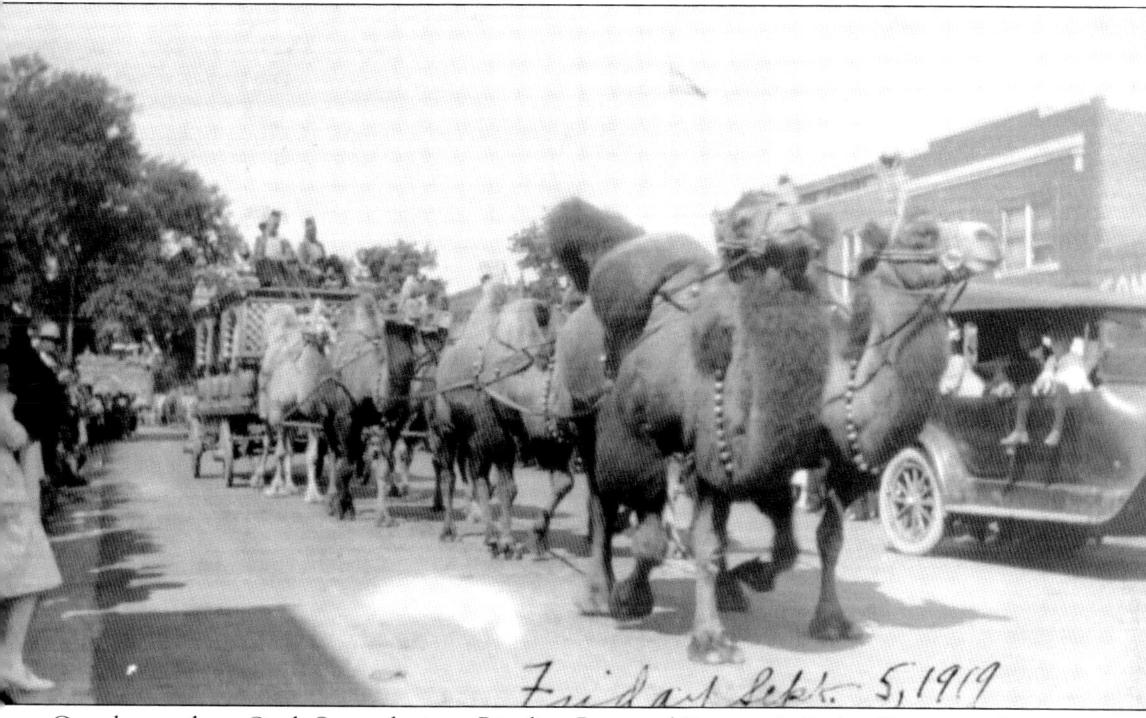

Camels pass down Sixth Street during a Ringling Bros. and Barnum & Bailey Circus parade in 1919. Concordia was once a regular stop for circus companies. A reporter for the *Kansan* newspaper attending the September 5, 1919, performance wrote of "cars parked in every available space," and said, "Many hundreds were denied admission to the big tent for lack of space to accommodate them." A circus business manager told the reporter receipts had not been added yet but, "You may say that it was the biggest crowd ever seen inside a tent to see a circus." When asked, "In Concordia?" he replied, "Anywhere." 16,000 people had attended a single performance in a town with about 7,500 residents. The record stood until 1922 and was shattered again in 1924 by another Concordia crowd numbering 16,680. (Courtesy of Guy Chizek.)

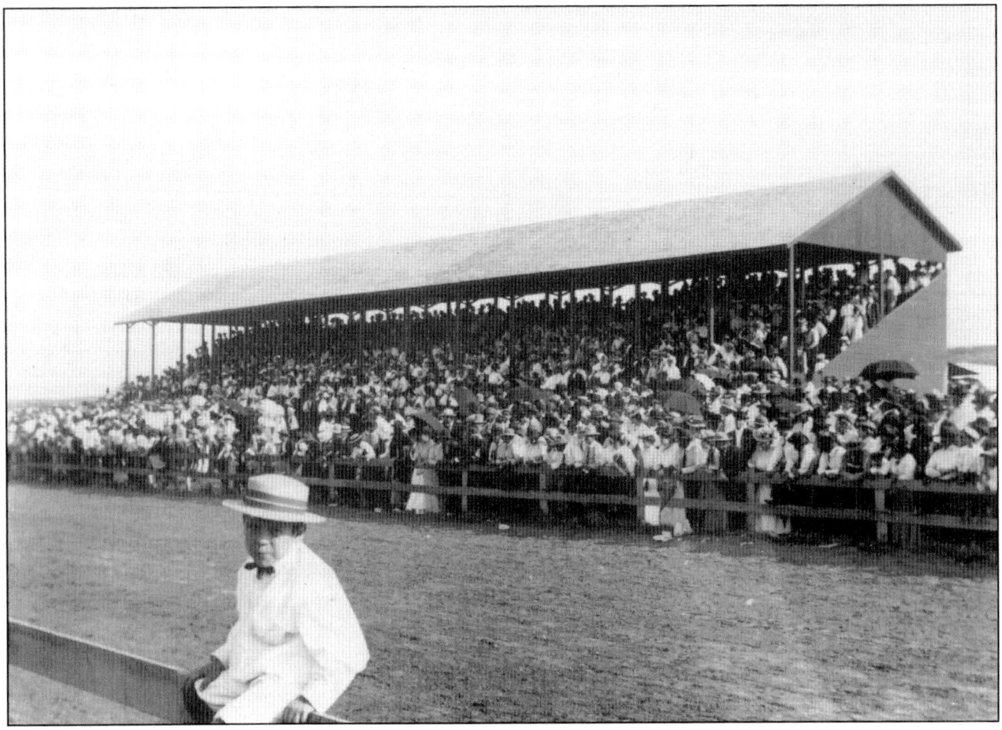

Above, a fairgrounds crowd, including the young railbird in the foreground, anticipates the next race at the fairgrounds. Below, in the 1920s, cameras could not stop action very well, and the horses in this photograph look as if they are really speeding by. In the late 20th century, the Erickson family operated a horse-racing track near the Camp Concordia site for a few years, but closed it when Kansas changed rules governing such establishments. (Both courtesy of Cloud County Historical Society Museum.)

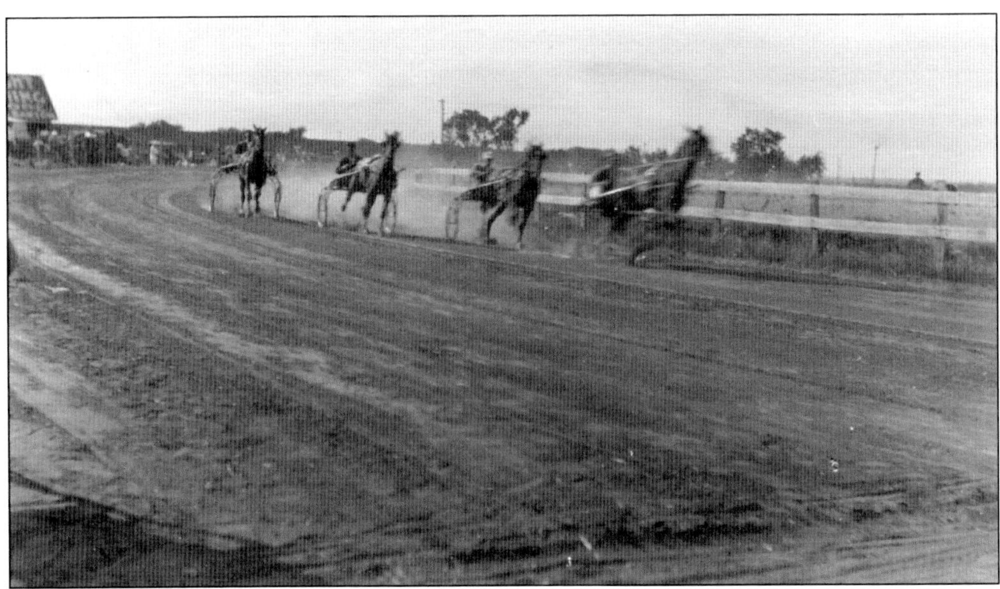

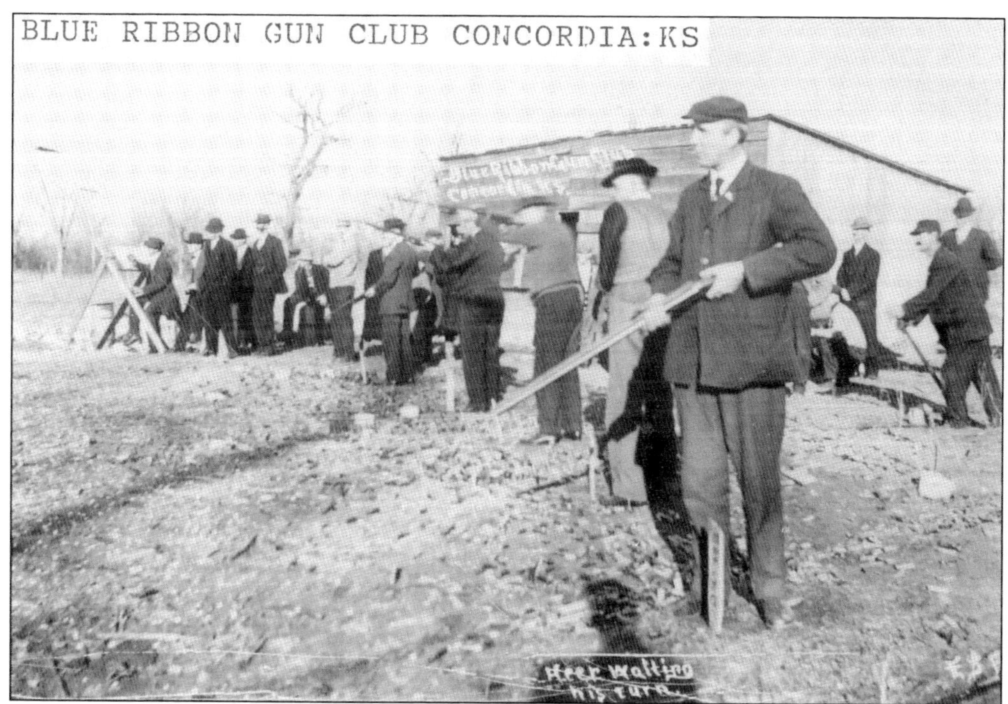

Members and guests of the Blue Ribbon Gun Club await their turns at a shoot. The club was one of the many organization founded for enthusiasts of particular hobbies in the early 20th century. (Courtesy of Cloud County Historical Society Museum.)

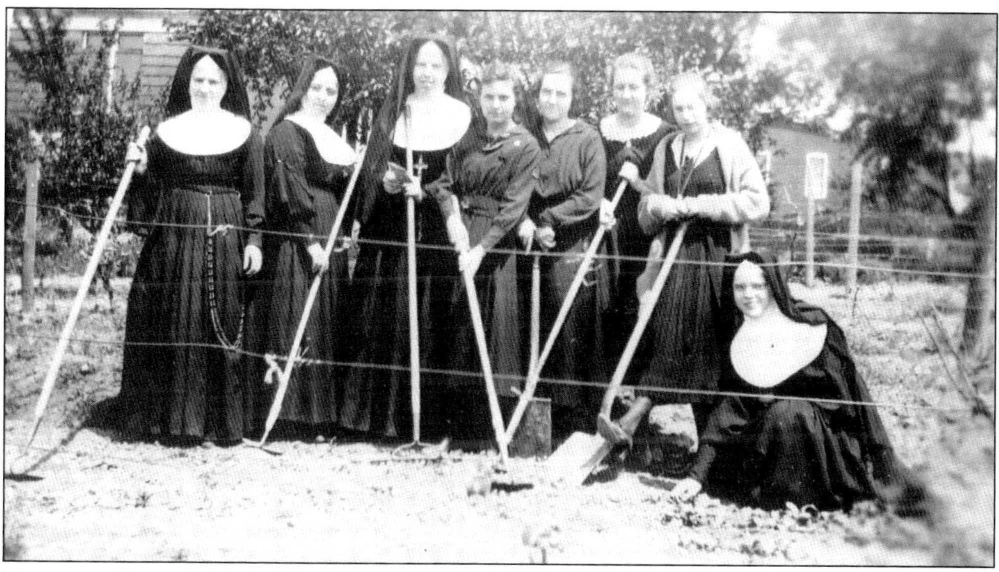

Novices and postulates at Nazareth Convent pause to have their photograph taken while gardening. Today, the Sisters of St. Joseph provide a community garden on convent property. The ground is prepared each season and local residents can sign up for a plot to grow vegetables and flowers using organic methods. (Courtesy of Sisters of St. Joseph Archives.)

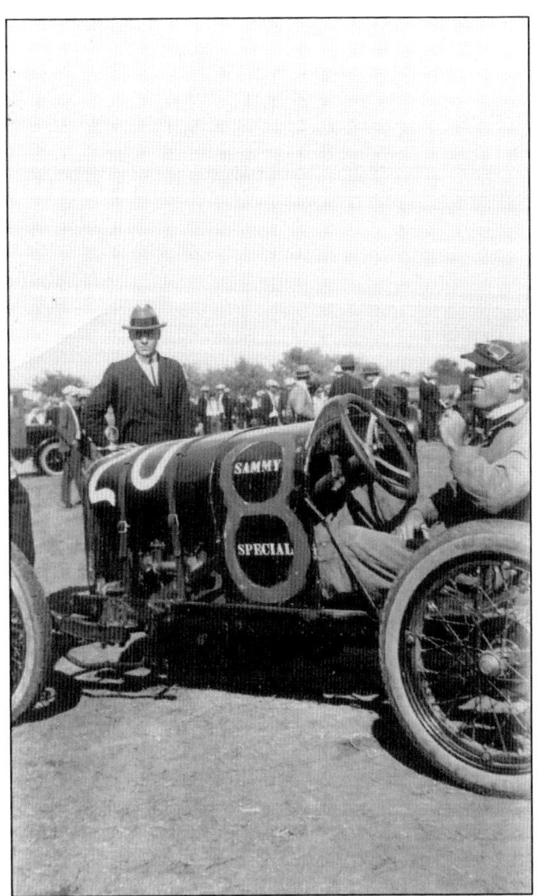

Auto racing was popular almost from the time cars became widely available, and this October 8, 1924, photograph shows a driver chatting before a race. Although the men are not identified, the car was the "No. 8 Sammy Special." In those days, racing teams often consisted of a driver and a mechanic. (Courtesy of Cloud County Historical Society Museum.)

Back when children enjoyed simpler pursuits, scenes like this were popular subjects for photographs. Enjoying a ride in a pony cart are Evelyn Eleanor Lewis (left), Aline Lewis (right), and Audrey Ball (front). Aline remembers that this picture was taken in the late 1930s. (Courtesy of Aline Luecke.)

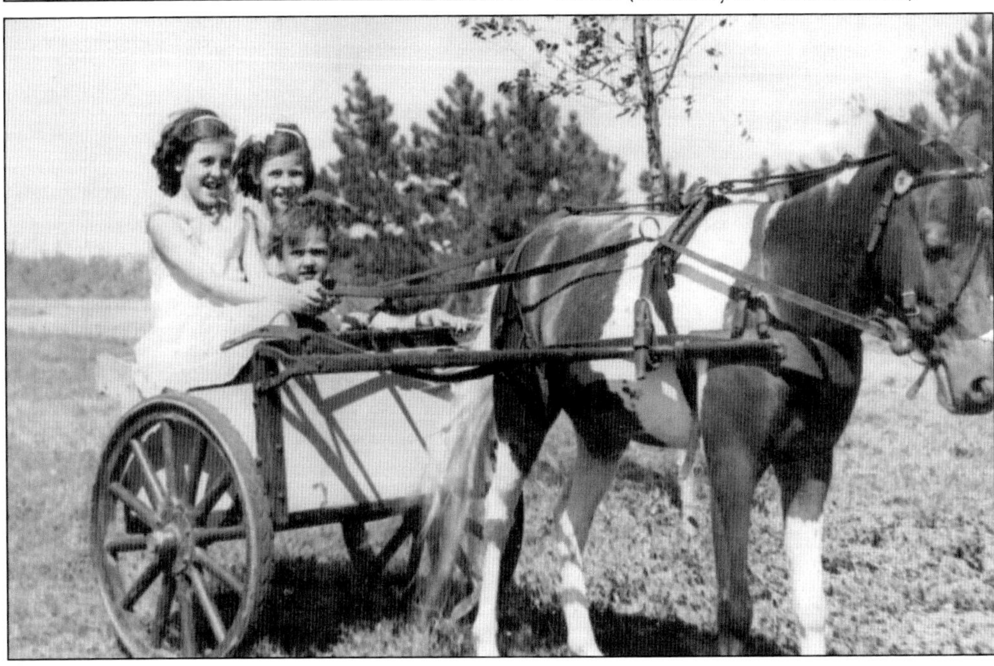

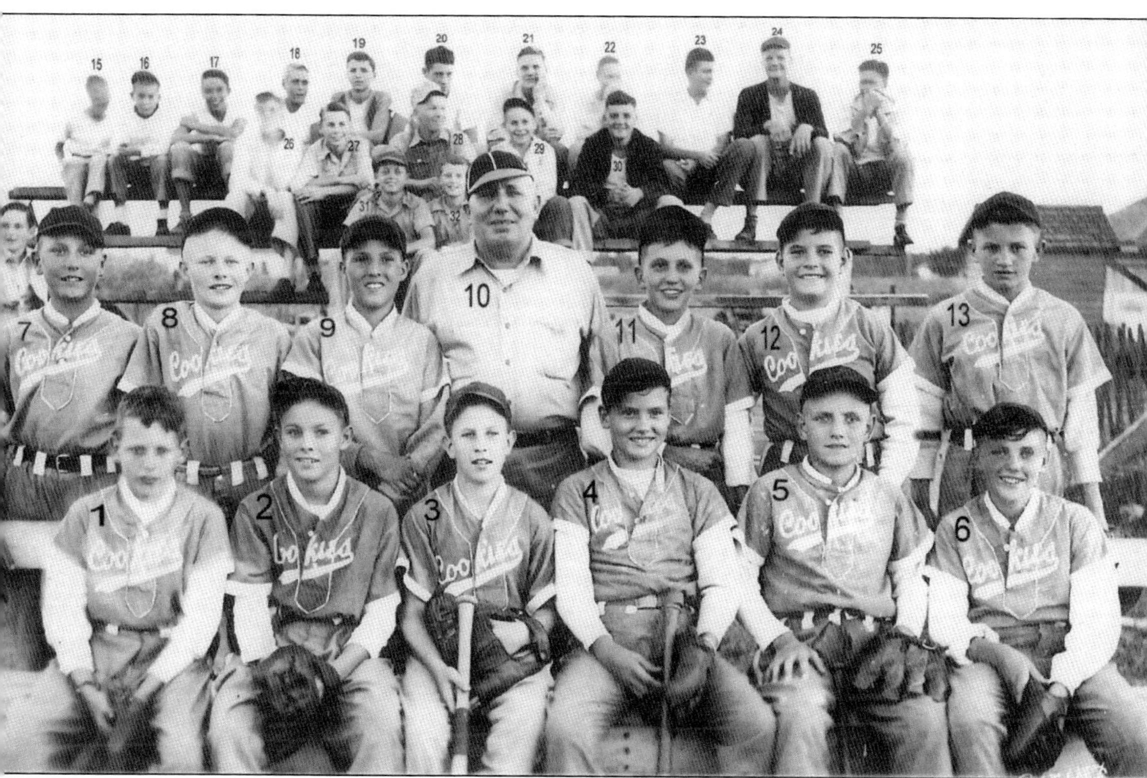

The first Concordia Cookies baseball team in 1945 included, from left to right, (first row) Norman Chartier, Tom Walker, Muryl Laman, Mickey Bethel, Larry Bowling, and Tom Edquist; (second row) Harold Scott, Dean Snavely, Gene Sterling, Coach Dick Taff, Bill Taff, Nathan Harris, and Bob Hanson. Spectators in the bleachers behind the team include, from left to right, (first row) Jerry Wilcox; (second row) Wayne Chartier and Richard Chartier; (third row) unidentified, Gene Johnson, Clayton Kempton, Leo Johnson, and Don Lowell; (fourth row) unidentified, Larry Stamm, Darrell Zohn, unidentified, Ted Hanson, Merrill Stanley, Harold Wilkie, unidentified, John Forsberg, Bill Matthew, and Don Day. (Courtesy of Tom Walker.)

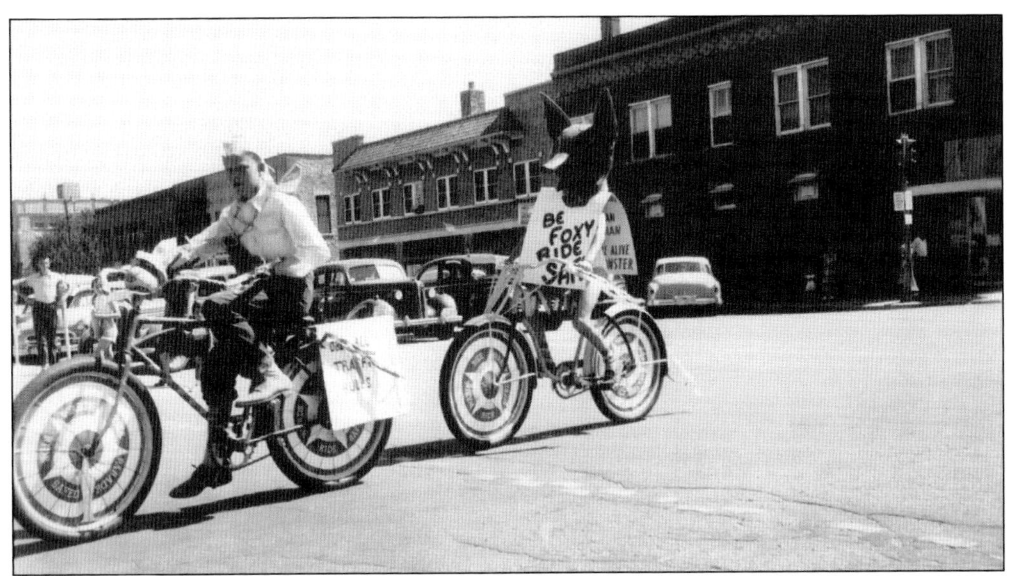

In 1954, hundreds of Concordians came downtown to watch Kenny Switzer, dressed as Old Father Time, win the annual Bike Safety Parade with his entry featuring the slogan, "Ride Safely All the Time." He won a new three-speed bicycle. Second- and third-place winners Susan Wassenberg and Marla Morgan, respectively, and fourth- and fifth-place winners Doug Rogers and Jeanie Ferman won merchandise certificates. At right above, Ferman rides her entry, "Be Foxy, Ride Safe." Lester's Sweet Shop treated the children to free ice cream cones. Below, at center, Janet Limbach, a *Blade-Empire* reporter, talks with F.P. Lundmark, Bike Safety Campaign chairman and manager of Montgomery Ward, which sponsored the event with the Summer Playground Program. Between them, the man wearing the hat is Dean Grimm. About 75 riders entered. (Both courtesy of Charles Switzer.)

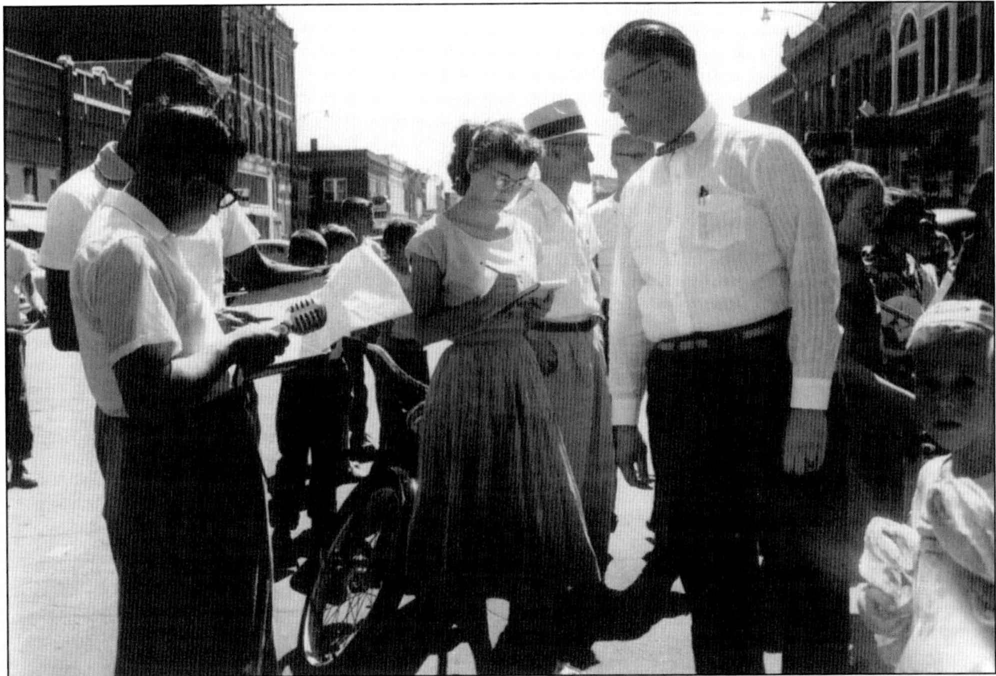

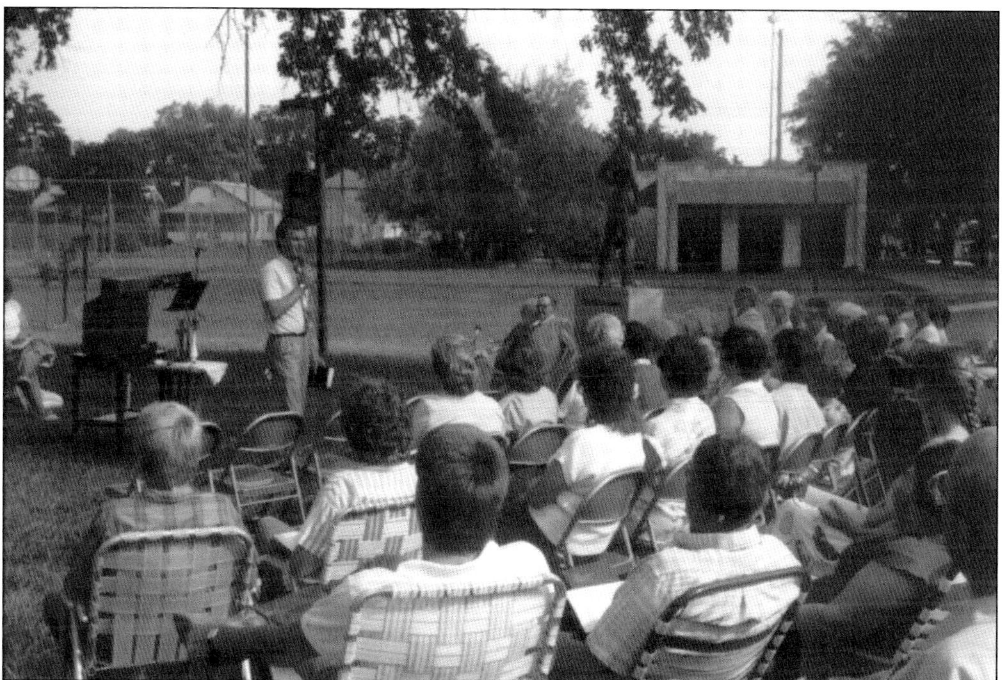

Concordia City Park has been the site of many events, including the annual fall festival. The festival started as a market day in the 1800s and has continued each year, coinciding with school reunions that bring many former residents back to town. This picture is from 1985. (Courtesy of Charles Switzer.)

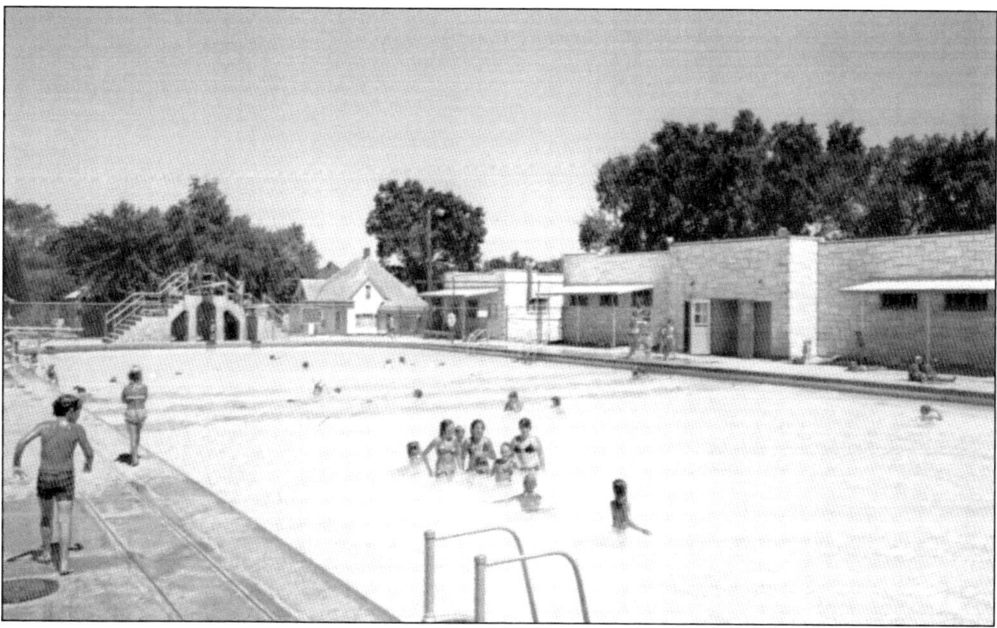

This postcard photograph of children playing in the swimming pool in city park was taken about 1958 by Wayne Switzer. This was the second public pool in town. Later, this pool was filled in and a new one was constructed, but the shelter house was preserved. Coauthor Dena Bisnette's father, Eddie Bisnette, worked as a lifeguard at this pool. (Courtesy of Charles Switzer.)

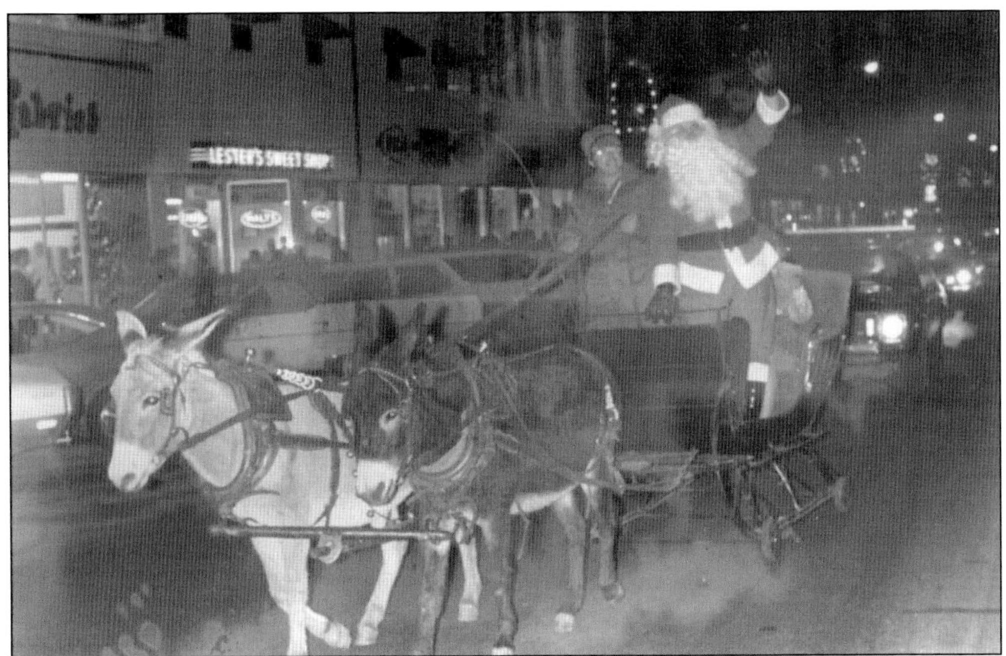

Santa Claus rides down the street in a sleigh converted to roll on lawnmower wheels during a Christmas parade in 1975; Santa is passing Lester's Sweet Shop's neon sign. Driving is Guy Chizek. Wally Carlson, who coached for many years at Cloud County Community College, plays Santa. (Courtesy of Guy Chizek.)

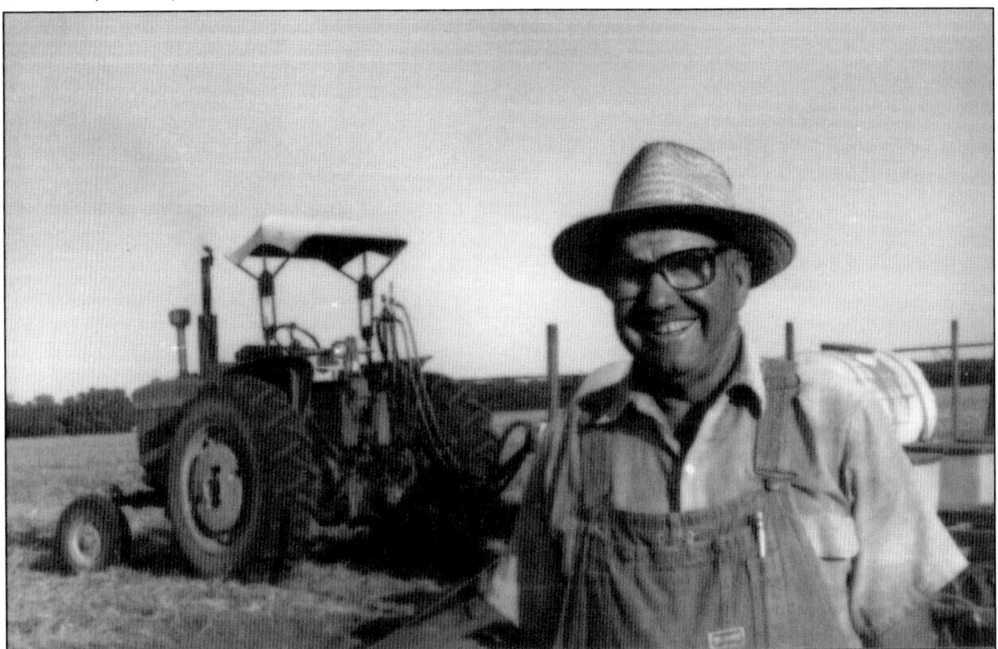

Part of the fun of fairs is competition. This photograph of local farmer and cattleman Elmo St. Pierre with his tractor was taken by his granddaughter Lisa Palmquist, who entered it in 4-H competition in the 1981 Cloud County Fair. She won a purple ribbon. St. Pierre, who was born in 1919, died in 2001. (Courtesy of Mary Ann Palmquist.)

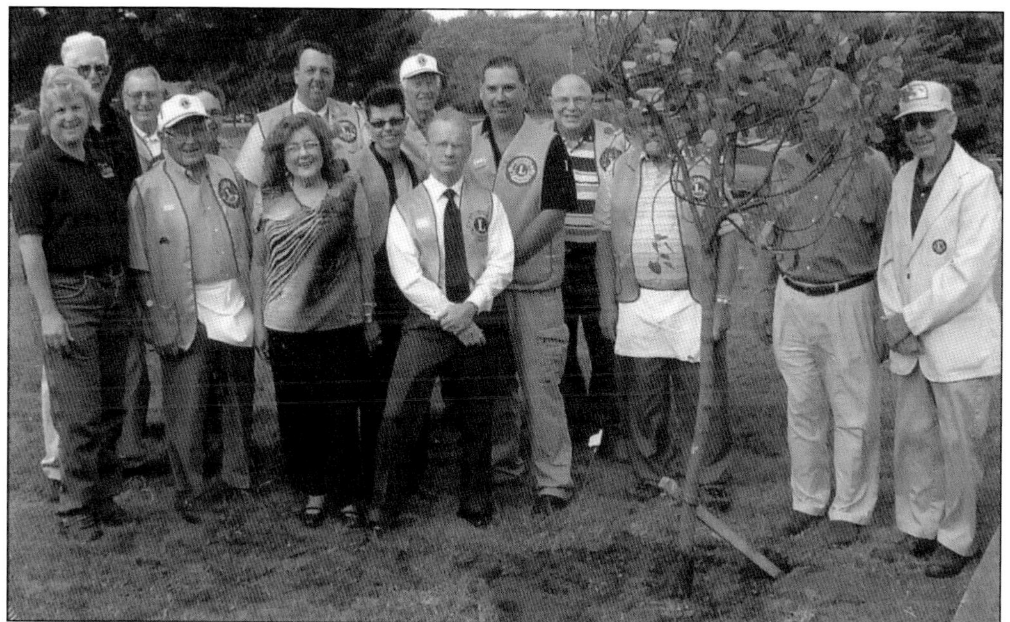

Concordia Lions Club remains active. Here, members participate in a tree replanting at Pleasant Hill Cemetery in 2011, replacing trees lost to disease and blight. Pictured are, from left to right, Kim Brewer, Mel Davenport, Dallas Nading, Devine Montoya, Marilyn Sorenson, Bruce Nutter, Susan Sutton, Bill Thompson, Bryan Marks, Marvin Petersen, Tim Holt, Eugene Leon, Al Uhric, and Gene Johnson. (Courtesy of Dallas Nading.)

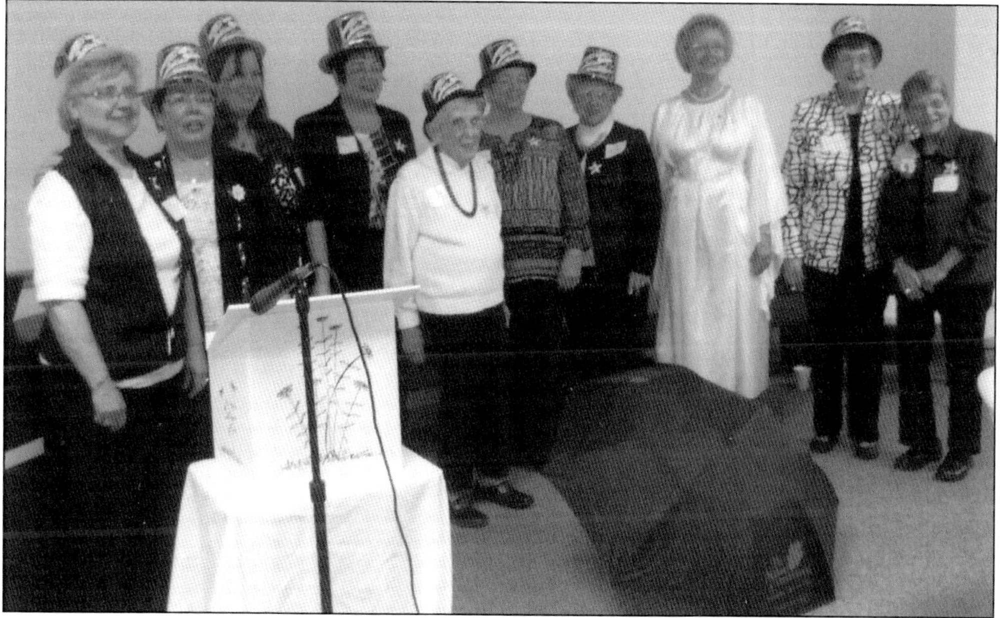

The Philanthropic Educational Organization, or PEO Sisterhood chapter in Concordia started about 100 years ago when Chloris Anderson learned about the club from a friend in Nebraska. It is the town's oldest non–church affiliated women's club still active. In 2014, the PEO chapter celebrated 100 years of history in music and speeches, and Sue Regan modeled a replica of a ceremonial uniform the original officers wore. (Courtesy of Jean Leon.)

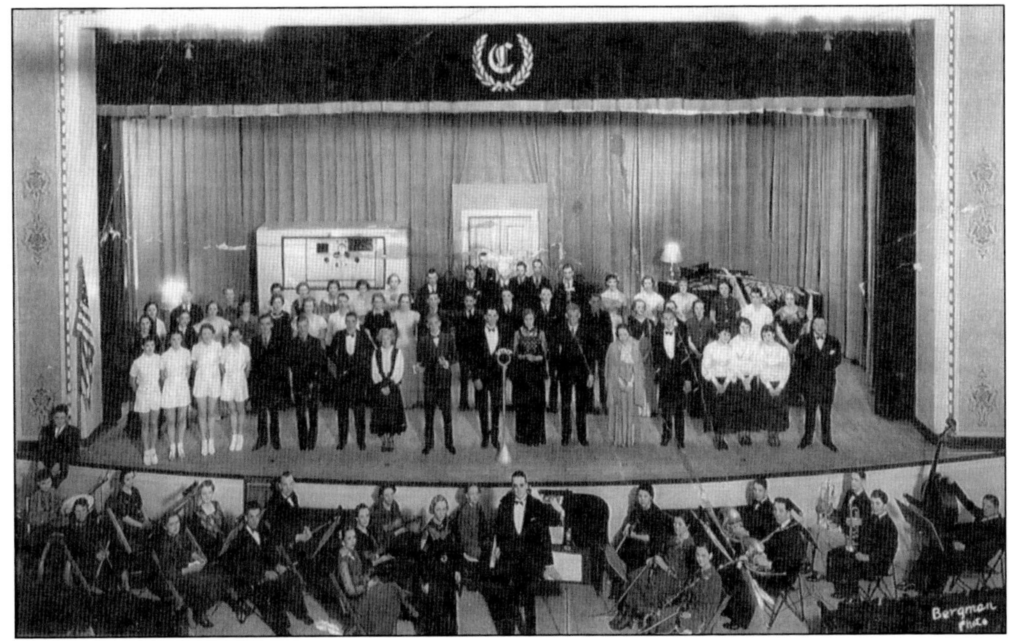

Radio stars toured to promote their programs in the 1930s, and groups of them made stops in Concordia, visiting with fans and performing. The large "C" monogrammed on the valance over the stage shows that this event happened in the auditorium in Concordia High School. (Courtesy of Tom's Music House.)

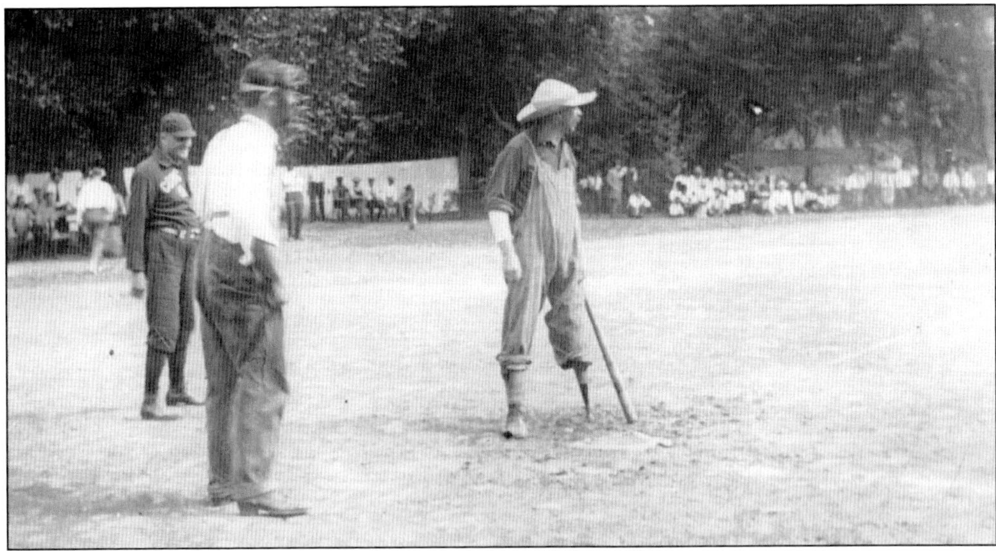

Gomer Davies steps up to the bat during a baseball game in the early 1900s. Davies probably lost his leg in a mining accident, since he worked in that trade before becoming a newspaper editor. However, he liked to make up stories about his wooden leg. Janet Pease Emery recounted one story in her book, telling how Davies had had a bit too much to drink at the Elks Club one evening and had started down the boardwalk to his home. He did not live far from the club and was puzzled when he seemed unable to get there. In the morning, he said he discovered that his wooden leg had become stuck in a knothole, and he had been walking in a circle all night. (Courtesy of Dallas Nading.)

Six

Concordia Has Unforgettable Residents

Unforgettable characters have wandered in and out of Concordia's history from the very start, beginning with founder James Manny Hagaman. There were so many, in fact, that when Janet Pease Emery wrote a book in time to publish it before the centennial in 1971, she decided to call it *It Takes People to Make a Town*.

Some of these people were what Emery called "Factotums," men and a few women who arrived during the town's infancy and became involved in nearly everything going on, from business and social events to politics. Some of them have been discussed previously. Others were known for specific professions or avocations or even by particular adventures they had.

A retired attorney, Clarence Paulsen, wrote a column for the *Blade-Empire* for many years called "Trivial History of Concordia and Environs" and many of his columns concentrated on personalities as well. Some of these people were highly placed in society, and some were not, but they all contributed to Concordia's unique character.

And they were characters indeed, the kind whose stories are told over and over, until the tales are sometimes so decorated it becomes hard to sort the truth from the legends.

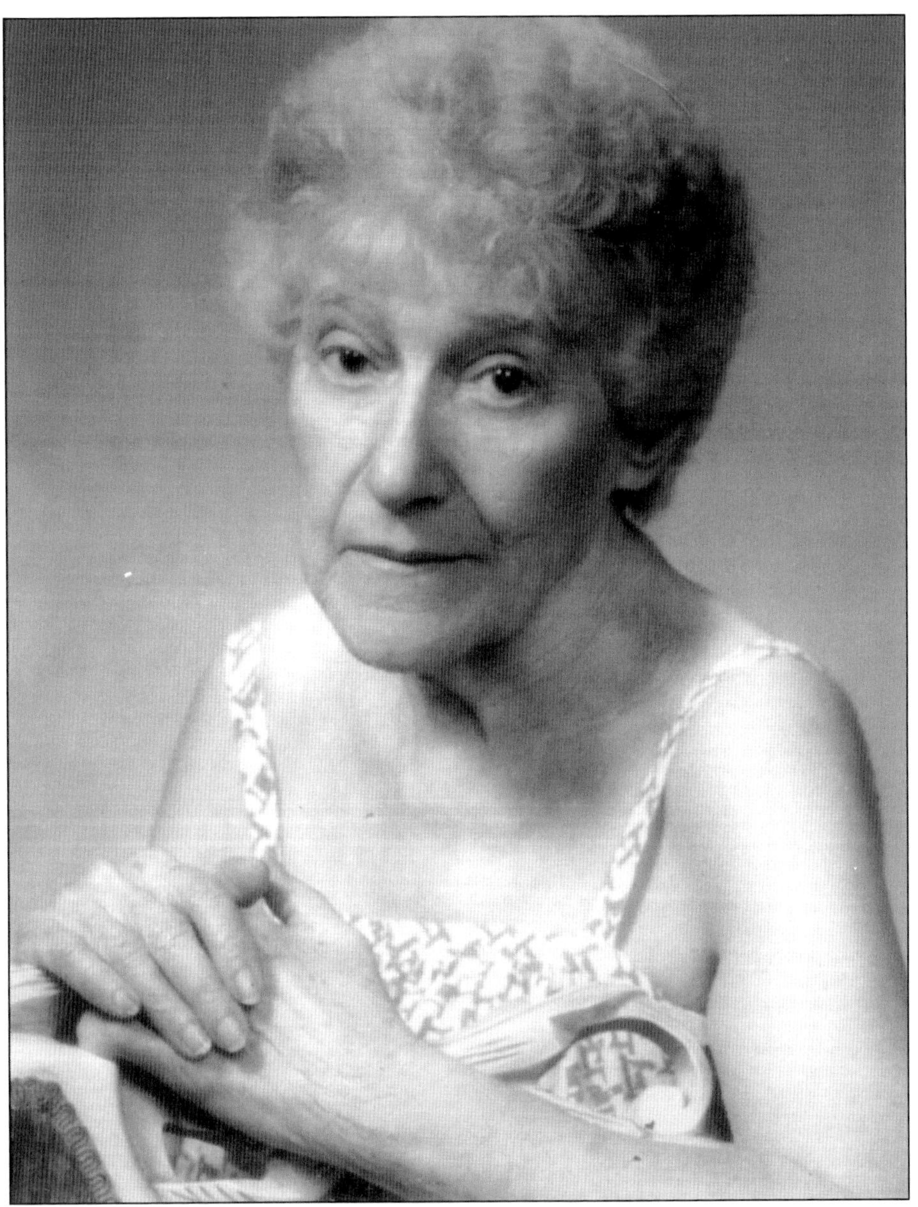

Marion Ellet, journalist for more than 70 years, turned in her last column to the *Concordia Blade-Empire* just four years before she died on August 26, 1996, at age 97. Ellet graduated from Smith College and traveled widely, paying her way by writing. She left Kansas in 1921 to write for the *Brooklyn Eagle* and the *New York Times*, returning five years later to the *Blade*. Her column "Mugwump Musings" was a regular feature in the *Blade*, *Emporia Gazette*, *Topeka State Journal*, and *Great Bend Tribune*. She covered the state legislature for the *Blade* and *Kansas City Journal-Post* and became known as politically astute. Declining jobs that would have placed her in the national spotlight, she was honored as one of the state's 10 outstanding editors by Sigma Delta Chi (now the Society for Professional Journalists) and received writing awards from the Kansas Press Association and Women's State Press Association. Ellet was granddaughter of a Concordia pioneer, Judge Frederick Sturges, and lived in her grandfather's home. (Courtesy of Cloud County Historical Society Museum.)

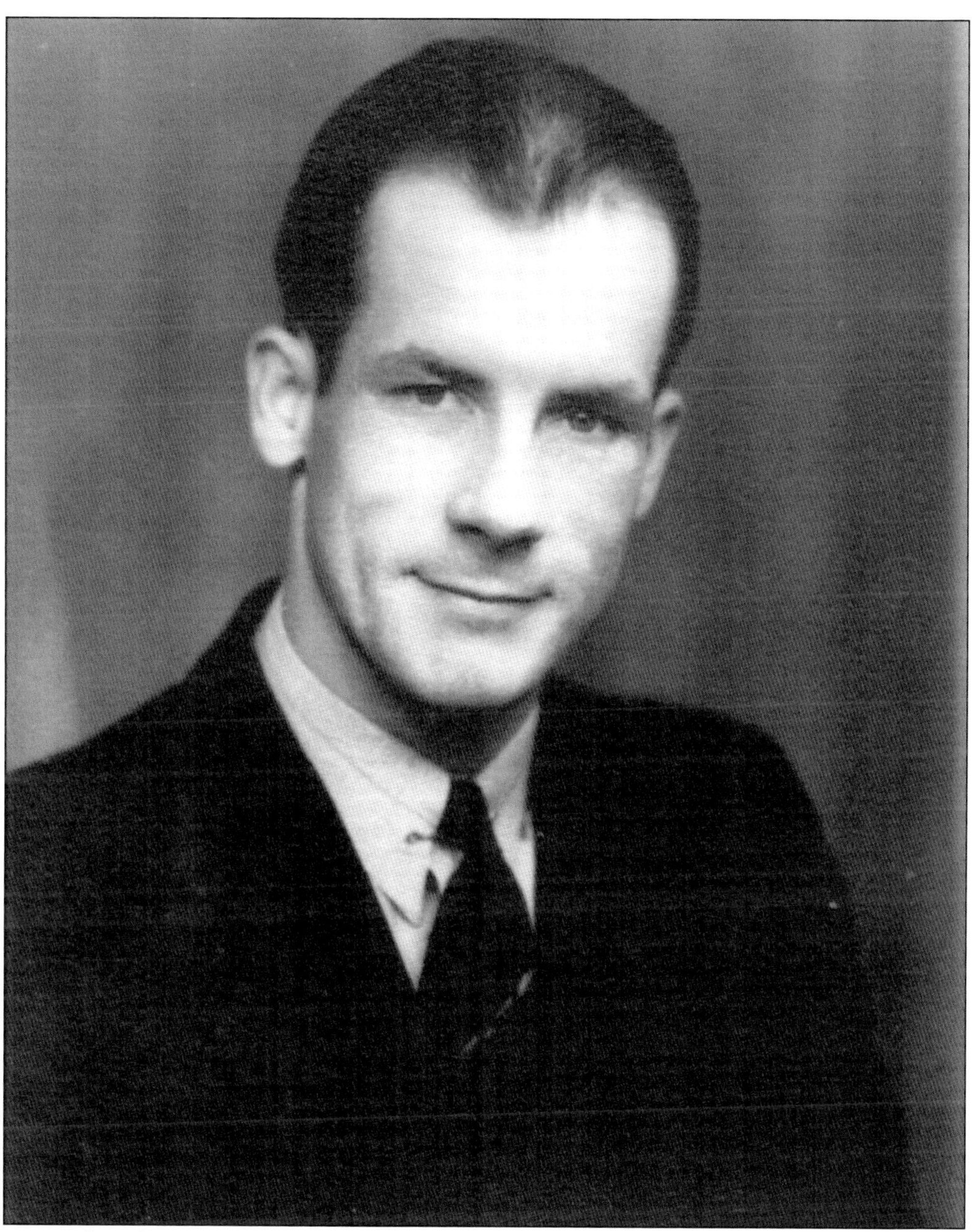

Concordia pilot Valta Lewis landed in the Guinness Book of World Records in 1929 when he flew Dr. Leo E. Haughey and nurse Frances Ring more than 100 miles to Alton during a blizzard. Lewis, in Wichita with his plane when he was called, flew above the storm, then dropped low to follow the Republican River to Concordia. Visibility on the way to Alton was still bad. Lewis used the Solomon River as his landmark, navigating with altimeter, watch, and compass. Landing in a cornfield, he approached a nearby farmhouse, which was the right one. The doctor performed a caesarian section using the mother's dining table for an operating table, with nurse and pilot assisting. The mother had refused to go to the hospital because it was run by nuns. Dr. Haughey left Ring to care for mother and baby, and upon discovering that the nurse was Catholic, the new parents paid her and ordered her to leave. (Courtesy of Aline Luecke.)

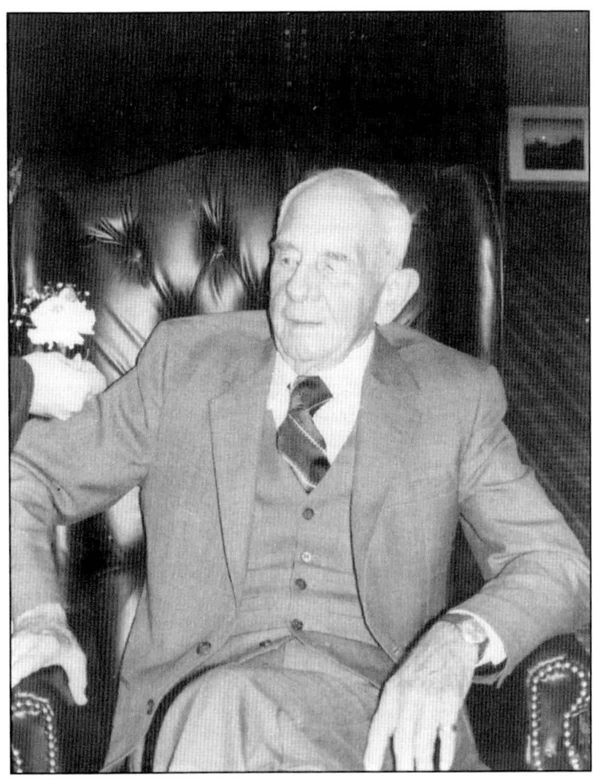

Frank Carlson, son of Swedish immigrants, grew up on a farm near Concordia. He became the only Kansan to serve as governor, US representative, and US senator. He was an advisor to Pres. Dwight D. Eisenhower and a delegate to the United Nations. He was state representative before running for governor, a position he held for two terms. Carlson, known for his strong Baptist faith, established the annual Presidential Prayer Breakfast. He served as chairman of Concordia's Centennial Committee, and the public library is named for him. He died in 1987. During his political career, Carlson always said he was a farmer first and a politician second. The painting below of the farm where Frank Carlson grew up was done by local genealogist Marilyn Johnston. (Left, courtesy of Dallas Nading; below, courtesy of Marilyn Johnston.)

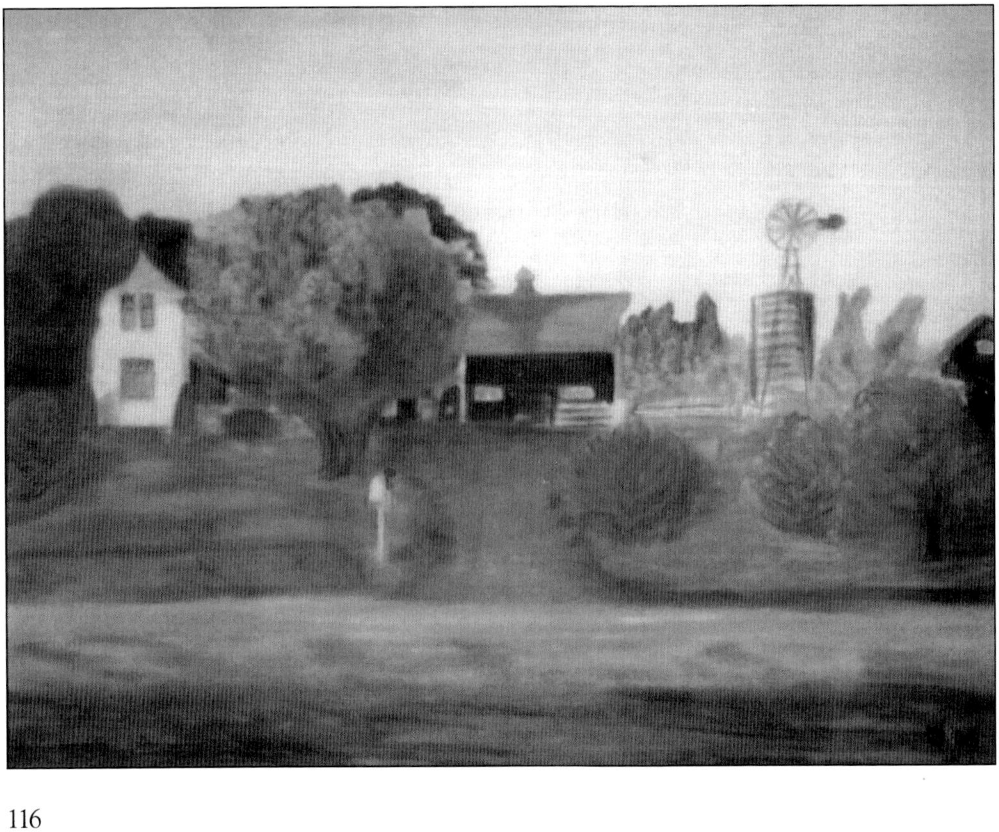

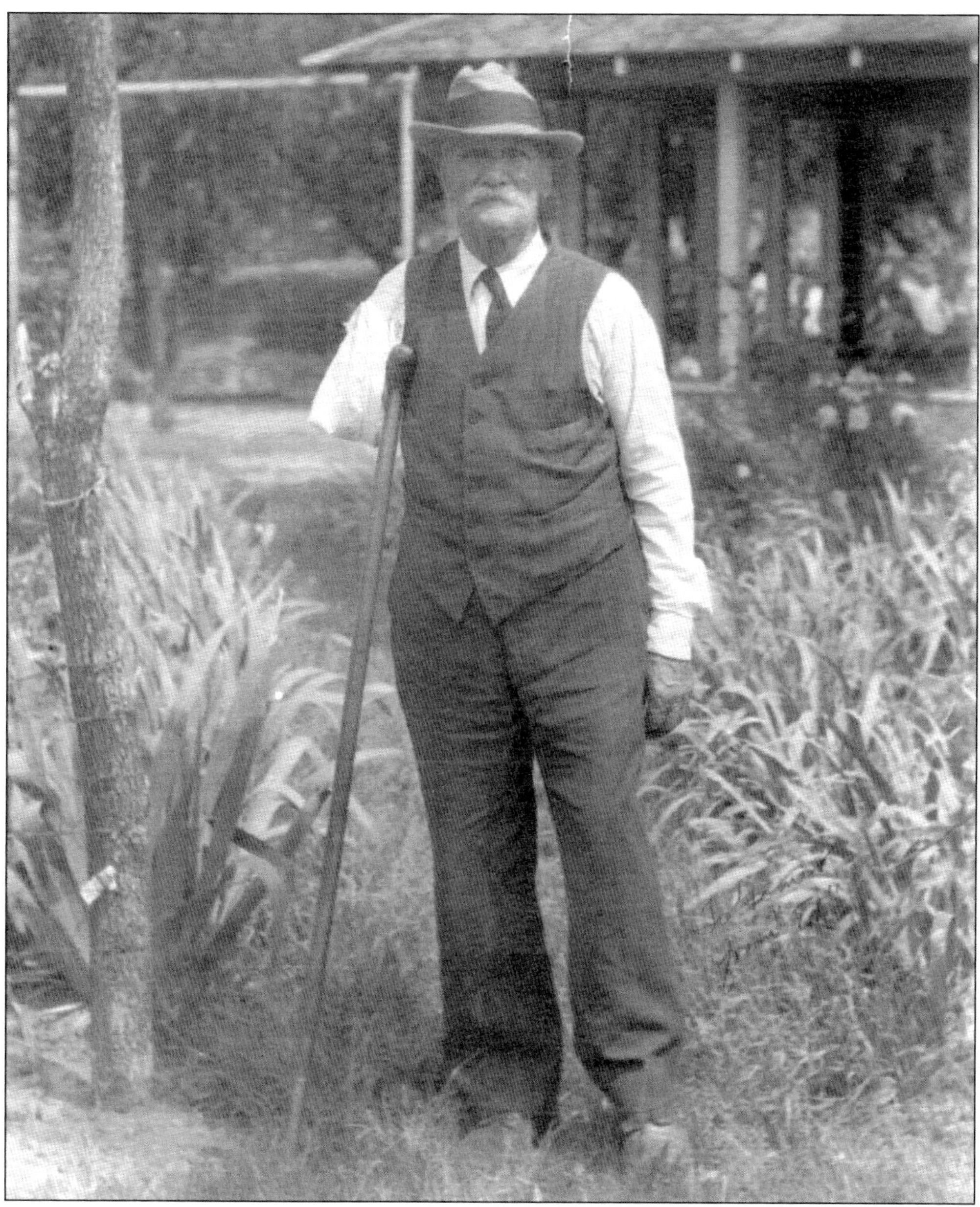

James Albert Gushwa, known as Popcorn Jim, sold popcorn on the street in Concordia for more than 40 years. He came to Cloud County in 1877 to work in Minersville and was a widower with two young daughters by March 1892, when he and some friends decided to hop a ride on a Missouri-Pacific train. Gushwa was caught under a wheel. Two men who had stayed with the horse and wagon rescued him, but the accident permanently shortened his right leg and cost him his right arm. Addicted to his morphine prescription, he tried to quit on his own and was sent to the state asylum for treatment. Returning to Concordia, he bought his first popcorn machine in September 1893. He served as police judge from 1895 to 1901 and then returned to the popcorn business and the informal free employment bureau he had established. He continued working until the late 1930s, when his health began to fail. He was 88 years old when he died on January 14, 1942. (Courtesy of Cloud County Historical Society Museum.)

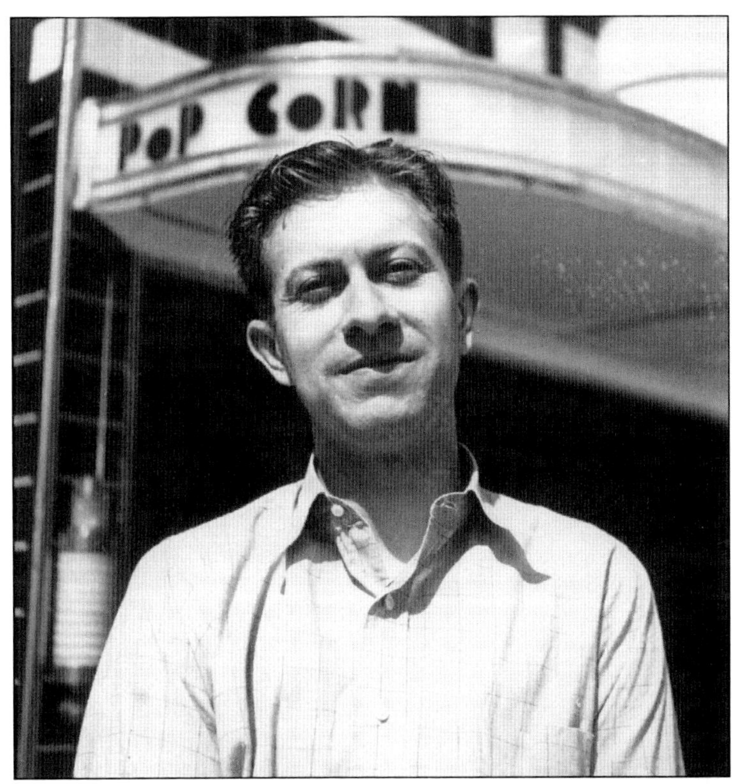

Concordia's other popcorn man was Vernon Stewart. Stewart started his business when he was a teenager, making home deliveries of popcorn. His business expanded, and he opened a shop next to the Strand Theatre. His popcorn stand was damaged along with the Strand in a fire, but both reopened. He closed in 1961 after 35 years in business. (Both courtesy of Cloud County Historical Society Museum.)

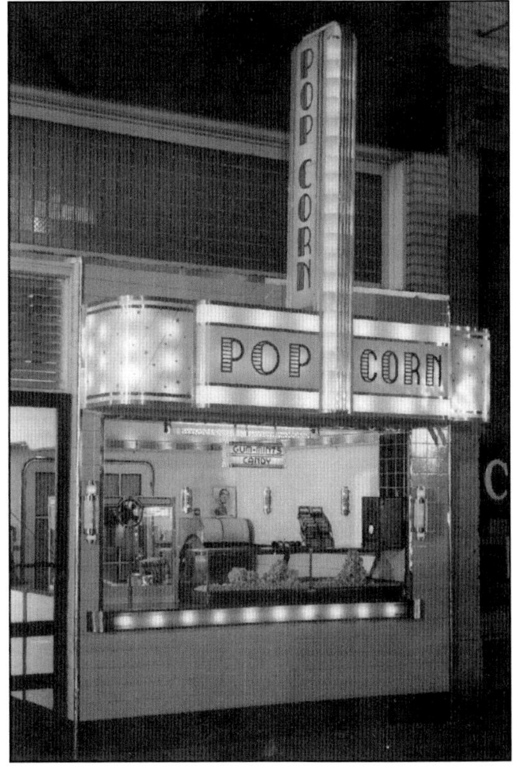

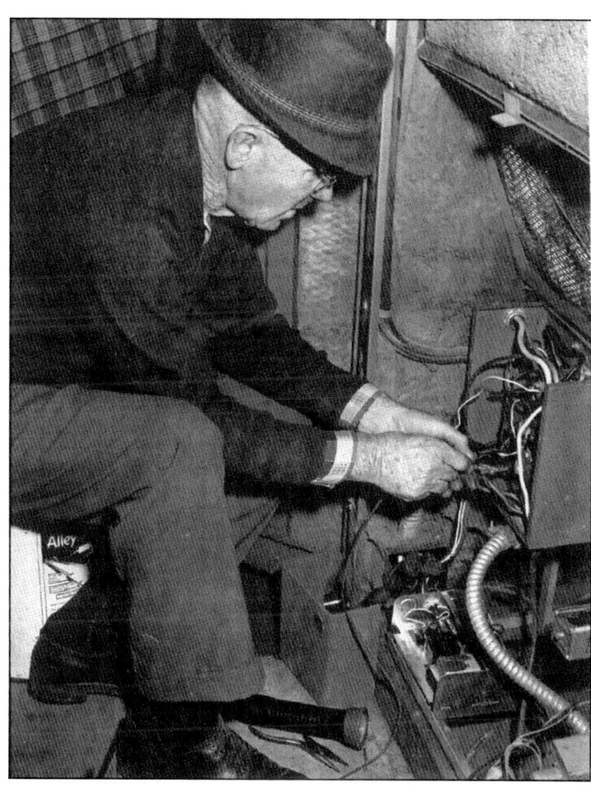

"When no one else can fix it, Arthur is called" was the headline to a newspaper feature about Arthur Lewis. Lewis was known around Concordia for his ability to repair all kinds of devices and was especially adept with electricity, having retired from Kansas Power and Light. At right, he solves a heating problem. He was also known for his hobby, artistic woodworking, which he often showed at the Senior Center, as seen below. (Both courtesy of Aline Luecke.)

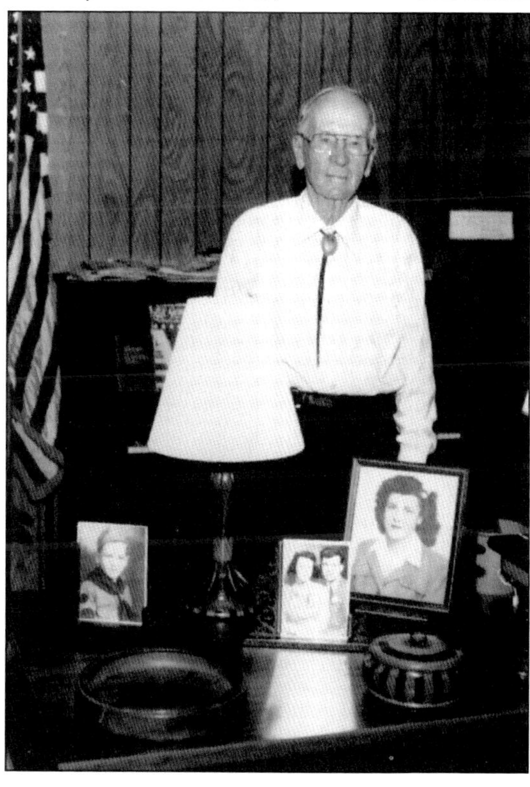

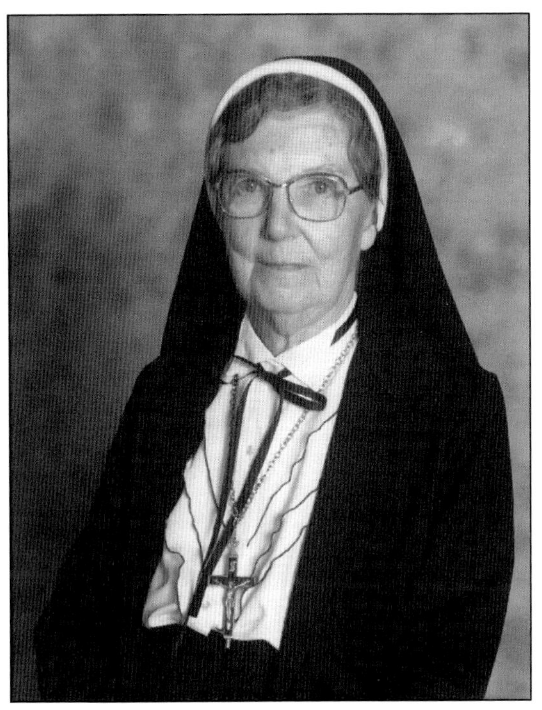

Sr. Frances Joanne Bonfield took charge of the business office at St. Joseph Hospital in 1933. Writing about her work, she described hanging wet sheets over windows and doors for surgeries during Dust Bowl days, bartering during the Depression, and battling polio in the 1940s and 1950s. She remembered the 1935 flood victims, including 28 men stranded on part of a washed-out bridge and others found clinging to trees. (Courtesy of Cloud County Community Health Center.)

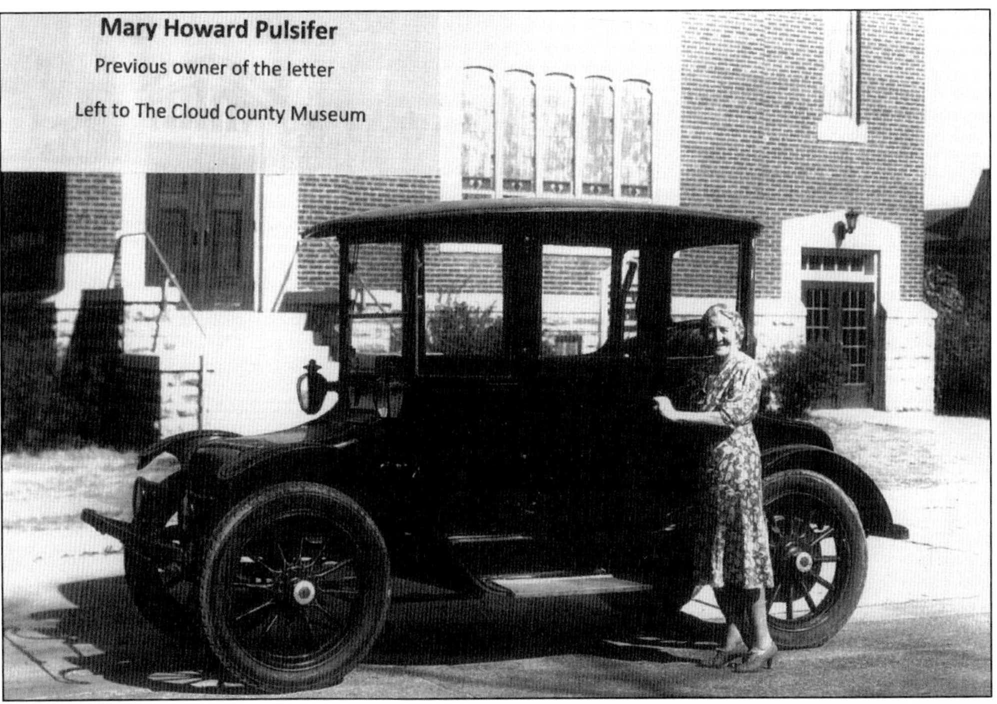

Mary Howard Pulsifer chauffeured people in her electric car during World War II because it used no gasoline. Before she died in 1949, she instructed a friend that, when Concordia established a historical museum, she was to donate a certain letter on Pulsifer's behalf. The letter was from Martha Washington to her niece and still belongs to the museum. (Courtesy of Cloud County Historical Society Museum.)

Seven

Concordia Looks to the Future

As Concordia looks to its future, the town faces the same problems small towns all over Kansas and across the Midwest have, including an aging population, young people leaving for jobs elsewhere, and businesses closing or moving due to changing market conditions.

But Concordia is adapting instead of dying like some other towns in the region. Concordia retains many things other towns have lost, including a thriving downtown district with a grocery store and a post office. Chains like Walmart and McDonald's are almost exclusively out on Highway 81, leaving downtown its unique character. Empty buildings and lots are being rehabilitated. Even a downtown soda fountain has reopened.

A daily newspaper, the *Blade-Empire*, still keeps track of things. A descendant of the *Empire* founded in 1870 and J.M. Hagaman's own *Blade*, the paper is an endangered species in the Internet age, but it is still quite alive. The *Kansan*, its weekly competitor, closed in 1988, but local residents still have another choice for news, KNCK Radio.

Concordia also boasts some long-lived businesses. A few are retail stores like Tom's Music House, which has been downtown for more than 50 years. More industrial examples include Cloud Ceramics, Farhas and Anderson, Peltier Foundry, Alston's, Champlin Tire Recycling, and George Hankins Steel. There is also Cloud County Health Center. And the need for higher education has been filled by Cloud County Community College since the 1960s.

The town adapted to the four-laning of Highway 81 and still sometimes must deal with Mother Nature, such as the storm that made permanent changes in one part of town in 1994.

Visitors are more welcomed than ever. The town has always attracted a small tourism base of hunters, and now has six attractions: Nazareth Convent, Brown Grand Theatre, National Orphan Train Complex, POW Camp Concordia Museum, Cloud County Historical Museum, and the outdoor art installation called the "Whole Wall Mural."

Yes, Concordia has plans for the future.

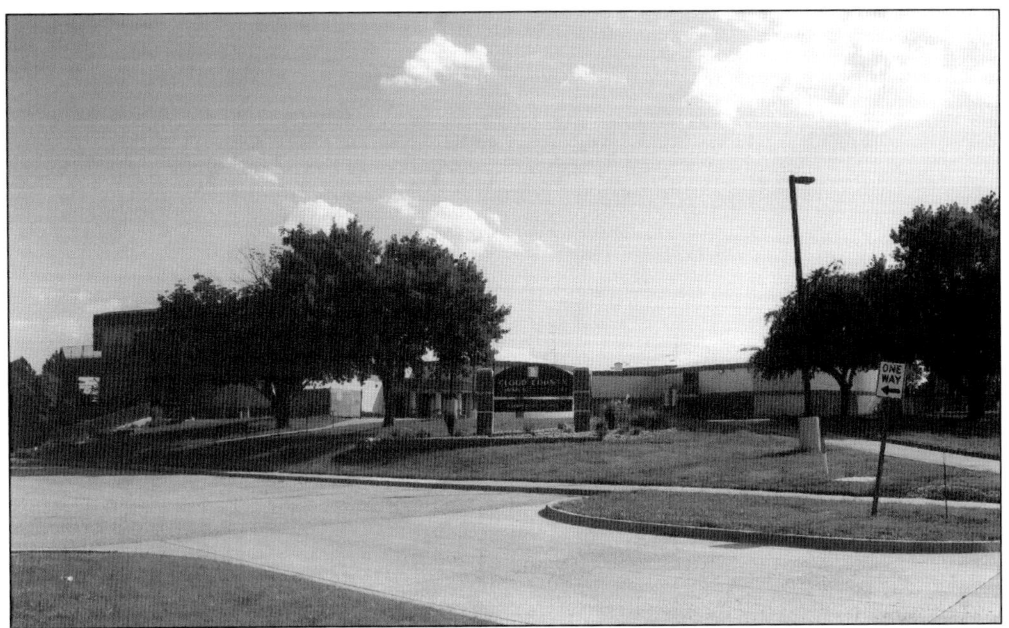

Cloud County Community College opened in 1965 with classes at Concordia High School. The first campus building was constructed in 1968. Everett Miller, a teacher there for more than 40 years, said the school's mission today remains the same as the day it opened: providing area students with an affordable higher education. This is the original section of the campus as it looks today. (Photograph by Dena Bisnette.)

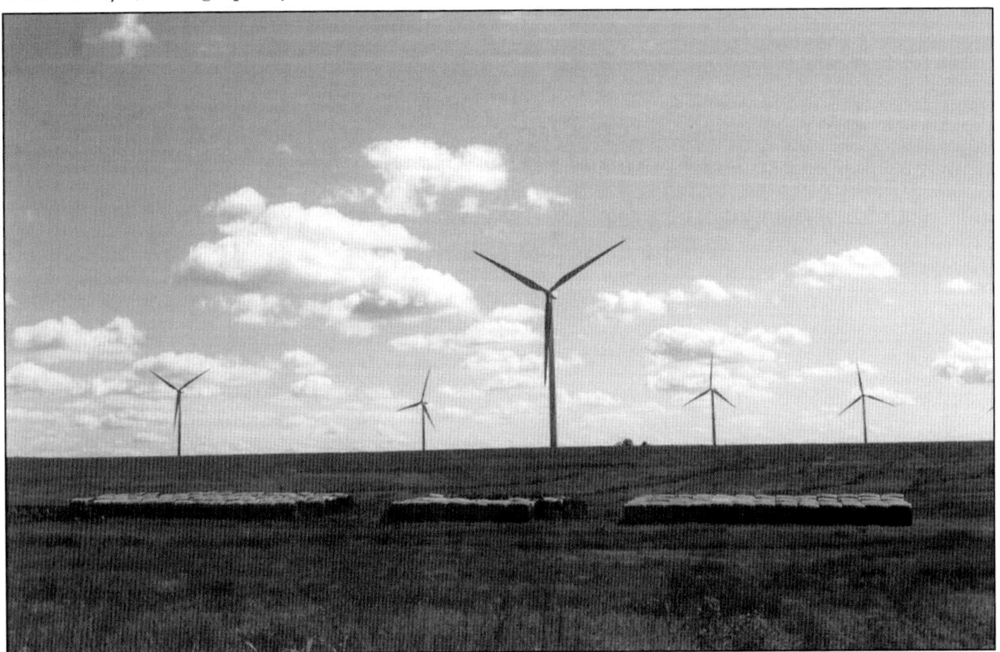

Cloud County Community College had the first program in the state for students wanting careers in wind energy technology, like the turbines producing electricity on this wind farm about eight miles south of town. More wind farms are appearing in Kansas and provide extra income for farmers who rent land to the companies installing the turbines. (Photograph by Dena Bisnette.)

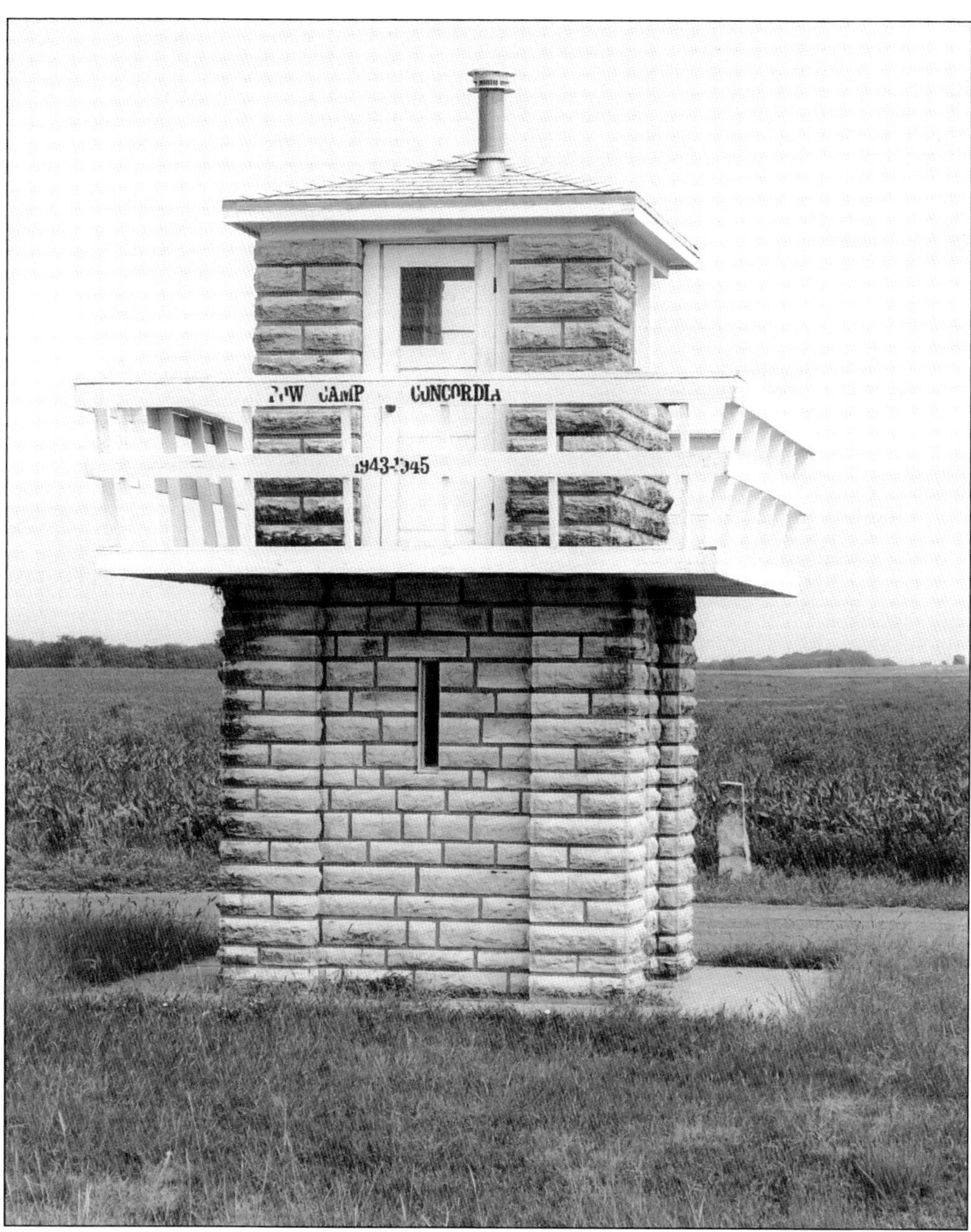

POW Camp Concordia Museum came from an idea introduced by now-retired Cloud County Community College professor Everett Miller, who decided to try to organize a reunion of everyone involved with the camp, including the Germans who had been prisoners there during World War II. "Celebration 95" was staged by volunteers using money raised from advertising on coffee cups, and 14 former prisoners were among the guests. According to Miller and Paul Rimovsky, the museum is an ongoing project, but visitors have already included several children and grandchildren of prisoners of war. This stone tower built by prisoners, including some who were skilled stonemasons, is one of the few structures that still exists at Camp Concordia. There were two, but one was falling in, so the stones from it were salvaged and used in the Brown Grand Theatre restoration. (Photograph by Dena Bisnette.)

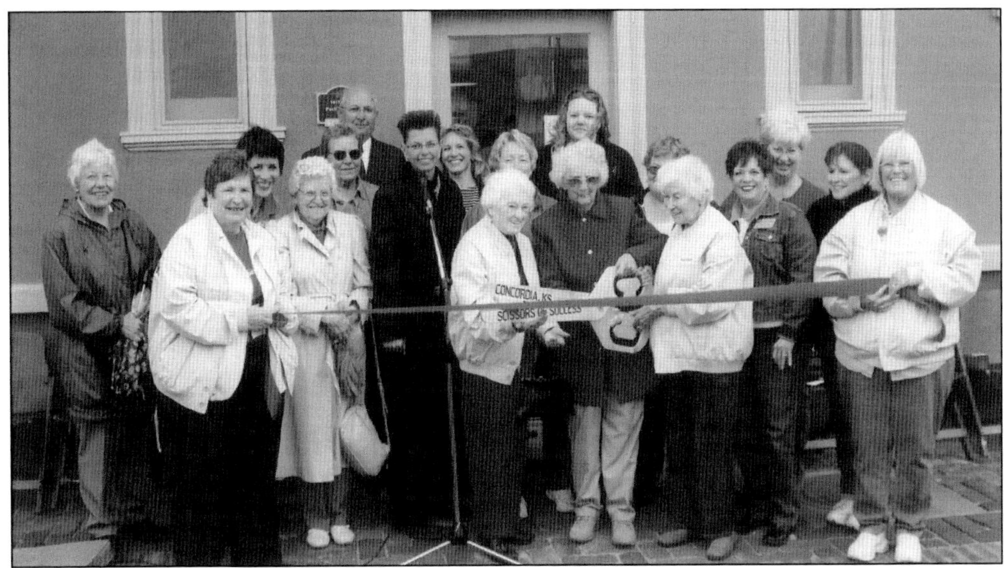

Between 1854 and 1926, orphan trains brought approximately 250,000 orphaned, abandoned, or homeless children to rural communities for adoption. They did not stop in Concordia, but in nearby communities, and some of their descendants still live in Concordia. When Mary Ellen Johnson founded the Orphan Train Heritage Society of America in 1987, she assembled an archive to help surviving riders and their descendants find out about their original families. She retired in 1993 and chose Concordia from several cities applying for the archive. A museum in the old Union Pacific Depot opened in 1993. Shown here at the ribbon cutting ceremony are, from left to right, (first row) Lois Gillette, Genny Jones, Mary Ellen Johnson, Gertrude Breault, Susan Sutton, Lela Newcombe, Anne Harrison, Linda Houser, and Becky Higgins; (second row) Holly Andrews, Ledona Dowell, Sen. Elaine Bowers, Joan Fraser, Judy Hill, Roberta Lowrey, Wanda Phillip, Charles Johnson, and Stephanie Haier. The depot is pictured below in 1966. A grant was secured to rehabilitate the building. (Above, courtesy National Orphan Train Complex; below, courtesy of Cloud County Historical Society Museum.)

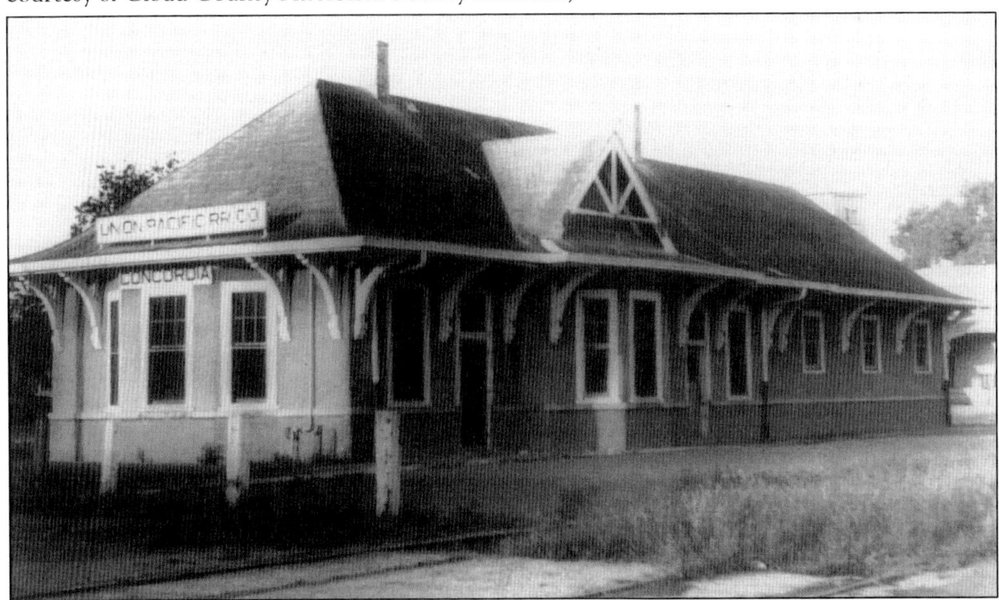

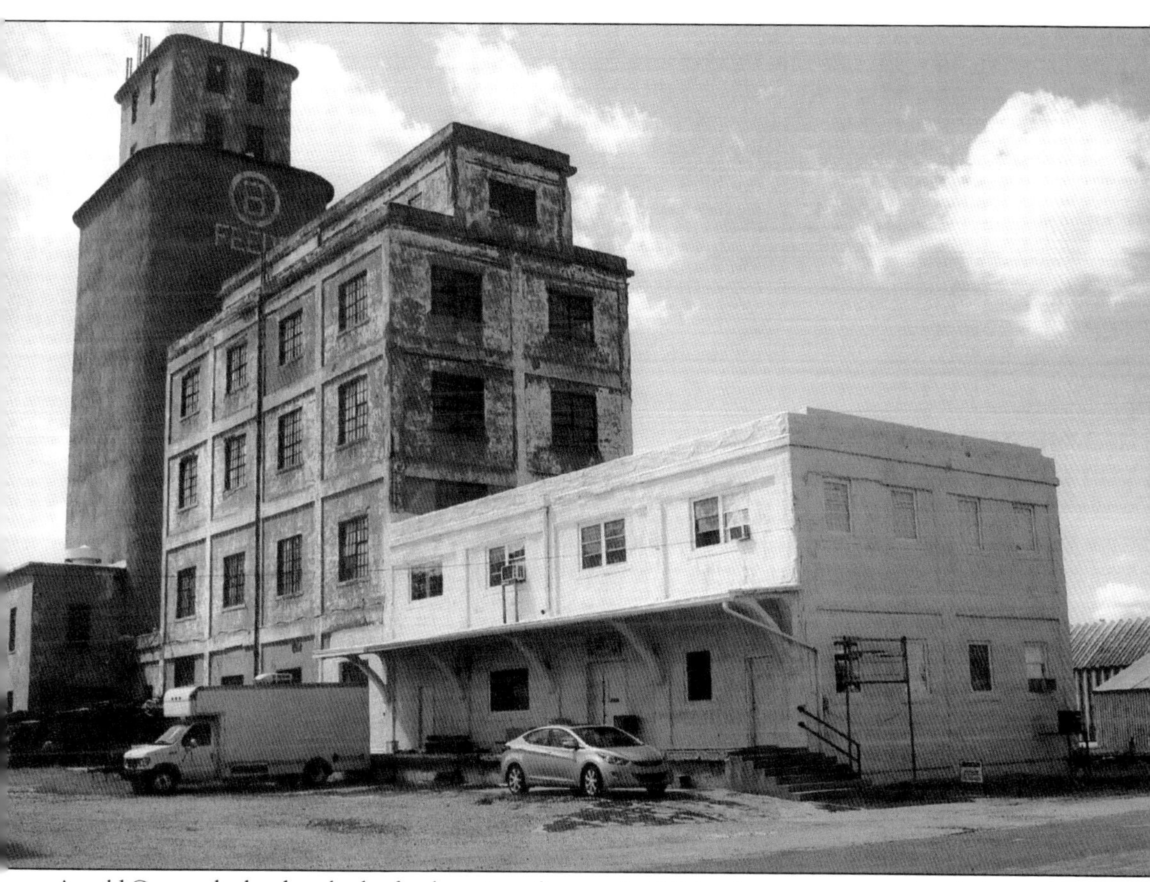

An old Concordia landmark, the final version of Lanoue's Mill, has become an example of adaptive reuse of an industrial building, a way of preserving the past while finding a practical, modern use for a structure. The lower section is now occupied by David Erickson, who uses it for the office for his business and as his residence. The square silo with the circled letter B is actually pink in color, a remnant of a company called Circle B Feeds; the owner thought the unusual color would draw attention to his business. Erickson said that that part of the building is empty, but cellphone companies rent space for their antennas on it. (Photograph by Dena Bisnette.)

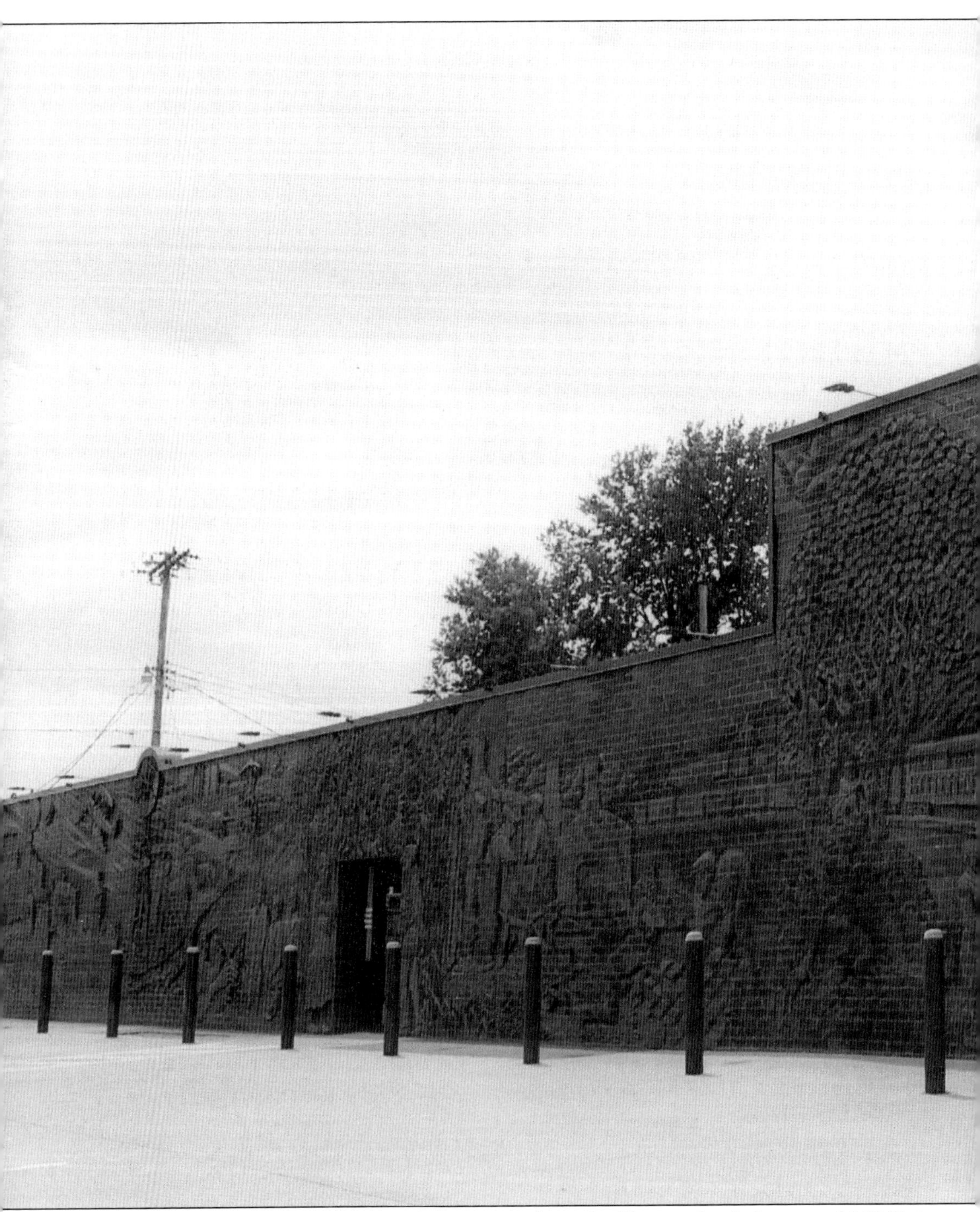

The "Whole Wall Mural" on the old Everitt Hardware building at Sixth Street and US-81 in Concordia celebrates the town's past. Artist Catharine Magel designed it and chose Mara Smith as her lead assistant. Work began in 2007, and the mural was completed in 2009. Cloud County Community College's art department assisted with the project. Cloud Ceramics constructed a giant easel for the design, which had to be eight percent larger than the finished project to accommodate

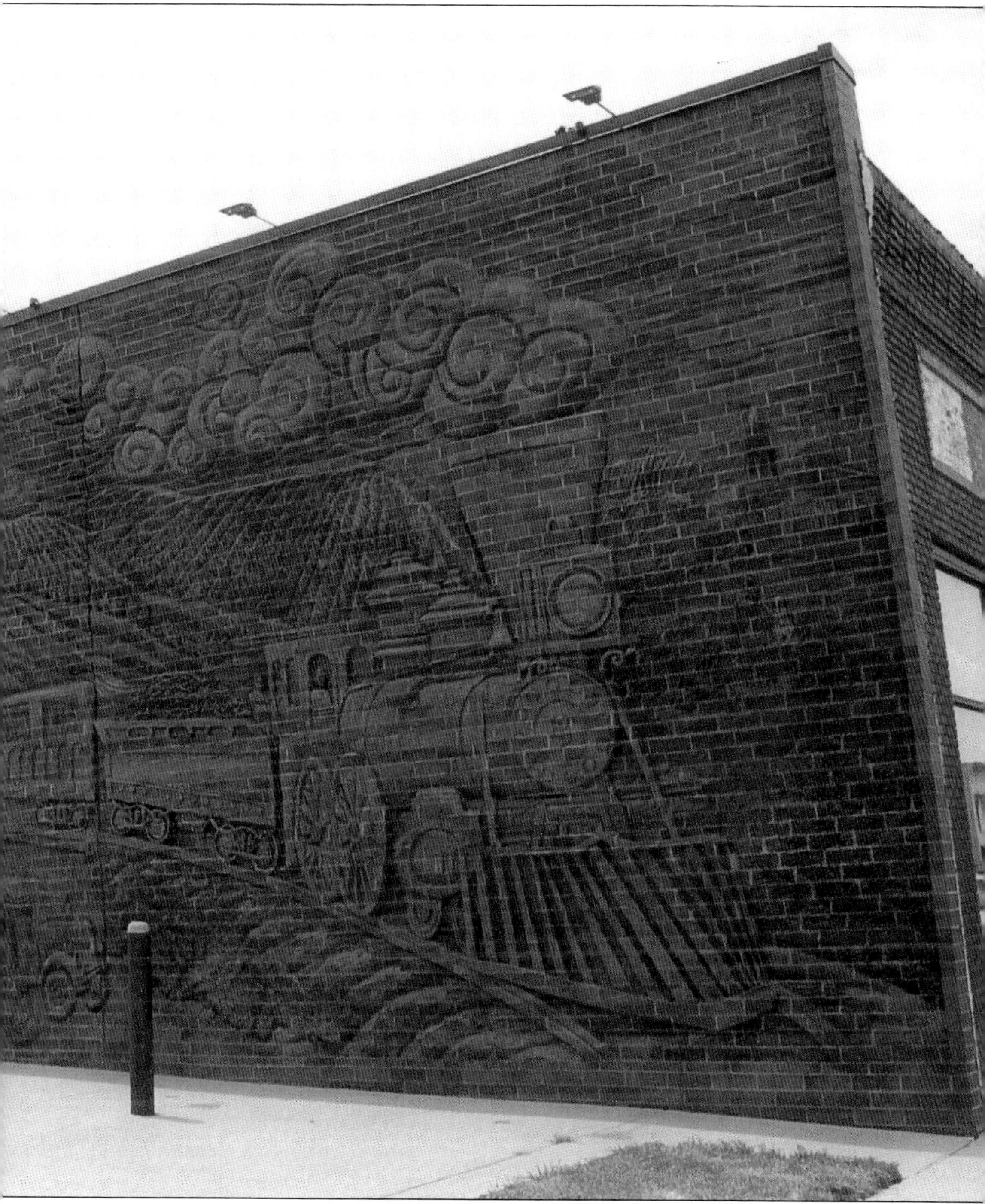

brick shrinkage during firing. After the design was divided into individually numbered sections and carved into 6,400 green bricks made by Cloud Ceramics, the bricks were fired and applied to the wall. Brick masons included Concordia High School graduate David Fleming and Brian Blase with Tyler Kuhn as brick tender. (Photograph by Dena Bisnette.)

Consistent with our mission to preserve history on a local level, this book was printed in South Carolina on American-made paper and manufactured entirely in the United States. Products carrying the accredited Forest Stewardship Council (FSC) label are printed on 100 percent FSC-certified paper.

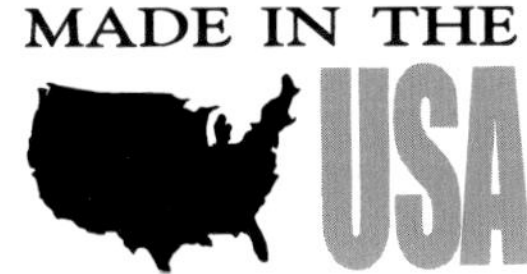